THE FILMS OF
ARNOLD
SCHWARZENEGGER

THE FILMS OF
ARNOLD
SCHWARZENEGGER

John L. Flynn

A CITADEL PRESS BOOK
Published by Carol Publishing Group

A CITADEL PRESS BOOK
Published by Carol Publishing Group
CITADEL PRESS is a registered trademark of
Carol Communications, Inc.
Editorial Offices: 600 Madison Avenue, New York, NY 10022
Sales & Distribution Offices: 120 Enterprise Avenue, Secaucus,
  NJ 10194
In Canada: Canadian Manda Group, P.O. Box 920, Station U,
  Toronto, Ontario M8Z 5P9
Queries regarding rights and permissions should be addressed to
Carol Publishing Group, 600 Madison Avenue, New York,
  NY 10022

Carol Publishing Group books are available at special discounts for bulk purchases, for sales promotions, fund raising, or educational purposes. Special editions can be created to specifications. For details, contact: Special Sales Department, Carol Publishing Group, 120 Enterprise Avenue, Secaucus, NJ 07094

Designed by Andrew B. Gardner

Manufactured in the United States of America

10 9 8 7 6 5 4 3 2 1

Library of Congress Cataloging-in-Publication Data

Flynn, John L., 1954–
    The films of Arnold Schwarzenegger / by John L. Flynn.
    — Rev. and updated ed.
        p. cm.
    "A Citadel Press book."
    Includes bibliographical references
    ISBN 0–8065–1645–3 (pbk.)
    1. Schwarzenegger, Arnold. I. Title.
PN2287.S3368F58   1995
791.43'028'092—dc20
                                        94–25287
                                          CIP

To
the memory of my father,
John J. Johnston,
who died much too young,
and to
Mike Robbian,
Steve Friedman,
John Zsittnik,
and Lenny Provenzano
for being there,
at various times in my life,
with your special friendship.

CONTENTS

FOREWORD

In this book about Arnold Schwarzenegger's career in motion pictures and the impact he has had on entertainment, no attempt has been made to tell the story of his personal and professional life beyond the biographical sketch and the information related to his films. While Arnold's personal life (with his wife, Maria Shriver, his family, and friends) and his professional one as bodybuilder, actor, entrepreneur, and political activist are enormously interesting (and provide their own special kind of amusement), such material falls outside the scope of this project. Mr. Schwarzenegger has written about his early years, as well as it will likely be done, in his autobiography, *Arnold: The Education of a Bodybuilder.* It is recommended reading should anyone desire to know the more intimate details of his youth. Two other books, *The Biography of Arnold Schwarzenegger* by George Butler and *Arnold: An Unauthorized Biography* by Wendy Leigh, provide separate, biased accounts of his life.

What has concerned me the most with *The Films of Arnold Schwarzenegger* has been factual accuracy in dealing with his cinematic appearances. Naturally the many pros and cons of writing about a person who is still active in films have been considered. Many readers may feel the author is constrained from telling all that he knows or from making certain critical evaluations about the performer's life. But by limiting my subject to his films, I purposely intended to avoid speculation or a discussion of unsubstantiated rumors about the public and private personas of Mr. Schwarzenegger. I therefore conceived the book around a very specific format. For each chapter and title I provide credits, release information, a plot synopsis, and background information as it relates to the

project, concluding with an appraisal of Schwarzenegger's contribution and the film's overall impact as well as its importance today.

The film entries—found throughout the book—represent a complete listing of all the motion pictures in which Arnold Schwarzenegger has appeared. They have been arranged chronologically (whenever possible) to accompany the text. Certain films—most notably those from independent producers—that were rereleased under different titles are noted by their alternate ones whenever possible. The date next to the film title represents the year of its general release. Without the kind assistance of many friends in the motion-picture industry, this book could never have been written. Especially helpful have been the public relations staff at Tri-Star Pictures, Carolco, and 20th Century-Fox, which own rights to many of Schwarzenegger's feature films. I am particularly grateful to Terry Erdmann, of Pros and Cons Publicty, for providing me with assorted press kits from the Schwarzenegger films and for that once-in-a-lifetime look behind the scenes in 1984. I am also thankful to my close friends and family (notably Susan Flynn) for sharing their invaluable time in hunting down precious leads and rare information. Special thanks to my agent, S. James Foiles, at Appleseeds Management, for his patience, understanding, and commitment.

PREFACE

THE PHENOMENON OF ARNOLD SCHWARZENEGGER

Arnold Schwarzenegger—known simply as "Arnold" to millions of his fans around the world—epitomizes the image of the self-made man, one whose unyielding determination has made him a legend in his own time. From bodybuilding champion, bestselling author, and real-estate tycoon to political activist, film director, and box-office superstar, he has excelled in just about his every endeavor. In fact, his twenty-five-year rise to fame represents one of the great immigrant success stories. Like Horatio Alger or F. Scott Fitzgerald's fictional Jay Gatsby, Arnold has achieved what many fantasize but few often realize—the riches of the American dream. His irresistible charm, charisma, talent, and fierce ambition have yielded wealth, power, adulation, notoriety, and success. He has married into one of the most influential families in the United States, befriended presidents and other world leaders, and affected the commercial output of America's dream factory. His ubiquitous presence in our popular culture does, however, raise several provocative questions: Why have filmgoers worldwide embraced this Austrian bodybuilder with the cartoon-hero bulk, pronounced accent, and long, almost unpronounceable name as their number-one box-office favorite? How has Arnold Schwarzenegger managed to make such an amazing transition from athletics to superstardom when other athletes, like Paul Robeson, Buster Crabbe, Reg Park, Steve Reeves, Jim Brown, Fred Williamson, O. J. Simpson, and Merlin Olsen, have found only limited success? What is the secret behind the phenomenon of Hollywood's biggest star?

Over the years many critics and film historians have attempted to answer those questions in an effort to discover the unique combination of elements that have contributed to his winning formula. But since most ticket buyers have simply accepted the worldwide stardom of Arnold Schwarzenegger as such an inevitable part of our popular culture, few actually find those questions relevant to a discussion of his career. Even fewer recall that long, difficult road to superstardom.

In the beginning Arnold seemed an unlikely figure to become a cultural icon. In his first major motion-picture appearance (*Hercules in New York* and *The*

Schwarzenegger, pictured here in his office in Venice, California, surrounded by symbols of his success, epitomizes the image of the self-made man. (Courtesy Cinema Archives)

Long Goodbye notwithstanding), Schwarzenegger played a thinly disguised version of himself in *Stay Hungry.* Exploiting the Austrian bodybuilder's muscular physique, the most obvious and unimaginative way to utilize him, writer-director Bob Rafelson introduces the character of Joe Santo as a one-dimensional athlete. Devoted—like some Buddhist monk—to a celibate life of bodybuilding, Schwarzenegger's Santo happily relinquishes the romantic advances of Sally Field to Jeff Bridges, then stands by (with a silly grin on his face) while Bridges's family and friends make fun of his athletic prowess. Given the limitations of this role, any other actor with big muscles and a foreign accent would have probably failed to make any impression at all. But Arnold had two secret weapons: He was smart, and he had a sense of humor. Those winning qualities helped elevate his performance above the commonplace and garnered him a Golden Globe Award in 1977.

Just as Schwarzenegger had used his muscles and reason to gain access to Hollywood, he summoned the same force and determination that he had once used to build his body to market himself a film star. Recognizing that his image didn't fit ordinary life situations, Arnold chose motion pictures that had an element of fantasy or science fiction for early starring vehicles. He then surrounded himself with beautiful women (Sandahl Bergman, Linda Hamilton, Rae Dawn Chong, and Sharon Stone), top-notch special effects, nonstop action, and a selection of hot, young directors (John Milius, James Cameron, John McTiernan, and Paul Verhoeven). Schwarzenegger reasoned that by making technology-driven motion pictures, audiences would accept him as the ultimate hard body in hardware movies. That intelligent reasoning has produced one successful project after another. In fact, during the last ten years, Arnold's films have generated more than a billion dollars in total revenues, making him one of the industry's most bankable stars.

And though Schwarzenegger's business acumen has made him possibly the most expensive talent in Hollywood today, he hasn't taken a flat fee for his work since the beginning of the nineties. Instead he accepts expensive perks (like a $12 million jet for *Terminator 2: Judgment Day*) from studio executives and a percentage of the worldwide gross of his movies. In 1989, *Forbes* magazine listed Arnold as one of the ten wealthiest entertainers in America, estimating that his gross income for the year would be $35 million. By 1991, he ranked as one of the top-

Although he seems an unlikely figure to become a cultural icon, the Austrian's muscular physique propelled him to international stardom. (Courtesy Cinema Archives)

three best-compensated entertainers on its annual list. Part of being a successful businessman in a town like Hollywood means becoming as rough as the competition, but Arnold refuses to give into the isolation or toughness of the industry. After all, his success in the motion-picture business was achieved in large part by hard work, determination, and pragmatism, not manipulative backstabbing. He prefers to maintain a nonthreatening, friendly disposition, because that's the person Arnold Schwarzenegger really is.

"I don't want to be taken overly seriously by anybody, because I'm not a very serious person. I'm having fun making movies that entertain people." Clearly, few other screen actors have established such a personal audience rapport or pioneered such revolution-

Schwarzenegger lounges comfortably at his luxurious home. (Courtesy Cinema Archives)

ary changes in the style of action films as Schwarzenegger. Early in his career, in *Commando*, he learned a valuable lesson about quality control: Anyone can make an action movie and sell tickets in the short run. But in order to keep filmgoers coming back for more, Arnold would have to offer them

Conan the Barbarian made Schwarzenegger a plausible movie star because he looked like the muscular hero from the comic books. (Courtesy Universal Pictures)

something other than nonstop violence. He said:

> I always felt it was best to build up stock with an audience out there that will always go to see your movies. If you want to keep those people loyal, you have to provide them with what they enjoy seeing. But that doesn't mean you can't add on every time ten percent of new stuff and gradually make them see a new side of you.

Throughout his film stardom, Schwarzenegger has certainly demonstrated that he knows how to pick good material and surround himself with talented professionals, but he has also shown an incredible sense of timing. He was in the vanguard of the high-tech, action-adventure genre, leading the way for the likes of Jean-Claude Van Damme, Bruce Willis, Dolph Lundgren, and—to some extent—Sylvester Stallone.* The screen has been slow in catching up with his lead; but each time it has, Arnold has surprised audiences and critics alike by attempting something unconventional. *Conan the Barbarian* made Schwarzenegger a plausible movie star because he looked just like the muscular hero from the comic books and pulp magazines. Ticket buyers were so impressed with his performance that they made the

*Few film historians will deny the importance the original *Rocky* (1976) had on Arnold Schwarzenegger's career. Stallone's performance as a semiliterate, muscle-bound boxer altered the public's perception of bodybuilders and paved the way for the Austrian's later success. However, without the Conan films and *The Terminator* (1984), there would have been no *Rambo II* (1985); without *Raw Deal* (1986) and *Red Heat* (1988), there would have been no *Cobra* (1986) or *Tango & Cash* (1989). Indeed, had audiences not so readily accepted Schwarzenegger in the lighthearted *Twins* (1988) or the equally likable *Kindergarten Cop* (1990), Stallone would have been (and in fact was) totally out of his league in *Oscar* (1991).

Like John Wayne and Clint Eastwood, Schwarzenegger has come to represent the image of a hero for the eighties and nineties. (Courtesy Dino De Laurentiis Entertainment)

By portraying a killer robot in *The Terminator* (1984) and *Terminator 2: Judgment Day* (1991), Schwarzenegger played against typecasting and became an even bigger movie star. (Courtesy Tri-Star Pictures, Inc.; Carolco Home Video)

Schwarzenegger as a man of few words who speaks through his actions. (Courtesy Tri-Star Pictures, Inc.)

film one of the top box-office winners of the year. But if Arnold had continued making Conan movies or feeble spin-offs like *Red Sonja* (1985), audiences would have eventually grown tired of his image. Cleverly, while his contemporaries were making inferior rip-offs (in the sword-and-sorcery genre), he turned villainous as *The Terminator*. By accepting the role of the killer cyborg from the future, he played against type and became an even bigger star. Less than one year later, Schwarzenegger showed his tender side by playing a single, if very self-sufficient parent in *Commando*, then used his sense of humor (which he had demon-strated in several action films) to again reinvent his image for *Twins* and *Kindergarten Cop*. Charisma, adaptability, and sheer force of will have helped Arnold outlast his so-called competitors. He also has both outlived and outgrown his image of a cult celebrity of the bodybuilding craze and has attained a level of respectability as Hollywood's biggest star.

Social historians regard his extraordinary life, motion-picture roles, and the hero worship they arouse as being indicative of the world in which we live. Because Schwarzenegger tends to play characters that are physically superior or larger than life, his popularity might be also linked to our yearning for strong, authoritative leaders. In *The Hero With a Thousand Faces*, Joseph Campbell explained his treatise on the power of myth in popular culture, that man typically celebrates tales of heroes and their deeds in order to understand his own place in the universe. The Greeks used mythological metaphors about Hercules and other famous titans to define heroic ideals; the Romans depended on biographical archetypes, drawn from Plutarch and other great historians, to give their culture meaning; the Middle Ages relied on hagiography (or writings about the saints). But Campbell further reminds us that modern man lives in a society in which most old myths have lost their power and that there exists in the contemporary world a cultural imperative to invent new stories and create new heroes. Post-industrial America,

13

The many faces and sides of Arnold Schwarzenegger. (Courtesy Universal Pictures)

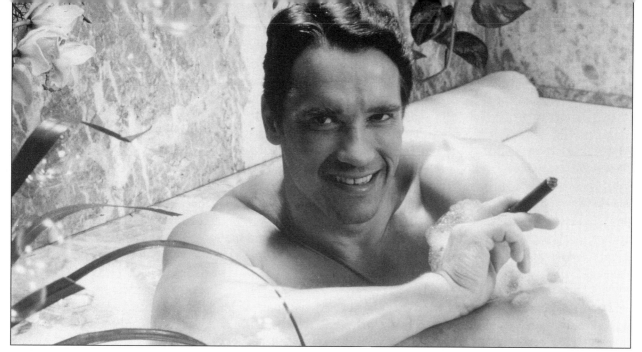

From bodybuilding champion, bestselling author, and real-estate tycoon to political activist, film director, and box-office superstar, Schwarzenegger has excelled in nearly every endeavor.

deliberately abandoning elements from previous periods, has thus embraced a new type of hero, a celluloid figure of few words who speaks through his actions. Without much doubt, the men of action played by John Wayne, Clint Eastwood, *and* Arnold Schwarzenegger represent the archetypal or symbolic ideals of a masculine, mythopoeic culture.

John Wayne's Rooster Cogburn or Clint Eastwood's Dirty Harry Callahan are, in fact, forerunners of Arnold's many film creations. Cogburn, the hard-drinking marshal in Henry Hathaway's *True Grit*, is an archetypal loner who must reluctantly venture forth (with allies) into the dark wilderness, achieve a decisive victory over the forces of evil, and return from his mysterious adventure with the strength and wisdom to empower other men. Callahan, the fascistic police inspector in Don Siegel's *Dirty Harry*, represents a force for justice in a world that has rejected the traditional values of law and order. Their actions, though often violent and vigilant, restore a sense of balance to the universe. Like Wayne's Cogburn, Schwarzenegger's Conan, Ben Richards, Douglas Quaid, and Dutch Schaefer all must undergo journeys into the heart of darkness to defeat superior adversaries in order to save their society from ruin. Like Eastwood's Dirty Harry, Schwarzenegger's Ivan Danko, John Matrix, Mark Kaminsky, and John Kimble all must take justice into their own hands

because the system has failed to protect the innocents (they love) from harm. Regardless of whether they struggle against a powerful sorcerer, drug dealers, totalitarian regimes, or an alien predator, the result is the same. Their mythic quest both uplifts and empowers modern man to action, freeing him from a society in which most individuals have been held hostage by a hostile environment.

Thematically, many of Arnold Schwarzenegger's motion pictures also concern another type of journey—that of the individual toward self-enlightenment. In *The Hero Within*, Carol S. Pearson defines six archetypal stages that the hero typically passes through on his way toward wholeness. From Innocent, Orphan, and Wanderer to Warrior, Martyr, and Magician (or King), the journey represents a universal quest for personal identity that every human being should undertake but few actually complete. Through his varied film roles, Arnold's cinematic Everyman functions as both a model hero and surrogate for that dangerous journey within. For example, the young Cimmerian in *Conan the Barbarian* must confront the terror of abandonment, the loss of love, and the reality of death after his parents are murdered by Thulsa Doom. When he is finally freed from the slave pits, he begins the task of defining himself by wandering the Hyborian Age in search of the Riddle of Steel. Conan soon becomes a warrior in order to defend himself, then a martyr to sacrifice for others, and finally achieves the wisdom and power of a king. Similarly, Julius Benedict, in *Twins*, follows the same progression from loss and suffering to self-definition, a struggle to retain identity, sacrifice, and love. Other characters, like Dutch Schaefer in *Predator*, John Kimble in *Kindergarten Cop*, and the Terminator in *Terminator 2: Judgment Day*, must undertake similar inward journeys to rediscover a part of themselves that they have long since abandoned. Somehow these familiar stories of larger-than-life heroes, who not only struggle toward self-awareness but also must learn to balance the boy (or primitive) within the man, have helped make Schwarzenegger very accessible to modern audiences.

Today Arnold Schwarzenegger stands in a class by himself as a talented performer, thoroughly gifted in projecting whatever image he elects to project. Hence, with one good look at him and his body of work, the distinction between superstar and actor becomes blurred. Even though Arnold's physical distinctiveness often lends itself best to motion pictures that feature the sleek high-tech look of special effects, he purposely uses a penchant for self-deprecating one-liners to humanize his heroic he-men as well as soften the on-screen violence. In fact, his sense of humor is what separates him from the other big action stars like Eastwood or Stallone, and yet the former Austrian bodybuilder has always been very conscious of walking that fine line between being bigger than life and becoming a self-parody. Arnold Schwarzenegger may look funny, with his cartoon-hero-like bulk, and he may sound funny, with his prominent accent, but he always maintains the image of a consummate professional. One can talk of few other performers in a like manner, and perhaps that's the real secret behind the phenomenon of Hollywood's biggest star. By embracing the traditional values of hard work, persistence, and adaptability—the very cornerstones that America was built upon—Arnold has achieved a much deserved place in our popular culture.

INTRODUCTION

ARNOLD SCHWARZENEGGER:
MUSCLEMAN TO SUPERSTAR

Arnold Schwarzenegger (a literal translation of the family name means "black plowman") was born on July 30, 1947, in the small, medieval village of Thal, approximately four miles from the city of Graz, Austria, to working-class parents. His father, Gustav, was a former military officer turned police chief,* and his mother, Aurelia, was a hausfrau (a housewife). Together with Arnold's older brother, Meinhard, the Schwarzenegger family lived above the father's police station in Spartan-like surroundings that lacked heat, indoor plumbing, and a refrigerator. Raised in a strict, Catholic home, Arnold learned from his father the value of self-discipline, a quality which facilitated his extraordinary success in later years. Gustav, a dominant, sometimes tyrannical figure in the youngster's life, encouraged both his sons to pursue a vigorous schedule of athletics. From the time the boys were old enough to understand him, he drilled them with household chores and exercise, then pitted them against one another in private competitions. A former European curling champion, the elder Schwarzenegger wanted his sons to

Arnold, as a young schoolboy (front row, second from the left), was educated at the Hans Gross School in Thal.

be world-class athletes and expected that Arnold would one day be a professional soccer player.

The superstar attributes his strategy for success to the "healthy upbringing" he received from his parents. "The only thing we didn't have was money," Schwarzenegger recalled. "I had a lot of attention from my parents, a lot of love, and enough food—even though growing up after the war was tough...."

When Arnold was six years old, his father took him into Graz to see the former Olympic swimmer turned Hollywood actor Johnny Weismuller, who was there to dedicate a swimming pool. The youngster marveled at the star's muscular physique and redoubled his own efforts to become a champion athlete. Skating, swimming, skiing, hiking, and table ten-

---

*Journalist Wendy Leigh, in *Arnold: An Unauthorized Biography* (Chicago: Congdon and Weed, Inc., 1990), suggests that Arnold's father, Gustav, an ardent admirer of Adolf Hitler, joined the Nazi party in 1938 for both political and economic gain. Although Austrians were not permitted to join the party between 1933 and 1938, she alleges that Gustav's Nazi party membership (number 8439?80) is a matter of record at the Berlin Document Center's Archival Records. Clearly, if Gustav had joined to take advantage of the party's prosperity, the Schwarzenegger family's lifestyle would have improved significantly. In July 1993, a London Court ruled that Arnold had been libeled in the Wendy Leigh books, and the case was settled in his favor for an undisclosed sum of money.

By age thirteen, Schwarzenegger began looking for role models and discovered the muscle-bound surrogate supermen of the Hercules movies. (Posters courtesy Warner Bros., above, and Woolner Brothers, right)

nis were often more important to the boy than the fundamentals of reading, writing, and arithmetic that he studied at the Hans Gross School in Thal. (He did possess an unusual appreciation of art and enjoyed drawing pictures to pass cold winter days.) Because Arnold and his brother were very competitive, the boys spent much of their leisure time trying to best one another while vying for the attention of their father. Unfortunately, Meinhard was always the favorite.

"We were only a year apart. We tried to outdo each other when it came to sports and school," Schwarzenegger confessed in a 1989 interview, although to this day he readily dismisses speculation that the boys were competing for their father's love. "That's a bit too heavy for a kid to think about." Arnold still maintains enormous respect for his late brother. Had he not died in an automobile accident in his early twenties, Schwarzenegger believes, Meinhard might have become a successful athlete or a renowned electrical engineer.

By age thirteen, Arnold had grown weary of his father's obsessive desires to make him a world-class

18

soccer player, dropped out of the sport, and began looking for other role models to emulate. The teenager turned to muscle-bound surrogate supermen; first a comic-book hero named Sieguard, then legendary Teutonic figures from mythology. Within a few months, however, Arnold discovered the flesh-and-blood superheroes of the silver screen in films like *Hercules* (1957), *Hercules Unchained* (1959), *Hercules Against Rome, Hercules in the Haunted World, Hercules and the Captive Woman,* and *Hercules Against the Moon Men.* He watched those B movies over and over again and vowed that one day he would be more famous than Reg Park or Steve Reeves. Admiration for these stars led Schwarzenegger to begin collecting bodybuilder magazines, from which he clipped photographs and pin-ups of musclemen. Disregarding objections from parents and friends, he covered his walls with these photos and devoured mythical stories about Park and Reeves while dreaming of America.

"Within a year, I had a very clear vision of where I wanted to go," he remembered more than thirty

years after the fact. "I began to work out, and from that moment on, my goals were clear!"

While swimming with his brother in the Thalersee River in July 1961, Arnold met Kurt Marnul, the former Mr. Austria and one of the most celebrated bodybuilders in Europe. Marnul was impressed by the fourteen-year-old's strong, bulky frame and invited Schwarzenegger to train with him at the Athletic Union in Graz. With the help of several other bodybuilders, Arnold trained seven days a week, abandoning school, church, and the normal pursuits of boys his own age. (To pay for the expensive steroids and anabolics which helped contribute to his massive physique, he began a three-year apprenticeship as a carpenter.) His body sculpting netted a six-foot-two-inch body that (at its peak) featured a fifty-seven-inch chest, a thirty-one-inch waist, twenty-two-inch biceps, and twenty-eight-inch thighs. At the age of seventeen, Arnold took part in his first bodybuilding contest in Graz's Hotel Steirer Hof and was named runner-up in the competition.

Schwarzenegger enlisted in the Austrian army on October 1, 1965, just a few months after his eighteenth birthday, and began his compulsory one-year service. While attending a special school to learn how to drive tanks, Arnold went AWOL to participate in his first international competition in Stuttgart. "I thought I was King Kong," he mused aloud years later, but the judges took Schwarzenegger serious

Arnold Schwarzenegger's muscle-building netted a six-foot two-inch body with (at its peak) a fifty-seven-inch chest, thirty-one-inch waist, twenty-two-inch biceps, and twenty-eight-inch thighs.

enough to award him the title Junior Mr. Europe. (In addition to winning the competition, Arnold met his lifelong friend Franco Columbu there.) He was caught sneaking back onto the military base and was promptly jailed, spending nearly a week in the stockade. His victory, however, not only earned him a prompt release but the encouragement of his superiors to continue bodybuilding.

One year later, after he had been named Mr. Germany, Arnold traveled to London to compete in his first Mr. Universe contest, sponsored by the National Amateur Body Builders Association. Although he came in second to America's Chet Yorton, Schwarzenegger renewed acquaintance with Rolf Putziger, a publisher and bodybuilding promoter. Putziger was so taken by the eager teenager that he offered him a job as a manager-trainer at his gym in Munich. Schwarzenegger accepted his offer, then began practicing for the next competition.

At age twenty, Arnold snatched the Mr. Universe title (becoming the youngest Mr. Universe in history) and was invited by his lifetime idol Reg Park to visit

Admiration for Steve Reeves (pictured) and Reg Park led Schwarzenegger to begin collecting bodybuilder magazines. Within a year he began working on his own muscular physique. (Courtesy Warner Bros.)

Schwarzenegger flexes his perfectly sculpted body.

a direct result of "the American spirit" to which he had become "addicted."

"I always felt I had an American mentality," he explained, defending his seemingly overnight success. I was born in the wrong country. When I came here, I was immediately sucked into the notion that everything was possible and that people were open-minded. I loved it. Americans don't start out with negative attitudes, as they do in Europe. People think big about achieving and making money and improving themselves—the whole idea of continuous progress.

Fulfilling a lifelong fantasy to play a mythical hero for the silver screen, Schwarzenegger accepted the lead in the low-low budget *Hercules in New York* (1970); he then followed his inauspicious film debut with a small role as a mob enforcer in Robert Altman's *Long Goodbye* (1973). Between film projects and while training for the Mr. Olympia competition, Arnold received word that his father, Gustav, had died at age sixty-five. The bodybuilder took his death "badly, because I knew how much he had done for me ..." but did not attend the funeral, which was held one week later, preferring to grieve privately for the man who had endowed him with the drive to succeed.

him in South Africa. That same year, Joe Weider, publisher of *Muscle & Fitness* and the world's foremost proponent of bodybuilding, brought Schwarzenegger to the United States for business reasons and set him up in Santa Monica, the mecca of bodybuilding. (Arnold was paid a small weekly salary to lend his name, face, and physique to any advertisements and public appearances that Weider could dream up for "the Austrian Oak.") He also arranged to have Arnold's closest friend, Franco Columbu, join him; the two bodybuilders moved into the same apartment and daily worked out together at Gold's Gym.

Even as Schwarzenegger was modeling his perfectly sculpted body for Weider's promotional schemes, he began marketing a line of mail-order bodybuilding aids under the name "Arnold Strong." Then Arnold invested whatever monies he earned from the mail-order enterprise in California real estate. Within a few years, while still in his twenties, he became a millionaire. Schwarzenegger contends that his prosperity was

Arnold competed and won the Mr. Universe title five times, the Mr. Olympia title six times, and the Mr. World championship once before retiring in 1975.

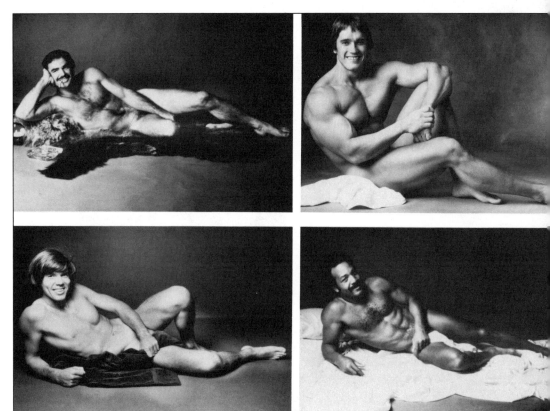

Schwarzenegger appeared (among distinguished company) as the August 1977 celebrity centerfold for *Cosmopolitan*. (Photo from *Cosmopolitan*'s 25th anniversary issue.)

At the 1972 Mr. Olympia contest, in Brooklyn, New York, Arnold was introduced to George Butler, then a free-lance photographer for *Oui*. Butler and his partner, writer Charles Gaines, were impressed by Schwarzenegger and suggested that he should be featured in a book (and possibly a documentary) about bodybuilding. Arnold agreed. Two years later, after encountering stiff resistance from the establishment (which maintained the homophobic attitude that all bodybuilders were gay), *Pumping Iron* was finally published by Simon and Schuster; it became an immediate bestseller, and Arnold Schwarzenegger became a household word. Prior to the book, the bodybuilding superstar had been treated like some sort of freak that people would laugh at behind his back. But the book lent credibility to the sport, and Arnold's professionalism made him more accessible to millions of Americans.

Schwarzenegger told Joan Goodman in a 1988 *Playboy* interview that he

made the sport more acceptable when I promoted bodybuilding in the mid-seventies .... In the old days bodybuilders talked about eating two pounds of meat and thirty eggs a day, how they had to sleep twelve hours a day and

couldn't have sex, and so on. And I said to myself, "Who the fuck wants to be part of that kind of sport?" First of all, it was not accurate; and second of all, if you want to make people join a particular activity, you have to make it pleasant sounding. It's like promoting anything. You make it fun. I talked about diet—but I said I eat cake and ice cream as well. I said I stay out nights and I have sex and do all the things that everyone says you shouldn't do. I said all you have to do is train three times a week for forty-five minutes to an hour and you will get in shape.

Arnold took advantage of his newfound notoriety and began to re-create himself with extraordinary finesse, hoping to grow beyond the public's perception that he was simply a gifted bodybuilder. Under the tutelage of Butler and Gaines, Schwarzenegger took ballet lessons. He was photographed by Robert Mapplethorpe, painted by Jamie Wyeth, and featured at a scholastic seminar at New York's Whitney Museum. He continued his education at UCLA and went on to earn a degree in Business and International Economics at the University of Wisconsin. He competed and won the Mr. Universe

Arnold Schwarzenegger says a few words to his fans during the ceremony honoring his Hollywood Walk of Fame star.

On June 2, 1987, Schwarzenegger received a star on the Hollywood Walk of Fame.

title five times, the Mr. Olympia title six times, and the Mr. World championship once before retiring in 1975 at an unparalleled height in the field. (He won the Mr. Olympia competition for a seventh time in 1980 and today coproduces the Mr. Olympia and Mr. Universe competitions out of Columbus, Ohio.) He also started writing books about fitness and bodybuilding, resulting in four bestsellers, including *Arnold: The Education of a Bodybuilder, Arnold's Bodyshaping for Women, Arnold's Bodybuilding for Men,* and *Arnold's Encyclopedia of Modern Bodybuilding,* a one thousand-page reference work, all published by Simon and Schuster.

Shortly before his retirement from professional competition, Arnold was invited by Lucille Ball to appear on a live television special with Art Carney entitled "Happy Anniversary and Goodbye." Even though he played the stereotypical role of an Italian masseur, Schwarzenegger demonstrated enormous charm and a natural penchant for comedy. Later, in 1974, Bob Rafelson hired him to play a bodybuilder for his adaptation of George Gaines's *Stay Hungry.* The role of Joe Santo, the gentle giant, won Arnold

"the Best Newcomer" award at the 34th Annual Golden Globe ceremony, sponsored by the Hollywood Foreign Press Association, in January 1977. Subsequent parts in the documentary *Pumping Iron* (1977), *The Villain* (1979), *Scavenger Hunt* (1979), and *The Jayne Mansfield Story* (1980) propelled him into a different spotlight.

Two years later, after many Hollywood producers had dismissed him as a muscle-bound freak, Schwarzenegger made *Conan the Barbarian* (1982) for Dino De Laurentiis. ("He was the King Kong of the industry at that time," Arnold said admiringly.) The film reportedly made $100 million worldwide ($41 million in the United States) and established him as a major box-office draw. Its sequel, *Conan the Destroyer* (1984), grossed more than $100 million worldwide. But the motion picture that forever altered the course of Arnold's career and proved that the Conan films were not flukes was *The Terminator* (1984). James Cameron's futuristic thriller, which cast Schwarzenegger in the title role as the relentless killing machine, catapulted him to international stardom.

The Terminator, according to Arnold, "automatically doubled my price." During the next few years, the former bodybuilder's popularity (and box-office draw) continued to increase in a diverse cross section of films, from *Commando* (1986), *Predator* (1987) and *The Running Man* (1987) to *Twins* (1988), *Total Recall* (1990), and *Kindergarten Cop* (1990). On

22

Arnold Schwarzenegger married Maria Shriver on April 26, 1986.

Arnold and Maria, the happy couple.

Enjoying one of his favorite cigars (a Cuban Davidoff), Schwarzenegger awaits an autograph session.

June 2, 1987, he was given a star on Hollywood Boulevard's "Walk of Fame." Later that year, Arnold was named "Star of the Year" by the National Association of Theatre Owners. (In the five years since then, Schwarzenegger's fee has risen from $5 million to $15 million a picture, earning him a place on *Forbes's* top-ten list of America's wealthiest performers.) "I have my reasons for working hard," he explained a few years ago. "I'm a capitalist in the truest sense. Because of that, I like to see my projects done correctly. I try not to disappoint my fans, who have come to expect a certain quality control in my movies."

During his amazing transition from athletics to superstardom, Arnold Schwarzenegger met and fell in love with NBC news correspondent Maria Shriver. Although their "chance" meeting at the Robert Kennedy Tennis Tournament in 1977 has been orchestrated by publicist Bobby Zarem, Arnold's charm and personal charisma prompted Maria to

invite him to Hyannis Port that following weekend. Once there, he met Rose Kennedy, Sargent Shriver, Ted Kennedy, and other key members of the Kennedy-Shriver clan. Arnold's relationship with Maria heated up the following year when she picked him up (at a Washington, D.C., hotel), dressed like a Gypsy, for a Halloween party and dinner. Schwarzenegger became a U.S. citizen in 1983 and, after an eight-year

Schwarzenegger was a presenter on MTV's 1992 Movie Awards show.

Arnold Schwarzenegger (outside the Dorothy Chandler Pavilion) attends the 62nd Academy Awards celebration with his wife Maria. His *Total Recall* (1990) won a special Oscar for Best Visual Effects.

courtship, married Maria on April 26, 1986 (with Franco Columbu attending as his best man). The couple's guest list read like a who's who directory, with important representatives from sports, Hollywood, high society, and politics.* Their first child, Katherine Eunice Schwarzenegger, was born three years later, on December 13, 1989. (The happy couple has since had two other children, both girls.)

Even though Arnold may have married into the ultraliberal Kennedy-Shriver family, the arch-Republican still maintains a close friendship with Presidents Reagan and Bush. His conservative views and popularity as a superstar have contributed much, over the years, to the political system in the United States. Arnold has promoted better working condi-

As the national weight-training coach for the Special Olympics, Schwarzenegger poses with hockey star Wayne Gretzky and athletes (seated from left) Matt Kiker, Ryan Muir, and Karl Kiker. (Courtesy Special Olympics)

tions for employees, accessible child care for everyone (regardless of economic status), and maternity leave for both parents. He favors a tough crime bill but has also worked on behalf of the National Rifle Association to preserve a citizen's right to bear arms. In addition to his lobbying work in Congress, he has actively campaigned for two presidents. In 1984, Schwarzenegger attended the Republican convention in Dallas and spoke on behalf of Ronald Reagan.

---

*Because the former bodybuilder had extended a wedding invitation to Austrian president Kurt Waldheim (who was just beginning to draw fire from the World Jewish Congress for an alleged involvement in Kozara massacre during World War II), several journalists accused Arnold of harboring sympathies for Hitler and Nazi Germany. (The suspicion that his father may have been a member of the Nazi party also contributed to their accusation.) Schwarzenegger responded to this issue during a 1989 *Penthouse* interview with journalist Sharon Churcher by stating, "I totally hate the Nazi period." To this day, Arnold works selflessly on behalf of, and contributes financially to, the Simon Wiesenthal Center in Los Angeles.

24

During the 1988 presidential race, while campaigning for George Bush, he was nicknamed "Conan the Republican." In early 1990, President Bush rewarded Arnold's hard work by naming him chairman of the President's Council on Physical Fitness and Sports. Unfortunately, his continued support of George Bush (and very vocal opposition to Bill Clinton) during the 1992 campaign cost him that valuable position. One of Clinton's first actions as president of the United States was to remove Schwarzenegger as chairman of the Physical Fitness Council. Another one of Bill Clinton's early legislative moves, an income-tax surcharge, has cost the superstar an additional 10 percent of what he earns annually and further widened the gulf between them.

Both the *New York Daily News* and the *Chicago Sun-Times* have run articles suggesting that Arnold's destiny lies in politics, possibly as governor or lieutenant governor of California. Schwarzenegger has remained disinterested. "I make great money. I have the perfect wife. I have freedom," he responded to suggestions about a future in politics. "How can it be seductive when you have a life that is already perfect?" He does believe that Colin Powell, the former chairman of the Joint Chiefs of Staff, would make a fine president and is willing to support him in a bid for that top office.

When he's not making motion pictures, campaigning for political causes, or promoting physical fitness, Arnold devotes much of his time and expertise to charitable causes. He is the national weight-training coach for the Special Olympics and founder of a pilot program for prisoner rehabilitation through weight-resistance training. (This program has not only proved immensely popular among inmates but has garnered high praise from penal authorities.) He is a sought-after lecturer, conducting seminars for executive groups and women's organizations or special classes for military personnel. He is also chairman of the board of the World Gym, a highly successful franchise, and coexecutive producer of the Arnold Schwarzenegger Classic, a major bodybuilding competition held annually in Columbus, Ohio. Arnold also continues with his education; his latest degree in business and international economics is from the University of Wisconsin—Superior Campus.

As an entrepreneur, Schwarzenegger continues to invest in real estate; his most profitable venture (with partners Sylvester Stallone and Bruce Willis) was an exclusive restaurant entitled Planet Hollywood, which opened in New York City in 1991. The restau-rant and entertainment complex was so popular the partners decided to open a worldwide chain. Planet Hollywood locations now include Manhattan, Los Angeles, Beverly Hills, Chicago, Washington, D.C., London, Minneapolis, Aspen, Phoenix, Las Vegas, Lake Tahoe, Reno, Dallas, Orlando, Atlanta, Hong Kong, and Maui, with Baltimore and San Francisco being considered as future sites. In the restaurants, which feature memorabilia from some of Arnold's (and Bruce's and Sly's) most famous films, customers are served delicious hamburgers and French fries; in the gift shops, located next door, visitors can purchase T-shirts, jackets, and pins, all emblazoned with the Planet Hollywood logo. Schwarzenegger has also opened his own private restaurant, Schatzi on Main, in Santa Monica; customers there can feast on a wide variety of gourmet food. The Austrian superstar sometimes works in the kitchen alongside his chefs.

This former bodybuilding champion keeps himself in shape through a daily program of running, bicycling, and lifting weights. Both Arnold and Maria Shriver enjoy skiing as well as other winter sports, and often vacation in Sun Valley; in fact, he recently built a getaway home there for his family and friends. He drives a $49,000 quasi-military vehicle, the Hummer, a civilian version of the Humvee, which was so effective during the Gulf War. Although Maria doesn't like the noise of the engine, and has publicly denounced the vehicle (while filming a cameo for *Last Action Hero*), his three children love it. Schwarzenegger has also recently developed an interest in golf, and purchased a unique set of MacGregor woods for $772,000. The clubs once belonged to John F. Kennedy, and Arnold acquired them in the April 1996 auction of the Jacqueline Kennedy Onassis estate. "I paid what I paid because I wanted them because I admired JFK and because I play golf," he said recently, perplexed by the loud coverage of his purchase in *Time* magazine and elsewhere. "It was something I could afford to do. Why is that such a big deal?" he also bought a leather desk set and a Norman Rockwell painting of Kennedy. These items will no doubt be just a part of the legacy that he leaves to his son and his two daughters. Truly a Renaissance man, Arnold Schwarzenegger continues to excel, through hard work and determination, in every aspect of life.

26

ONE

THE EARLY FILMS:
FROM *HERCULES IN NEW YORK*
TO *THE JAYNE MANSFIELD STORY*

Hercules in New York

(a.k.a. Hercules Goes Bananas; Hercules—The Movie), 1970. Unicorn Pictures in association with Lawrence F. Fabian Productions. *Director:* Arthur Seidelman. *Producers:* Arbor Weisberg and Lawrence F. Fabian. *Screenwriter:* Arthur Seidelman. *Starring:* Arnold Strong (Schwarzenegger), Deborah Loomis, James Karen, Taina Elg, Ernest Graves, Tanny MacDonald, and Arnold Stang. [75 minutes]

Considered a treasure by collectors of cheapie exploitation movies, *Hercules in New York* appears to have been made with so little thought or effort that the film belies its own ambitious pretenses. Originally conceived as both a parody and pastiche of sword-and-sandal epics, it is, in fact, an unfunny one-joke spectacle. The seventy-five minute, made-for-Italian-television movie remains noteworthy today for having first featured an actor who would transcend its limited $300,000 budget to become Hollywood's biggest star.

In his motion-picture debut, Arnold Schwarzenegger—then at the peak of his form as a Mr. Universe winner and Mr. Olympia contestant—fulfilled a lifelong fantasy to play the mythological hero he had embraced as a youth. Billed in Arthur Seidelman's 1970 ultra-low-budget motion picture as "Arnold Strong," the largely unknown Schwarzenegger followed in the footsteps of his boyhood

(Opposite) Fulfilling a lifelong dream, Arnold Schwarzenegger followed in the footsteps of boyhood heroes Steve Reeves and Reg Park as the legendary Hercules. (Poster courtesy Raf Industries, Inc.)

Hercules (Schwarzenegger) drives his chariot through the streets of Manhattan in *Hercules in New York.* (Courtesy Raf Industries, Inc.)

heroes Steve Reeves and Reg Park as the legendary Hercules. His American sponsor and the publisher of *Muscle & Fitness* magazine, Joe Weider, had arranged for the part by convincing producers Lawrence F. Fabian and Arbor Weisberg that Arnold was a well-known European stage actor. Fabian and Weisberg were dubious of the promoter's claims but later hired Schwarzenegger because of his athletically sculpted frame. Although teeming with muscular enthusiasm and youthful vigor, the Austrian body-builder was then given little opportunity to demonstrate his passion for the role. Stripped of his voice (through ineffectual dubbing), most of his clothes, and all of his dignity, Arnold was ineptly paraded through the piece like some cartoon figure.

Joe Santo (Schwarzenegger) embraces receptionist Mary Tate (Sally Field) in a tender moment from Bob Rafelson's *Stay Hungry*.

Even though Schwarzenegger now professes to choose his film roles with extreme care, he still maintains good-natured humor about his first motion-picture performance:

> Imagine coming to this country in late 1968 and then getting a phone call a few months later saying we want you to star in a Hercules movie.... I couldn't believe it, because this is only the kind of things you read about and you say this thing is fake. I was a farm boy coming off the boat from Austria, and here I was asked to star in a film. I thought this was a great beginning, even though I didn't know what I was doing....

Seidelman's fairy-tale plot finds Hercules (Arnold Schwarzenegger), the illegitimate son of Zeus, expelled from Mount Olympus by an angry, jealous god. Catapulted to earth, he lands in New York City

during the psychedelic sixties. Like a poor man's "Crocodile" Dundee, Hercules arrives with no money dressed simply in his native toga. The classic big lug is, at first, bemused by the teeming metropolis, but later he is chased by beautiful women, fight promoters, grizzly bears, gangsters, and an angry Zeus hurling thunderbolts. Eventually, in order to prove his mythological lineage, the Greek hero accepts a challenge to become a professional wrestler. This 250 pounds of lightweight entertainment culminates in a predictable chase through Times Square, with Hercules driving a white chariot.

Struggling with an uninspired script, feeble dialogue, and poor direction (all by Arthur Seidelman), Arnold manages to dominate each scene with his physical presence and innocent charm. His Hercules is a very likable guy, and even though Schwarzenegger had excelled with the "performance" aspect of bodybuilding through his very natural penchant for exhibitionism, his awkwardness in front of a movie camera contributes much to our acceptance of this "stranger in a strange land." While casting him as the mythological hero was a smart move, the producers should have hired an equally skilled screenwriter to adapt one (or all) of the twelve labors of Hercules for the screen. Audiences would have certainly found that story line to be much more palatable than the existing one. Ironically, Lou Ferrigno, one of Arnold's bodybuilding rivals and longtime friends, made his motion-picture debut in a 1983 Hercules movie from Cannon Films that was tailor-made (from the classic stories) for Schwarzenegger.

Hercules in New York is occasionally shown on late-night television, and every time it airs Arnold receives twenty or more calls from friends, laughing hysterically after viewing his abortive film debut. (The film is also currently available on MPI and Unicorn Home Video.)

The Long Goodbye

1973. United Artists/Lion's Gate Entertainment. *Director:* Robert Altman. *Executive producer:* Elliott Kastner. *Producer:* Jerry Bick. *Screenplay:* Leigh Brackett. *Based on the novel by* Raymond Chandler. *Photography:* Vilmos Zsigmond. *Music:* John T. Williams. *Editor:* Lou Lombardo. *Starring:* Elliott Gould, Nina Van Pallandt, Sterling Hayden, Mark Rydell, Henry Gibson, Jim Bouton, David Arkin, Warren Berlinger, and Arnold Schwarzenegger. [111 minutes]

Wearing a strange rubber Batman costume, Santo works out for the forthcoming Mr. Universe Contest.

Three years after debuting on-screen as Hercules, Arnold Schwarzenegger played a mob enforcer in Robert Altman's poorly received adaptation of *The Long Goodbye*. Actor and longtime admirer David Arkin had seen Arnold's disastrous acting debut but nevertheless recommended him to Altman for a decidedly minor role as an underworld hit man. Although many details about "Arnold Strong" were garbled or contradictory, the director hired him sight unseen. Nearly twenty years to the day after the film completed production, Robert Altman recalled that Schwarzenegger "was a likable guy, but I never would have forecast his success."

Based on the detective novel by Raymond Chandler, this ugly, boring film travesty finds Philip Marlowe (Elliott Gould) hired to locate the missing husband of a beautiful but dangerous heiress (Nina Van Pallandt). His investigation takes numerous twists and turns but predictably leads back to the person who hired him. Then, while helping another client who has been accused of murdering his wife, Marlowe is robbed, beaten, and generally terrorized by a group of thugs (including Schwarzenegger) who work for a local gangster.

Robert Altman's *The Long Goodbye* tries to be entertaining and stylish but ultimately fails as both a detective story and a tribute to film noirs of the forties. Even though the director had previously distinguished himself with *M*A*S*H* and *McCabe and Mrs. Miller*, critics of the time period were more or less split in their assessment of his work. *Sight & Sound* wrote that "Altman's fragmentation bomb blows itself up rather than the myths he has said he wants to lay to rest." Michael Billington of *Illustrated London News* complained that the film was "a spit in the eye to a great writer." Of course, since Schwarzenegger's performance was not much more than a bit, he wasn't mentioned by reviewers. Playing the role of a tall, deaf mute, he is really given nothing to do except look big and belligerent. Subsequent roles in *Stay Hungry* and *Pumping Iron* would help change that image and lend credibility to his desire to become a serious actor.

The Long Goodbye is available on video cassette from M-G-M/UA Home Video.

Dissatisfied with his rich existence, Craig Blake (Jeff Bridges) learns the secret of life from bodybuilder Joe Santo.

Bodybuilders parade through the streets and interrupt traffic in Birmingham, Alabama, in order to raise public consciousness.

Stay Hungry

1976. United Artists. *Director:* Bob Rafelson. *Producers:* Harold Schneider and Bob Rafelson. *Screenplay:* Charles Gaines and Bob Rafelson. *Based on the novel by* Charles Gaines. *Photography:* Victor Kemper. *Music:* Bruce Langhorne and Byron Berline. *Editor:* John F. Link II. *Starring:* Jeff Bridges, Sally Field, Arnold Schwarzenegger, R. G. Armstrong, Robert Englund, Woodrow Parfrey, Joanna Cassidy, Ed Begley, Jr., Scatman Crothers, Fannie Flagg, and Robert E. Mosley. [102 minutes]

For several years, Bob Rafelson, the director of *Five Easy Pieces* and *The King of Marvin Gardens*, had been trying to make a film of Charles Gaines's novel *Stay Hungry*, but he had never found the right actor to play the bodybuilder opposite the two other leads. He had screen-tested Sylvester Stallone and other Hollywood musclemen but remained dissatisfied until someone mentioned Arnold Schwarzenegger. "I only fell into acting by accident," the Austrian native told *US* magazine. "Bob Rafelson needed a muscular actor and he couldn't find one. The slim look was the thing then, so he gave bodybuilders screen tests and I got the job."

Craig Blake (Jeff Bridges) and Mary Tate (Sally Field) fall in love, while Santo continues his quest to win the Mr. Universe contest.

In the film, Craig Blake (Jeff Bridges), a rich, disenchanted southerner and heir to property in Alabama, becomes involved in a real-estate deal that will net millions of dollars for a Mafia family. In order to collect, he must convince a gymnasium owner to sell his property so a high rise can be built. Once Craig visits the gym, however, he becomes so fascinated by the earnest bodybuilders and fierce female karate instructors that he soon forgets his underworld deal. One of the bodybuilders, Joe Santo (Arnold)—who likes to work out in a rubber Batman suit—befriends Blake, the poor little rich boy, and introduces him to club receptionist Mary Tate (Sally Field). Blake and Mary fall in love, but their plans to live happily ever after are spoiled by Blake's genteel cousins. (Apparently, Mary is a simple country type who doesn't fit in at a rich family gathering.) Uncle Albert (Woodrow Parfrey) scoffs at Craig's interest in bodybuilding and tells him that girls without breeding will lead him to ruin.

Meanwhile the mob's attempts to destroy the club's air-conditioning unit and muscle in on its little world are met with muscle of a different kind from Santo and his bodybuilding buddies. After parading through the streets of Birmingham to raise public consciousness as to their plight, the musclemen fight it out with their underworld counterparts. In the end Craig turns his back on his privileged family to establish his own life with Mary, and Joe Santo competes for the top prize in the Mr. Universe contest.

Critic Gene Siskel considers *Stay Hungry* his favorite Schwarzenegger film, while Roger Ebert called it a "quirky, funny, oddball movie with unlikely characters." Other reviewers were less generous with their praise and dismissed the piece as confus-

ing and disjointed. Despite its critical and commercial failure, *Stay Hungry* helped establish Schwarzenegger as a legitimate actor. It also won the former body-builder his first Golden Globe Award as Best Newcomer at the 1977 event hosted by the Hollywood Foreign Press Association. (Sylvester Stallone also won a Golden Globe for *Rocky*, and his astounding success convinced Arnold that physically fit men *could* become movie stars.)

Schwarzenegger explained his simple outlook:

When you win the world championships thirteen times, what's new about it. So I was basically very hungry to go on with life and just do something that is more challenging. To start all over again and work towards it is what makes life interesting. At that time Bob Rafelson was looking for somebody for *Stay Hungry* who had a Mr. Universe physique. He looked at many bodybuilders and also actors that may also have that kind of physique. He couldn't find anybody. And then I read with him, and he liked that. Then I did a screen test which he liked and hired me for the film. When the film came out, I got good reviews and that gave me the confidence to pursue a career in motion pictures.

Stay Hungry is currently available on videocassette from CBS/Fox Home Video.

The Streets of San Francisco

1977. ABC Television in association with Quinn Martin Productions. *Executive Producer:* Quinn Martin. *Director:* George McGowan. *Based on characters from the novel* Poor, Poor Ophelia *by* Carolyn Weston. *Starring:* Karl Malden, Richard Hatch, Diana Muldaur, Larry Mahon, and Bert Freed. *Guest Star:* Arnold Schwarzenegger. [60 minutes]

Through a mutual acquaintance, Arnold Schwarzenegger got a part in an episode of ABC's *The Streets of San Francisco* entitled "Dead Lift" (5/5/77). Mike Stone (Karl Malden), a twenty-three-year veteran of the force assigned to the Bureau of Inspectors Division of the San Francisco Police Department, and his college-educated partner, Inspector Dan Robbins (Richard Hatch), investigate a series of brutal murders of young women. They interview several suspects, including a European body-builder (Arnold Schwarzenegger) who has come to

Schwarzenegger pumps iron in the stylish documentary *Pumping Iron* (Courtesy Cinema Archives)

Based on the popular book of the same name, *Pumping Iron* is an intelligent and lively documentary about the subculture of bodybuilding. (Courtesy Cinema Archives)

America after winning some important contests. As the story unfolds, Stone and Robbins discover that the bodybuilder, unable to endure rejection, has killed any woman who dared refuse his advances. Arnold's performance is somewhat mediocre, considering his recent experience with *Stay Hungry*, but television executives were so pleased to learn that he could act before a camera that his modest appearance led to commentary for CBS Sports.

Pumping Iron

1977. Cinema Five. *Directors:* George Butler and Robert Fior. *Producers:* George Butler and Charles Gaines. *Screenplay:* Charles Gaines. *Starring:* Arnold Schwarzenegger, Mike Katz, Franco Columbu, and Lou Ferrigno. [85 minutes]

Building upon his success in *Stay Hungry*, Schwarzenegger played himself—one year later—in the stylish documentary *Pumping Iron*. The most famous motion picture of its time about physical fitness featured an intelligently written script, impressive direction, colorful locales as well as equally colorful characters, and sprightly good humor. But more important, the film introduced a charming and talented twenty-nine-year-old Austrian bodybuilder to millions of filmgoers around the world.

Based on the book of the same name, this lively documentary about the bodybuilding subculture follows behind-the-scenes action at the Mr. Olympia competition. The focus is on several competitors, including Franco Columbu, Lou Ferrigno (in pre–*Incredible Hulk* days), and Schwarzenegger, building genuine suspense as to who will win the titles of Mr. Universe and Mr. Olympia. By showing the tortuous demands and regimen required for world-class champions, *Pumping Iron* avoids the considerable temptation of making bodybuilding and those dedicated to the sport seem altogether grotesque. These muscle*men* may be exceptionally motivated, they may spend hundreds of hours lifting weights or watching their diets as they constantly strive toward perfection, but they are nonetheless men. They have the same fears, ambitions, and desires of other men. The documentary clearly illustrates both sides of the sport of bodybuilding, from the grueling training rituals to the more personal and intimate human side.

Arnold readily acknowledges his human side, in one of the more popular scenes, by comparing the

Arnold Schwarzenegger achieved celebrity status through George Butler and Charles Gaines's *Pumping Iron*. (Courtesy Cinema Archives)

effects of oxygen-rich blood racing through his biceps to a sexual orgasm. "The most satisfying feeling you can get in a gym is the pump," he confesses to the camera. "Muscles get a really tight feeling as blood rushes in...." He also admits to having a very large sexual appetite, decidedly heterosexual, and a penchant for playing practical jokes. Whereas the documentary compels us to watch Schwarzenegger perform, it also affords a deeply personal glimpse into the real man. Arnold is more than (using his own words) "a body sculptor"; he is an enchanting, sardonic, and humorous talent.

During the early seventies, even though Schwarzenegger had become a legend among his

Arnold Schwarzenegger appeared in his only Western to date,
The Villain, as the "handsome stranger," opposite Ann-Margret.
(Courtesy Viacom)

peers, bodybuilding was still an obscure and largely misunderstood sport. However, at the 1972 Mr. Olympia contest in Brooklyn, the Austrian muscleman was introduced to a free-lance photographer for *Oui* magazine who wanted to change the public's perception of bodybuilders. George Butler and his partner, writer Charles Gaines, suggested that Arnold be featured in a book (and possibly a documentary) about bodybuilding. "I wasn't interested in dispelling the image of bodybuilders that some people had," Arnold said in publicity material released in conjunction with the project. "I just told them what bodybuilders are and let them draw their own conclusions." After carefully considering their proposal and after much deliberation, Schwarzenegger finally agreed.

Butler recalled in a later interview:

It was particularly hard for Arnold because he was treated as a complete freak. Schwarzenegger was in a sport no one liked, or even understood, and he had a physique that people were repulsed by. For instance, if I was sitting opposite him at a restaurant, I could see people at the tables behind laughing at him.

Of course he noticed it, but he was never impolite.

Two years later, after enduring all manner of criticism from the press, which maintained the stereotypical impression that bodybuilders were gay, *Pumping Iron* was finally published by Simon and Schuster and became an immediate bestseller. The sport of bodybuilding was vindicated, and Arnold Schwarzenegger took advantage of his newfound notoriety by reinventing his public image. The documentary debuted three years later at the 1977 Cannes Film Festival, and Arnold's performance convinced many of his harshest critics that he was more than simply a gifted bodybuilder. *Time* magazine critic Richard Schickel, one of the first to recognize Arnold's cinematic appeal, wrote, "Cool, shrewd, and boyishly charming, he exudes the easy confidence of a man who has always known he will be a star of some kind...." Under the tutelage of Butler and Gaines, Schwarzenegger took ballet lessons. His likeness was captured by world-renowned photographers, he was painted by noted artists, and he was featured at important social events. By the end of the decade, the Austrian muscleman had been transformed into the ultimate action hero. All he needed now was the right vehicle in which to demonstrate his newly created persona, but he would have to wait five long years and suffer one disastrous film after another until *Conan the Barbarian* made him a star.

The acclaimed *Pumping Iron* is available on RCA/Columbia Pictures Home Video. A second feature, entitled *Pumping Iron II: The Women* (1985), did not have the benefit of the Schwarzenegger presence.

The Villain

(a.k.a. *Cactus Jack*) 1979. Columbia Pictures in association with Rastar. *Director:* Hal Needham. *Executive Producer:* Paul Maslansky. *Producer:* Mort Engelberg. *Screenplay:* Robert G. Kane. *Photography:* Bobby Byrne. *Music:* Bill Justis. *Editor:* Walter Hanneman. *Starring:* Kirk Douglas, Ann-Margret, Arnold Schwarzenegger, Paul Lynde, Foster Brooks, Ruth Buzzi, Jack Elam, Mel Tillis, and Strother Martin [89 minutes]

One of the worst films of the seventies, *The Villain* was an overextended, tedious, and crudely embarrassing spoof of the western genre. Hal Needham, the stunt coordinator turned director who scored big with the *Smokey and the Bandit* movies, had always dreamed of making a comic western like *Cat Ballou* and assembled some of the top stuntmen to accomplish that task. He also convinced Rastar to advance him a sizable sum of money ($3 million) to film on location in Tucson, Arizona. Regrettably, his three principal performers, including Arnold Schwarz-enegger, were forced to take a backseat to all the mindless, overstated action.

Cactus Jack (Kirk Douglas), an incompetent outlaw, arrives in a small southwestern town for the purpose of robbing the bank; instead he rides from one

disaster to the next. Another visitor to the town, referred to simply as the Handsome Stranger (Schwarzenegger), has been named marshal by the fearful inhabitants and asked to bring the "villain" to justice. Accompanying him in his one-horse buckboard is the town whore, Charming Jones (Ann-Margret). She also has a score to settle with Jack. The three encounter crazy Native Americans (led by Paul Lynde as Chief Nervous Elk), wild buffalo, runaway trains, and all manner of natural disasters along the way.

No doubt amusing in its conception, the film fails completely in its attempt to superimpose classic comic stunts (drawn from "Road Runner" and "Bugs Bunny" cartoons) onto live-action situations. The sequences, though impeccably staged, are simply unfunny and highly predictable, and the picture is also spoiled by poor timing, ludicrous scripting, and tiresome racial stereotypes. Although Needham was quick to rebuff critics for not understanding his tongue-in-cheek approach, that did not absolve him of guilt. He *alone* was responsible for this clumsy farce.

Kirk Douglas, Ann-Margret, and Arnold Schwarzenegger star in *The Villain.* (Courtesy Viacom)

Earlier that year, Arnold Schwarzenegger had turned down $200,000 to endorse tires and declined the part of Mae West's muscleman in the 1979 film *Sextette* in order to play opposite Ann-Margret and Kirk Douglas. However, when Schwarzenegger arrived in Tucson in October 1978 and was given the revised script, he was dismayed. Although he knew the motion picture would probably be a disaster, he reluctantly accepted the $275,000 for his part as the Handsome Stranger, a cowboy who prefers the company of his horse to women. Hal Needham remembers that

> Arnold was an absolute delight to work with. He's very funny and a nice guy. He is very professional and eager to learn. He played a straight man to Ann-Margret with all that cleavage. I think he did that very well.

Unfortunately, Schwarzenegger's only bit of business was to sit stone-faced on a buckboard beside Ann-Margret. His boyish charm, physical presence, and natural sense of humor are totally wasted by Needham; even worse, Arnold's movements on camera seem awkward, somewhat clumsy, and tentative.

Several critics who had praised his work in *Stay Hungry* and *Pumping Iron* not only were disappointed with Schwarzenegger but actually blamed him for the motion picture's failure. Janet Maslin of the *New York Times* identified him as "a weight on the movie," while *Newsweek*'s David Ansen quipped that Arnold's horse had more acting ability. A less caustic *Variety* critic wrote that "Arnold Schwarzenegger shows little development as an actor since *Stay Hungry*." But in fairness to him, reviewer Paul Taylor denounced Needham's direction, proclaiming that "timing is entirely absent from this limp, laughless fiasco, as is any evidence of imagination...desperation is the keynote." All reviews aside, Arnold knew he would have considerable ground to make up if audiences were to again take him seriously.

The Villain, which shares nothing in common with the 1971 British film starring Richard Burton, is currently on videocassette from RCA/Columbia Home Video.

Scavenger Hunt

1979. 20th Century-Fox. *Director:* Michael Schultz. *Executive Producer:* Melvin Simon. *Screenplay:* Steven A. Vail and Henry Harper. *Photography:* Ken Lamkin. *Music:* Billy Goldenberg. *Editor:* Christopher Holmes. *Starring:* Richard Benjamin, Ruth Gordon, James Coco, Scatman Crothers, Cloris Leachman, Cleavon Little, Roddy McDowall, Robert Morley, Richard Mulligan, Tony Randall, Willie Aames, Meat Loaf, Carol Wayne, Dirk Benedict, Vincent Price, and Arnold Schwarzenegger. [116 minutes]

After the critical beating he took for *The Villain*, Schwarzenegger agreed to appear in a cameo role in *Scavenger Hunt* without realizing he was repeating the same mistake. Eccentric game manufacturer Vincent Price wills $200 million to the member of his family who can collect the greatest number of useless objects on a list. Actors Richard Benjamin, Ruth Gordon, James Coco, Scatman Crothers, Cloris Leachman, Cleavon Little, and many others appear in brief, embarrassing roles in this largely absurd comedy. Schwarzenegger himself is seen briefly as an eager gym instructor turned masseur named Lars. Producer Melvin Simon hoped audiences would remember the screwball comedies of the thirties or Stanley Kramer's *It's a Mad Mad Mad Mad World*, but instead they wisely stayed away from the film *Variety* called "loud, obnoxious, and above all unfunny."

Scavenger Hunt is available on videocassette from CBS/Fox Home Video.

The Jayne Mansfield Story

(a.k.a. *Jayne Mansfield: A Symbol of the '50s*), 1980. CBS Television in association with Alan Landsburg Productions. *Director:* Dick Lowry. *Executive Producer:* Alan Landsburg. *Producers:* Linda Otto and Joan Barrett. *Teleplay:* Charles Dennis and Nancy Gayle. *Based on the book* Jayne Mansfield and the American Fifties *by* Martha Sexton. *Photography:* Paul Lohmann. *Music:* Jimmie Haskell. *Editor:* Corky Ehlers. *Starring:* Loni Anderson, Arnold Schwarzenegger, Raymond Buktenica, Kathleen Lloyd, G. D. Spradlin, and Dave Shelley. [100 minutes]

Arnold Schwarzenegger received his first real exposure to a large audience on network television (*The Streets of San Francisco* and commentary on CBS Sports, notwithstanding) by starring opposite Loni Anderson in *The Jayne Mansfield Story* (aired 10/29/80). To date it is his only made-for-television movie as an actor. While he was waiting for the start of filming on *Conan the Barbarian*, he had been contractually prohibited by Dino De Laurentiis from appearing in any motion pictures. But the legal document did not prohibit him from appearing on the small screen. His decision to play Jayne Mansfield's husband, Mickey Hargitay, a former Mr. Universe (1956) whom Arnold had met prior to shooting, was a smart one. Although the film was dismissed by critics as being factually questionable, Arnold received high marks for a charming and sensitive performance that demonstrated good range.

Like so many other biographical films, *The Jayne Mansfield Story* begins with the central character's death in 1967 (in a car accident outside Biloxi, Mississippi), then flashes through key events in Jayne Mansfield's life, thanks to the remembrances of her second husband, Mickey Hargitay. His narrative actually begins just prior to their meeting, when Jayne, with a five-year-old daughter in tow, was still waitressing in Los Angeles. Several days later, after getting photographed with a Hollywood chimp, she forces herself on talent agent Bob Garrett (Ray Buktenica) and demands he find her a job in motion pictures. Jayne soon learns that most casting agents are looking for a blond sex queen to take Marilyn Monroe's place. With her genius IQ of 162 and intense ambition, Jayne decides to exploit her body until she becomes famous. She quickly captures media attention with her brazen sexuality and lands a starring role in the long-running stage play *Will Success Spoil Rock Hunter?* (She repeated the role in the film version.)

Mickey is first introduced to Jayne while he is appearing in the Latin Quarter in New York as one of Mae West's boys (who, like all bodybuilders, were merely treated as meat) and she is performing on Broadway. The two immediately hit it off and begin a tumultuous love affair that would last through the fifties and sixties. Regrettably, while her star continues to rise, Hargitay's was already in decline. Mansfield is very quickly acknowledged as the most fabulous body in the world, but she persists in making one mediocre appearance after another in B-movies that never make money (except *The Girl Can't Help It* in 1956). Refusing to accept her typecasting as a dumb blonde, she turns to alcohol to drown her sorrows. For a woman who built a career as a great body with boundless ambition and a slightly higher intelligence, Jayne tries numerous stunts to start over. But ultimately she is reduced to being a second-rate stripper in a bar in Biloxi.

Even though the television movie was not well received critically, viewers had their first real opportunity to see Arnold Schwarzenegger in action. And to his credit, he turned in a remarkable performance, holding his own opposite Loni Anderson as the blond

Arnold Schwarzenegger received his first real exposure to a large audience on network television by starring as Mickey Hargitay opposite Loni Anderson in *The Jayne Mansfield Story*. (Courtesy Alan Landsberg Productions)

bombshell of the fifties. Ironically, the film also provided a strange parallel to Arnold's earlier screen career. Like Jayne Mansfield, he relied on his superior body to secure film roles, hoping to use his success (and self-promotional skills) to catapult him to superstardom. Schwarzenegger commented about what he had learned from Jayne Mansfield's career:

I learned that you have to establish yourself in an area where there is no one else. Then you have to create a need for yourself, build yourself up. While their empire goes on, slowly, without realizing it, build your own little fortress. And all of a sudden it's too late for them to do anything about it. And they have to come to you because you have what they

37

want. Because you're stable and your films always make money for the producer or the studio.

He was soon to put that simple philosophy to the test with *Conan the Barbarian.*

Other Projects

The Comeback

1980. *Director and Executive Producer:* Paul Graham. *Writer and Editor:* Geoff Bennett. *Starring:* Arnold Schwarzenegger. [78 minutes]

The Comeback (1980), not to be confused with the 1978 British horror film with American singer Jack Jones, was a lackluster, biased account of Arnold Schwarzenegger's attempt to win the 1980 Mr. Olympia title after he had retired from the sport.

Following five years away from competition, Arnold won the title for the seventh time in a contest some entrants claim was "rigged." Filmed in Australia against the backdrop of the competition, it was an attempt by Paul Graham and Geoff Bennett to make the seventy-eight-minute semidocumentary look like *Pumping Iron,* but it failed to capitalize on Schwarzenegger's worldwide fame and success.

Shape Up With Arnold

1982. Fitness video produced by Video Associates. [85 minutes] Video Associates produced an eighty-five-minute fitness tape entitled *Shape Up With Arnold* to capitalize on the home-video workout craze made into a multi-million-dollar industry by Jane Fonda. The video offers fitness instruction and three complete workouts, with weights and without, for men and women as directed and choreographed by Arnold Schwarzenegger. Fun—and perfectly timed to capitalize on the bodybuilder's big-screen debut as *Conan the Barbarian.*

Schwarzenegger's big break in motion pictures came as *Conan the Barbarian* in the Dino De Laurentiis production. (Courtesy Universal Pictures)

Two

ARNOLD THE BARBARIAN

Conan the Barbarian

1982. Universal Pictures in association with Dino De Laurentiis and Edward R. Pressman Productions. *Director:* John Milius. *Executive Producers:* D. Constantine Conte and Edward R. Pressman. *Producers:* Buzz Feitshans and Raffaella De Laurentiis. *Associate Producer:* Ed Summer. *Screenplay:* John Milius and Oliver Stone. *Based on characters created by* Robert E. Howard. *Photography:* Duke Callaghan. *Music:* Basil Poledouris. *Production Designer:* Ron Cobb. *Editor:* C. Timothy O'Meara. *Starring:* Arnold Schwarzenegger, James Earl Jones, Sandahl Bergman, Max Von Sydow, Valerie Quennessen, Gerry Lopez, Mako, Cassandra Gaviola, Ben Davidson, and William Smith. Released in United States on May 14, 1982. [129 minutes]

Conan the Barbarian, the film version of the pulp legend by Robert E. Howard, marked a decisive step forward in Arnold Schwarzenegger's career. By combining what he had learned about acting with the perfect screen vehicle (for his bodybuilder's frame), Arnold emerged as a charismatic film personality. The motion picture, which eventually grossed over $100 million and established him as a worthy action star, also blended the resources of Dino De Laurentiis, the directorial skills of John Milius, the celebrated set designs of Ron Cobb, an inspired script by Oliver Stone (who later would go on to bigger things as a director) and Milius, and the dedication of a cast and crew that labored long and hard under very difficult circumstances to create a wonderfully orchestrated piece of filmmaking that ranks as one of the best sword-and-sorcery movies ever.

Schwarzenegger told the *New York Post* in a 1982 interview:

This picture is a winner because Conan is a winner. Conan is a man of honor. His whole life revolves around strength—strength of body, mind, and spirit. He's the kind of person an audience can identity with. He never gives up. I think women appreciate Conan's vulnerability. He's an innocent, in a way. He doesn't win every time. He's not a Superman or a Hercules. Kids like the fact that he's strong. He's a fighting machine. Some other people respect him for his mental strength. He has a goal of revenge and he follows through with it. In the long run, there's no way he can ever lose.

The Screen Story

The motion picture opens with a shot of Conan as the sixty-year-old king of Aquilonia (Schwarzenegger) and a simple, off-screen narrative by Akiro, the Wizard of the Mounds (Mako).

Between the time when the oceans drank Atlantis and the rise of the sons of Ayras, there was an age undreamed of.... And unto this, Conan, destined to bear the jeweled crown of Aquilonia upon a troubled brow, came. It is I, his chronicler, who alone can tell thee of this saga. Let me tell you of the days of high adventure....

Through the history of mankind, the times that are most recorded in mythology and song are those of great deeds and fantastic adventures. Such a time was the Hyborian Age.

Cassandra Gaviola, as a mysterious woman who offers Conan warmth in her home, turns into an evil succubus.

In the small Cimmerian village, which is Conan's boyhood home, the Master (William Smith) forges a great sword in his blacksmith shop. Later, high atop a peak that overlooks the snow-covered huts, the Master bequeaths the mighty weapon to his son and imparts the Riddle of Steel. Young Conan (played by Jorge Sanz) must trust no one—not men, not women, not beasts—only his sword! The boy does not fully understand his father's words; but when his peaceful village is overrun by Vanir warriors, led by Thulsa Doom (James Earl Jones), he soon realizes the power that the mighty sword commands. His father wields the weapon with great expertise and manages to bring down many of Doom's fearsome raiders before he is ultimately killed. His mother, too, is murdered, decapitated by the evil sorcerer with Conan's sword. Filled with rage, young Conan memorizes the Vanir standard (two snakes coming together over a black sun) and vows that someday he will avenge his parents' murder.

Young Conan is led away, with the other children, to a life of slavery. He endures fifteen years of agony, first chained to the Wheel of Pain (an enormous grinding stone), then as a gladiator, while managing to forge a magnificent body and an indomitable spirit. Though he becomes victorious as a "pit fighter" and gains great wealth and riches for his owner, he begins to enjoy the crowds "who greet him with howls of lust and fury" for he knows his sense of worth. His victories soon can not easily be counted, and he is taken to the East to learn about swords, language, writing, philosophy, and women. When asked what is best in life, Conan replies, "To crush your enemies, to see them driven before you, and to hear the lamentations of the women."

Freed suddenly one day by his owner, Conan wanders through his strange Hyborian world in search of purpose and his own identity. Then, chased into a cave by wolves, he comes face-to-face with the skeletal body of his god Crom—actually the remains of some Atlantean king buried in a ceremonial tomb. All his life he has been told that Crom lives beneath the earth, and he views his chance meeting with the deity as having great significance in his life. He approaches "the thing in the crypt" and takes the slumbering god's sword. With his newly acquired Atlantean steel, Conan dispatches the wolves waiting outside the cave and runs headlong into their spiritual keeper, the Wolf Witch (Cassandra Gaviola). He takes shelter and warmth from her, but when she attempts to drain his strength (like an evil succubus), Conan throws the witch into the fire.

Following the Wolf Witch's demise, Conan flees along with her half-frozen captive Subotai (Gerry Lopez), a Mongol and a thief. The two warriors strike up a quick friendship and embark on a long series of adventures that take them across the exotic and primitive world of Hyboria. They eventually arrive in Shadizar, where an evil snake cult maintains control over the populace. (Conan believes the sorcerer who killed his parents and imprisoned him may be the leader of the cult.) Deciding to penetrate the Tower of Serpents, Conan and Subotai happen upon Valeria (Sandahl Bergman), queen of thieves, who is after the richest jewel in all Hyboria, the Eye of the Serpent. The two join forces with her and penetrate the snake-ritual chamber where Rexor (Ben Davidson), Thulsa Doom's henchman, is conducting human sacrifices. Just before all hell breaks loose, Conan snatches the priceless jewel from under the watchful eyes of a monstrous snake and hacks the thirty-six-foot-long creature to pieces.

After stealing the gem, the trio fight their way to the top of the tower and then, with their pockets stuffed with loot, repair to a local tavern. Conan, Subotai, and Valeria are soon arrested by the palace guard and brought before King Osric (Max Von Sydow). The aging king, who lost his daughter (Valerie Quennessen) to Thulsa Doom and his snake

Conan the Barbarian destroys a giant snake while attempting to steal a fabulous gem from the Tower of the Serpent.

cult, convinced by the trio's tenacity and daring that they are the only ones who can free her from the evil sorcerer, offers them a handsome reward to bring the princess back to him alive. Valeria and Subotai want nothing to do with Doom, but Conan knows that his god Crom expects the warrior to exact revenge for his parents and his village.

In the morning Conan leaves his companions behind to follow his destiny. That destiny leads to prehistoric burial mounds, tended by his chronicler Akiro (Mako), and Doom's own forbidding stronghold, the Mountain of Power. The Cimmerian infiltrates a large group of pilgrims on their way to the sorcerer's fortress, but because he makes an unlikely convert, Conan's disguise is revealed. He is captured by Doom's guards and taken to the Fountain Plaza, where he receives a savage beating at the hands of Rexor and Thorgrim (Sven Ole Thorsen). Doom then questions him about the stolen gems and his dead snake, but Conan only displays contempt for the man who murdered his parents and destroyed his village. At the sorcerer's whim, the Cimmerian is crucified on the Tree of Woe. Battered and bruised, nearly dying from his wounds, Conan is rescued by Subotai.

Conan is brought back to the mounds, where the Wizard calls upon the spirits of light and darkness to restore the barbarian to health. The cost is high, for it requires Valeria to offer her life in exchange for his. As Conan recovers, Valeria kisses him and promises that she will return from the dead, if necessary, to fight at his side.

Once he is fully recovered, Conan and his two camouflaged companions penetrate the mazelike interior of the Mountain of Power to rescue the Princess of Shadizar, being held captive in the Orgy Chamber by Thulsa Doom and his henchman. Subotai and Valeria decide to create a diversion while the Cimmerian battles Rexor and Thorgrim to the death in order to free the young woman. During the subsequent battle, Valeria manages to snatch the Princess from the evil clutches of Doom as he metamorphoses into a monstrous snake, and Conan brings the walls of the Orgy Chamber tumbling down. After escaping from the Mountain of Power, Conan and his cohorts must still battle Doom's Neanderthal allies before they can carry the Princess to safety. Valeria is mortally wounded and dies in Conan's arms, again vowing to return if he ever needs her help. In true pagan traditions, he burns her body on a funeral pyre.

His first love dead, Conan chains the Princess to an altar of stone that overlooks the mounds and awaits the hordes of Thulsa Doom. Subotai and the Wizard stand alongside their grieving friend as he prays to Crom for victory. A rousing battle ensues in which the three warriors stand up against a cavalry charge of twenty-five mounted riders among the ruins of the mounds. Slowly, deliberately, savagely, Conan, Subotai, and the Wizard take the raiders out one by one. During the battle Conan is caught between two warriors, and Valeria appears from the dead long enough to distract them. Doom realizes that the battle is lost and tries to kill the Princess with a snake arrow, but Subotai manages to deflect its deadly sting.

Surviving the attack, Conan leaves the Princess and a wounded Subotai in the care of the Wizard and follows the evil sorcerer back to his Mountain of Power to confront him before his followers. Conan takes back his father's (now broken) sword and beheads Doom. The Cimmerian then throws the head into the cult gathering before burning the massive structure to the ground. His revenge complete, Conan returns to the mounds for the Princess and Subotai.

So did Conan return the wayward daughter of King Osric to her home. And having no further concern, he and his companions sought adventure in the West. Many wars and feuds did Conan fight. Honor and fear were heaped upon his name. In time he became a king by his own hand…but that is another story.

Production Details

Conan the Barbarian began its long road to the screen in the imagination of its highly gifted creator, Robert E. Howard. Born in 1906 in Peaster, Texas, to a wealthy physician, Howard drifted into writing as a profession after failing as a farmer, tailor, and public stenographer. As a young man who kept mostly to himself, Howard had been the target of continual harassment from a local Texas bully and used a regi-

Rescued from the Tree of Woe by his love Valeria (Sandahl Bergman), Conan must undergo a strange religious ritual in order to regain his strength.

Valeria and Subotai (Gerry Lopez) battle the demons who attempt to steal the soul of Conan.

men of exercise and weight lifting to bulk out his six-foot frame. His experiences as a loner dealing with the bully ultimately led him to create one of his most popular characters, Conan the Cimmerian. Muscular, quick, incredibly ruthless, the thief who became king was the central figure in eighteen highly popular heroic fantasies set against the distant, glittering Hyborian Age. With "The Phoenix and the Sword," first published in the December 1932 issue of *Weird Tales*, Howard launched the sword-and-sorcery genre. Stories like "The Scarlet Citadel," "The Tower of the Elephant," "Black Colossus," and "Red Nails" not only helped expand the legend of Conan but also made Howard a small fortune. He tried to introduce other characters, including Solomon Kane, King Kull, Bran Mak Morn, and Red Sonja, but the Cimmerian remained the audience favorite. Howard might have continued writing Conan adventures had his semi-invalid mother not fallen into a coma. Intensely devoted, the thirty-year-old writer could not face a life without her and in 1936 committed suicide a few hours before she passed away.

The Conan stories did not die with Robert Howard; rather, they inspired other writers, for example, L. Sprague de Camp and Lin Carter, to keep the tradition alive through pastiches or completions of eight unfinished stories. In the mid-sixties, Conan reached a mass-market audience with the first paperback publications, featuring illustrations by artist Frank Frazetta. In the early seventies the Cimmerian had become such a cult figure that Marvel Comics decided to release the comic series *Conan the Barbarian*, illustrated by Barry Windsor-Smith, and later *The Sword of Conan* graphic magazine.

Interest in a film version of *Conan the Barbarian* began in 1970 when Lin Carter announced that negotiations were in process to bring the Cimmerian to the screen; unfortunately, Lancer Books, which published the Conan stories, was forced into bankruptcy, and all legal rights to authorize a film were tied up in several lawsuits. Carter lost interest and turned to writing stories about his own hero (Jandar of Callisto), but Ed Summer, the owner of a New York–based comic-book store, remained very enthusiastic about the project. So enthusiastic, in fact, he introduced film producer Edward Pressman to the Frazetta-illustrated novels and the Marvel Comics series. The soft-spoken movie producer and heir to the Pressman Toy Company was suitably impressed by the Conan stories to make several inquiries into the property. However, both he and Summer agreed that the biggest stumbling block wouldn't be the lawsuit but finding the right person to play Conan. That problem was quickly solved when Pressman attended a rough-cut screening of *Pumping Iron* and beheld five-time Mr. Universe and seven-time Mr. Olympia winner Arnold Schwarzenegger for the first time.

While Edward Pressman authorized literary agent Henry Morrison to purchase the rights to Conan (no matter what the cost or legal entanglement) and Summer began scripting a suitable scenario with Marvel Comics editor Roy Thomas, the producer arranged to meet Schwarzenegger at a health-food store in Hollywood for a high-powered lunch. He needed Schwarzenegger as Conan if the film was going to work. Arnold Schwarzenegger later remarked:

> People are coming up to me all the time pretending they're producers, and at first I didn't take Ed too seriously. But he gradually convinced me that I was right for the role and, more importantly, that he had the financial backing to get the film off the ground.

Pressman finally agreed to Schwarzenegger's terms, and the legal entanglements, which had prevented the first film version from reaching the screen, soon dropped away, with the principals agreeing to take a percentage of the motion picture's gross. Summer and Thomas completed an original screenplay (not based on any of Howard's stories or the subsequent pastiches), and John Buscema, one of Conan's comic artists, roughed out a number of preproduction drawings based on their script. A tentative budget of $2.5 million was set, and Pressman began shopping for the backing of a major studio. But in 1977, prior to the release of *Star Wars*, not a single studio was interested in committing funds to an unknown project like *Conan the Barbarian*. Pressman and Summer were crushed by the studios' lack of foresight and searched for independent financing.

Finally, Paramount Pictures, while sketching plans for a big-budget *Star Trek* film, acknowledged a tentative interest in the genre and authorized several million dollars in front money to Pressman for a new screenplay by their contracted writer Oliver Stone. Stone had just won an Academy Award for his script of *Midnight Express* and had proven to be both an accomplished writer and director with the 1974 horror film *Seizure*. Pressman reluctantly agreed, much

Conan, Valeria, and Subotai break into Doom's fortress and witness a sight incredible decadence....

to the dismay of Summer and Thomas, and Stone began work on his own film version. Basing his script on Howard's "Black Colossus," "Rogues in the House," and "A Witch Shall Be Born," Stone came up with a high-caliber effort that nicely reflected the violent Hyborian Age. He introduced Thulsa Doom (a character from Howard's King Kull stories) as the chief villain and, with his own share of bizarre fantasy touches, placed emphasis on Conan as a swaggering soldier of fortune and a humorless adventurer. Regrettably, Stone's script also departed from the familiar stories by placing the Hyborian Age in a postholocaust future. Once Pressman and production designer Ron Cobb reviewed the finished product, the producer's modest budget of $2.5 million mushroomed to a whopping $40 million.

Many directors, including Alan Parker, Ralph Bakshi, John Frankenheimer, Ridley Scott, and even Oliver Stone, were considered for the project; but Edward Pressman finally settled on John Milius, thanks to the encouragement of Summer and Cobb. Like Schwarzenegger, Milius was an imposing personality whose talent as a writer and director had been etched out in rugged action films featuring men in conflict. He had previously written and directed *Dillinger*, *The Wind and the Lion*, and *Big Wednesday* and provided the screenplays for *Dirty Harry*, *Jeremiah Johnson*, *Magnum Force*, and *Apocalypse Now*. Milius was the perfect choice to bring Howard's exotic world and violent hero to the

...Doom's decadent orgy.

big screen. Although Milius had already committed to directing the mountain-man epic *Half of the Sky* for Dino De Laurentiis, the Italian producer agreed to release him from his contract for a piece of the Conan pie. By this time, Paramount had become so involved in *Star Trek: The Motion Picture* that it had lost interest in the Conan project, and De Laurentiis used his influence to arrange a distribution deal with Universal Pictures (which brought $17.5 million to the film and another $12 million in advertising).

Because John Milius was a strong-willed perfectionist and an accomplished screenwriter, he extended Oliver Stone's script beyond the simple story that was written. Stone mentioned Conan's origin, but Milius chose to shoot the first third of the film as a full-fledged "origins" story. By using a series of lap dissolves, he planned to show the growth of Conan from young boy to man, first with his father, then later chained to the Wheel of Pain. Another series of dissolves would depict Conan's training as a gladiator, from a raw recruit to a seasoned fighter. Milius also felt that the early pit-fighting scenes were inspired by Howard and highly reminiscent of the art of Frank Frazetta. Three drafts and nearly two years later, he was finally ready to begin work on *Conan the Barbarian*.

During the two-year interim, contractually bound to *Conan* and not able to take on any roles without the permission of Pressman or De Laurentiis, Schwarzenegger continued to build his body. (The Italian producer had briefly flirted with the idea of casting Arnold as the lead in *Flash Gordon* but later chose Sam J. Jones for the part.) Schwarzenegger remained philosophical about the loss and concentrated on Conan. He told reporters in 1982:

I had a good combination of the acting and physical development and athletic abilities, and they were the requirements for the job. Conan wasn't supposed to have a very healthy-looking body in the sense of a perfect body, with muscles just sticking out everywhere. So it was a matter of toning down the muscle size and making it look like the muscles were there from hard work rather than from organized training—there is a difference in physique. So I had to reshape my body by doing more running, bicycling, and other athletic activities and tone down the weight training to about an hour a day and train with lighter weights rather than heavy weights.

He also spent numerous hours learning how to sword fight from master Kiyoshi Yamazaki, training with the samurai sword and kendo sticks. He studied horseback riding and rock climbing and practiced lines from the first draft with an acting coach. By the time Milius had completed the script, Arnold's 250-pound frame was scaled down to a leaner, more sharply defined 228.

Before the cameras could begin rolling, however, a great deal of imaginative planning had to go into *Conan the Barbarian*. The bulk of designing and coordinating the overall look of the Hyborian Age fell on Ron Cobb's shoulders. Cobb had already produced hundreds of drawings and sketches for Pressman during the early stages, and when he returned to the production, Ron brought a much more sophisticated look. Born in 1937, the young Los Angeles native learned to draw and paint on his own. After a short stint in the service, Cobb became a political cartoonist and free-lance designer in 1974 for John Carpenter's *Dark Star*. He later contributed alien designs to the famous cantina sequence in *Star Wars*, redesigned the interior of the mother ship in Spielberg's *Close Encounters of the Third Kind: The Special Edition*, and provided extensive design work for *Alien*, including the look of the Nostromo. Prior to being assigned as production designer for *Conan*, he had worked briefly on *Raiders of the Lost Ark*. He said:

> My basic attitude in designing *Conan* was to undo history. We wanted the film to have a realistic, historical look, but at the same time we were always trying to invent our own fantasy history.

Ed Summer recalled:

> Ron Cobb worked wonders in designing the sets. He used natural formations as the basis of his sets as much as possible. There were some sets that were built into a niche in a rock. On the Wolf Witch set, he used a bizarre stone formation to great advantage. The mound set was built near the ocean to make use of some incredible sand suns. When you see the finished film, you get the impression that you're seeing massive expanses, but really, it's just Ron being clever.

With most of the other details (related to location scouting, design, and set construction) falling into place, the final step in preproduction was filling the motion picture's key roles. While Arnold Schwarz-

enegger had been cast from the beginning as Conan, various other casting suggestions were made then later discarded. Several Universal executives wanted to see Raquel Welch as Valeria and Sean Connery as Thulsa Doom. Persis Khambatta was, at one time prior to her role in *Star Trek: The Motion Picture*, considered as the Princess, and John Huston was seen as either the Wizard of the Mounds or Thulsa Doom.

Ultimately John Milius settled on a cast that did not bring many preconceived notions with their performances.

Sandahl Bergman, who at the time had little film experience beyond a brief appearance in Bob Fosse's *All That Jazz*, was chosen to play Valeria, Queen of Thieves. The character had been modeled after both the lead in Howard's "Red Nails" and Belit in "Queen of the Black Coast." Gerry Lopez, a champion surfer Milius had met while filming *Big Wednesday*, was enlisted as Subotai the Mongol. The character was not based on any Howard incarnation but rather the "Subotai" character Toshiro Mifune had played in *The Seven Samurai*. James Earl Jones was hired to portray the evil sorcerer Thulsa Doom (drawn from the King Kull stories). Although he doesn't resemble the character from the story, he conveys many of the literary character's qualities. Max Von Sydow, who had appeared in several De Laurentiis films, including *Flash Gordon*, signed on as King Osric, while William Smith, Ben Davidson, and Sven Ole Thorsen were cast for their athletic prowess. French actress Valeria Quennessen contributed great sexual appeal as the Princess. (Buzz Feitshans and Raffaella De Laurentiis would serve as line producers, Terry Leonard would handle the stunts, and Nick Allder was hired to produce the film's special effects.)

Although the start of principal photography was still several months away, Milius and Schwarzenegger flew to England's Shepperton Studios in October 1980 to create a special film trailer that would be released at Christmas with Dino De Laurentiis's *Flash Gordon*. (The footage was unfortunately never included as a trailer with the science-fiction comedy.) In the sequence, later incorporated as a framing device for the movie, Schwarzenegger sits on the throne of Aquilonia as its sixty-year-old king, reciting lines from Howard's "Nemedian Chronicles" and inviting audiences to join him on a journey back to his younger days. The barbarian-as-king footage is very good and greatly encouraged both star and director.

The cast and crew of *Conan the Barbarian* arrived in Spain during the Christmas break, and

In a final confrontation with Doom's forces, Conan and Subotai battle overwhelming odds for the safety of a princess.

principal photography began on January 7, 1981, with Schwarzenegger as Conan fighting off a pack of wolves. The shooting schedule, which would take nearly five months, had been divided into two parts. For the first part, interiors would be filmed in an aircraft hangar in Torrejon, while exteriors would be shot on locations in and around Madrid. For the second part of the shoot, exteriors would be lensed in the small southern coastal area of Almeria. Milius had used those locations for *The Wind and the Lion*, and even though he would have preferred to work in Yugoslavia, the director knew that the death of Marshal Tito (and the subsequent political unrest in Yugoslavia) made Spain an ideal second choice.

During that first day of shooting, Schwarzenegger suffered a serious injury when an attack by one of the dogs (playing the wolves) nearly ended the production. However, realizing that everything was riding on his performance, Arnold insisted, much like his cinematic counterpart, that he was fine and that filming should continue. "One of them hit me too soon," Schwarzenegger revealed, laughing about it months later.

It caught me off guard and I went right over the ledge. I fell ten feet and landed on my

back. I was covered with scratches and bruises. It was probably a pretty good beginning for this movie, though. It set the tone for the whole time we were there. This was going to be fun...but dangerous.

Regrettably, the political turmoil that broke out in Spain in mid-February caused Milius and his crew to realize the dangerous position and precarious situation in which they had all been placed. Fearing that they might not be able to finish the shoot, the crew began to hurry through several important sequences. The scene that features Conan's battle with a giant serpent (controlled by hydraulics) posed numerous problems and retakes, and as the political climate worsened, the film unit's tempers flared. With less than three days to complete a sequence that should have taken weeks, Milius settled for something that was less than perfect. When right-wing sympathizers took over two hundred hostages in Barcelona, the company shut down filming in Madrid and quickly moved south to Almeria. There, under conditions much more primitive, the crew found itself facing some of the production's more spectacular scenes. These included Conan's assault on Thulsa Doom's Mountain of Power and the climactic battle of the mounds. During one of the key fight sequences, Terry Leonard's stuntmen were so hurried that Sandahl Bergman was hit with a sword and had a finger cut to the bone.

By the time *Conan the Barbarian* wrapped in May, the cast and crew were exhausted from the five-month shoot. In fact, everyone involved in the production had taken their share of knocks, including Schwarzenegger.

> I was attacked by dogs, I tore a ligament falling off a horse. I had my neck sliced by an ax handle. I jumped into a lake and smashed my head open on a rock. I was thrown off a camel. None of the actors minded risking injury, though, because of John [Milius]. He made *Conan* the best working experience that I have ever had. John and I are alike in many ways. He had a vision about this movie. I also have that type of vision. When I teach my bodybuilding seminars, I tell people that you must have a very clear vision of something in order to attain it, to make it a reality. People without this type of vision wind up drifting around aimlessly. John knew exactly what he wanted, and we were there to see that it was accomplished.

With the principal photography completed, John Milius returned to California to begin the postproduction process. Opticals by Peter Kuran and Jim Danforth were added, and the final score by Basil Poledouris (who had done the music for *Big Wednesday* for Milius) was recorded with a full orchestra. Although the film had been scheduled for a Christmas 1981 release, some additional trimming was required to pass inspection with the Motion Picture Association of America (MPAA), which objected to several violent scenes. The release date was rescheduled for February, then April, before Universal finally settled on May 14, 1982. (Following several very successful sneak previews in February and March, the studio realized the film's potential as a major summer blockbuster.) The extra time allowed Milius, always the perfectionist, to respond to preview audiences' suggestions by adding a few polishing touches. Regrettably, the extra time also afforded Albert Pyun's low-budget rip-off, *The Sword and the Sorcerer*, the perfect opportunity to upstage his multimillion-dollar production by two weeks.

A Critical Commentary

Following its nationwide release in May 1982 to anxious masses, *Conan* grossed a whopping $9 million in its first week and remained on the top of the box-office charts for several more weeks until it was displaced by Steven Spielberg's *E.T. The Extra-Terrestrial*. During the balance of the summer season, *Conan* battled for second place with *Star Trek II: The Wrath of Khan*, *Cat People*, *Blade Runner*, *Krull*, *The Road Warrior*, and Pyun's *The Sword and the Sorcerer* and finished with a respectable $50 million. Its subsequent release in the foreign markets by 20th Century-Fox brought in an additional $50 million, easily outdistancing all competitors to become the foreign champion. Even though *Conan* was very popular with ticket buyers, most critics viewed the motion picture with distaste. They either complained about its excessive gore and violence or sneered at Milius's attempts to endow it with a macho philosophy. One reviewer called Schwarzenegger's performance "silly," while Vincent Canby of the *New York Times* summed up the other critical complaints by terming *Conan* "the archetypal escapist film, a kiddie fantasy for grown-ups." The negative criticism did not apparently hurt the movie's appeal, for audiences went on to make it one of 1982's top summer hits.

Even though some reviewers were critical of his performance, Arnold Schwarzenegger *is* Conan the Barbarian. He embodies both a ruggedness in his portrayal and a roughness as an actor that make him very convincing as the Cimmerian, and his intense screen presence transcends any preconceived notions about the Robert E. Howard character. As Conan, he probably gives his most professional and sincere performance of his then twelve-year career. While his accent comes through stronger in this film than in any of the others, Arnold portrays Conan with the same coolness and assurance that Clint Eastwood gave Dirty Harry or Sean Connery lent to James Bond. Peter Ranier of the *Los Angeles Herald Examiner* wrote that "Arnold's not given much opportunity to demonstrate anything except his physique," but that is simply not true. Exuding toughness, Schwarzenegger not only plays Conan as a hardened, dedicated warrior who epitomizes machismo but also demonstrates great tenderness in his love scenes, first with the gladiatorial whores, then with Valeria. (He is particularly sensitive to her during her death scene on a funeral pyre.) Arnold also shows his vulnerability, eliciting great sympathy

Poster art from *Conan the Barbarian*. (Courtesy Universal Pictures)

from the audience, when he is beaten and crucified by Thulsa Doom. Schwarzenegger clearly demonstrates his acting skills, and while he may have been purposely given few lines, his darkly handsome persona dominates nearly every scene. He even looks like the artist's conception of Conan, and his Teutonic accent is actually an advantage.

Director John Milius also skillfully handles our first introduction to Conan as an adult in just one of many marvelous sequences. Audiences are first introduced to the Cimmerian lashed to the Wheel of Pain. The camera purposely does not reveal Conan's face until a key moment. Only his shoulders, the back of his head, and his hands are actually seen. When the camera finally reveals Schwarzenegger as he tilts his head upward, the pain and suffering are expertly communicated through his rugged features. Milius had wanted to create a modern legend, like Beowulf or Hercules, and his craft as both a writer and filmmaker produce the archetypal fantasy hero in Conan. His homage to Masaki Kobayashi's *Kwaidan*—notably the Wolf Witch scene and Conan's resurrection from the dead, John Ford's *The Searchers*, with its revenge fable, and Kurosawa's *The Seven Samurai*, with the climactic battle of the mounds, also help to further delineate Milius's vision of a legendary hero. Conan is the direct descendant of Tarzan and Flash Gordon and the spiritual stepchild of *Hercules*, *The Giant of Marathon*, *Colossus of Rhodes*, or any number of the other sword-and-sandal epics of the late fifties and early sixties. His individual shots are purposely constructed like frames from a Marvel comic, one of the film's principal sources, and succeed in emphasizing the pulplike nature of the story. Admittedly, Milius's zen philosophy and references to Friedrich Nietzsche, whom he quotes liberally throughout the film, are unnecessary and burden the plot with an intellectual tone that never quite seems to work.

Conan the Barbarian is also a triumph of production design, set decoration, special effects, costumes, and makeup. Credit for the distinctive look of the film belongs entirely to the gifted Ron Cobb. Although many of his designs seem somewhat familiar today, they established a pattern that would be copied in other films throughout the decade. Readers of the pulp novels (or comic series) can easily recognize his very expressionistic work. Particularly effective is the extraordinary way in which Cobb used local Spanish sites to project the exotic Hyborian Age. The film as a whole is surprisingly low on special effects, but Cobb's

work and the genius of Peter Kuran's visual concepts stand head and shoulders above what was currently being offered on the screen. (Perhaps the only negative point in *Conan* relates to Nick Allder's hydraulic snake. While the creature looks frighteningly real, it moves much too lethargically to be taken seriously. Conan's triumph seems hardly fair, under the circumstances.) Basil Poledouris's rousing score, which is a combination of symphonic and choral music, contributes to the overall atmosphere.

Sandahl Bergman as Valeria is striking as the Nordic beauty who wins Conan's eternal love, revealing a considerable depth of character with both the budding romance and the violent swordplay. She is truly Arnold Schwarzenegger's equal, and not simply "love interest," and subsequently would have made an exceptional *Red Sonja* (see Chapter Five: "She-Devil With a Sword"). James Earl Jones also performs wonders as the evil sorcerer Thulsa Doom. While most science-fiction and fantasy fans remember him as the sonorous voice of Darth Vader from the *Star Wars* films, Jones is also a veteran stage actor. In fact, when *Conan the Barbarian* was first released, Jones was appearing on Broadway opposite Christopher Plummer in Shakespeare's *Othello*. Both Bergman and Jones provide a perfect balance for Schwarzenegger, who does attempt to command every scene.

After the arduous struggle to get Robert E. Howard's pulp creation to the screen, Arnold Schwarzenegger was pleased with the final product. He even referred to the character as his own personal Rocky Balboa (in reference to Stallone's debut character in *Rocky*) and looked forward to playing the Cimmerian again. In 1982 he told reporters:

> I have a contract for five more Conan films, but it depends on the success of the first one. In general I like fantasy movies, adventure movies—action. John Wayne– and Clint Eastwood–type movies—they are much more fun to do than pictures that have heavy messages.

Conan the Barbarian is currently available on videocassette from MCA/Universal Home Video. A special letter-boxed edition is also available on laserdisc.

(Opposite) *Conan the Barbarian* made Schwarzenegger a plausible movie star because he looked like the muscular hero from the comic books. (Courtesy Universal Pictures)

50

THREE

RETURN TO CIMMERIA

Conan the Destroyer

1984. Universal Pictures. *Director:* Richard Fleischer. *Producer:* Raffaella De Laurentiis. *Executive Producer:* Stephen F. Kesten. *Screenplay:* Stanley Mann. *Based on an original story by* Roy Thomas and Gerry Conway *and characters created by* Robert E. Howard. *Photography:* Jack Cardiff. *Music:* Basil Poledouris. *Editor:* Frank J. Urioste. *Starring:* Arnold Schwarzenegger, Grace Jones, Mako, Wilt Chamberlain, Tracey Walter, Olivia D'Abo, Jeff Corey, Pat Roach, Ferdinand Mayne, Sven Ole Thorsen, and Sarah Douglas. Released on June 29, 1984. [103 minutes]

Returning to the fantastic—almost mythic—roots of the pulp stories and novels by creator Robert E. Howard, Richard Fleischer's *Conan the Destroyer* was decidedly different from its predecessor. Even though writer-director John Milius had turned out one of the screen's most successful sword-and-sorcery epics (worldwide grosses for *Conan the Barbarian* topped the $100 million mark), many longtime fans of the book or comic series were disappointed by his handling of Conan's character. They also objected to Milius's zen-existential slant as well as his overall contempt for supernatural events. The new film represented a step back to the barbarian's bloody basics. Audiences that had become accustomed to the obligatory shock elements, the gore of the previous production, were instead treated to nonstop action and adventure. While some may consider it flawed and faded today, the motion picture was at the time one

(Opposite) Schwarzenegger returned to the fantastic (almost mythic) roots of the Cimmerian sword-wielder in the big-budget sequel *Conan the Destroyer*. (Courtesy Universal Pictures)

of the most expensive productions mounted by Dino De Laurentiis. In fact, when viewed in retrospect, Fleischer's tribute to the genre actually represents yet one more high point in Arnold Schwarzenegger's early film career.

The actor said a few months before the release of *Conan the Destroyer:*

> I think Conan's character was set up very well in the first film. Milius really did his homework and created an incredibly realistic world for Conan to live in. But the people behind *Conan II* thought this film should not get too heavy philosophically. Instead, Conan really gets into action, battling it out in every corner he ventures. Conan has no patience for dialogue; it is a waste of time for him. The only thing that counts, the only way he gets rid of his problems, is by getting physical.

The Screen Story

Picking up several years after the events of the first film, this direct sequel finds the Cimmerian (Schwarzenegger) still deeply mourning the death of his only love, Valeria. Now an accomplished thief and mercenary, Conan finds that the riches of his conquests do not satisfy the emptiness he feels within. While his comic sidekick Malak the Quick (Tracey Walter) sits counting the booty of their latest score, the barbarian kneels before his makeshift shrine. An unseen army hides in the hills beyond them, awaiting the signal to attack from their leader Bombaata (basketball great Wilt Chamberlain). He, in turn, waits for a nod from his hooded commander.

53

Before Conan can escape from the field of combat, Bombaata (Wilt Chamberlain) arrives with Queen Taramis (Sarah Douglas), his mysterious hooded commander.

Before Conan and Malak can leave, the army attacks. But the two warriors cut a wide swath through men and nets before finally being overwhelmed by sheer numbers. Bombaata's hooded commander is soon revealed to be Taramis, queen of Shadizar (Sarah Douglas), one of the most powerful leaders of the Hyborian Age. The evil sorceress uses her magical powers to find the one weakness within Conan. His great grief for the loss of Valeria is all that she needs to control him.

Queen Taramis promises to revive Valeria *if* the brawny barbarian agrees to lead an expedition to fulfill an ages-old prophecy. He must accompany Taramis's niece, the virginal princess Jehnna (Olivia D'Abo), who bears a birthmark indicating her destiny, to steal the fabulous Heart of Ahriman, a gemstone jealously guarded by the powerful wizard Thoth-Amon (Pat Roach). This gemstone unlocks the crypt containing the horn of the god Dagoth, which, when placed in the ancient statue at Shadizar, will restore the living god to his people. "What good is a sword against sorcery?" Conan asks, and little does he know how prophetic his words really are. The evil queen plans to sacrifice Jehnna and her party to

Dagoth upon their return.

After Taramis wins the Cimmerian's confidence, he takes Jehnna, Bombaata (who is sworn to protect the virtue of the princess), and Malak on the quest, uncertain of their direction and relying solely on Jehnna's instincts. They journey first to the castle of Thoth-Amon, the sorcerer who holds the key and will destroy any who attempt to steal it.

On their way Conan enlists the aid of his friend Akiro (Mako), feeling the need for a competent wizard to battle the forces of evil, and Zula, a fierce warrior-woman (played by New Wave disco singer Grace Jones). Both need rescuing from overwhelming numbers—one from hungry cannibals and the other from a half-dozen bloodthirsty soldiers—and Conan uses his prowess with the sword to free them. Even though the two swear allegiance to Conan, Bombaata chooses not to trust either of them.

When they finally reach Thoth-Amon's castle, the virginal princess is kidnapped during the night by a giant bird of smoke. Conan and the others awake to find her missing and engage in a monstrous physical and mystical battle with the evil sorcerer. Jehnna, who has been shielded from the outside world until this journey, finds herself awed by the Cimmerian's death struggle with the ape-demon (one incantation of Thoth-Amon). She also discovers romantic feelings stirring for the first time in her life.

The victorious group leaves the shattered castle and searches for the horn in a series of caverns. Once they find the arcane artifact, Akiro reveals the terrible truth about Dagoth from the sacred writings. Conan is at first skeptical of the writings but, when betrayed by Bombaata, begins to believe the terrible truth. Jehnna is to be put to death as a virginal sacrifice to Dagoth so that the god may rule the world. Suddenly, with orders to kill Conan, four elite guards (from Taramis) descend on their small party.

Conan, Zula, Malak, and Akiro survive the challenge of the Four Elite, but Bombaata manages to ride off with Jehnna, who remains unaware of her impending fate. Angered, the Cimmerian swears vengeance to Crom and, with the others, sets off for Shadizar to save Jehnna and repay Taramis's treachery. Meanwhile, at the castle, Jehnna is drugged and

prepared for the sorcerous ceremony by Taramis. It begins with the entire congregation standing before the temple to watch the rebirth of the god Dagoth.

Arriving not a moment too soon, Malak guides Conan and the others through a secret passageway that leads into the castle. As the group nears the altar, Bombaata bars the way, and the Cimmerian, his blood lust rising, accepts the deadly challenge. While the two hulking figures duel, Zula and Malak try to save Jehnna from the queen, but not before the sleeping god awakens. As Dagoth rises, he reveals his true form, posing a much more deadly threat than any of them realized. If Jehnna now dies, the god of Shadizar will rule the world through a mystical stranglehold that cannot be broken. Conan knows that he must destroy the god and save the beautiful heiress to the throne in order to preserve all their lives.

Finally, in a climactic hand-to-hand confrontation, Conan takes on the horned demon Dagoth. The barbarian first battles the creature with his sword; then, recognizing the horn holds all the power, Conan

Queen Taramis, an evil sorceress, promises to revive Valeria *if* Conan agrees to lead an expedition to fulfill an ages-old prophecy.

jumps onto its back and tears the arcane artifact from its head. The god Dagoth dies.

In tribute to the Cimmerian and his friends, Jehnna awards the positions of captain of the guard to Zula, court counselor to Akiro, and fool to Malak. The new queen also offers to make Conan her king, but he declines. He wants to rule his own kingdom. "Conan mourned his lost Valeria. At length he sought adventure in distant lands until, at last, he found his own kingdom...."

Conan escorts Jehnna (Olivia D'Abo) on a dangerous journey.

Production Details

With *Conan the Barbarian* a surprise hit, Universal Pictures (the film's American distributor) got together with Dino De Laurentiis on a sequel. The studio's only concern was that the Italian producer soften the violence in order to make the movie more accessible to general viewers. (The first film's bloodshed had been cited as a reason for its relative lack of merchandising spin-offs and its limited number of under-eighteen admissions.) In anticipation of a PG rating, De Laurentiis opted to tame the savage sword-slinger by removing most of the bloody violence. The producer

also brought on board most of the same production people from the first *Conan* and turned the day-to-day operation over to his daughter Raffaella. The result is one of the best from a production standpoint. In fact, many Schwarzenegger fans consider it superior to the first film even though it is considerably lighter.

It originally was entitled *Conan—King of Thieves*, and coproducer Raffaella De Laurentiis first commissioned a script from Roy Thomas and Gerry Conway (two Marvel Comics writers responsible for helping revitalize interest in Robert E. Howard's pulp hero in 1970). They labored long and hard, concocting many unsuitable screenplays which had expensive, overfanciful (and largely unproducible) details. De Laurentiis rejected these treatments and ultimately hired Stanley Mann to draw elements together from the various scripts to produce *Conan the Destroyer*. (Mann had recently penned *Firestarter* for Dino De Laurentiis.) Sources close to the production reported that Mann's script also underwent several revisions in order to keep the barbarian linked to a PG rating.

At first, Arnold Schwarzenegger had strong feelings against playing a less savage Cimmerian. He said prior to the start of actual filming:

I think it's a mistake. I know Sylvester Stallone made an extra $20 million because he got a PG rating for *Rocky III*, but it's a matter of how much you want to stay within the character's reality. Can you slaughter people and never see blood? Is it possible? You must have battles. That's part of life, war, and the world of Conan.

But as the muscleman became more involved in the production, he realized that they had no intention of stripping Conan of his violent actions. They simply planned to add a dimension of vulnerability and humor to the barbarian's character in order to provide audiences with some degree of accessibility.

Planning and preproduction began in Mexico City's Churubusco Studios, a sprawling complex where Raffaella was already heavily involved in staging *Dune*. Both Dino De Laurentiis and executive producer Stephen Kesten maintained that they would be getting more spectacle on-screen for $16 million in inexpensive Mexico than was purchased with the $19.7 million spent in Spain on *Conan the Barbarian*. The coproducer admitted during an early press conference:

> It's cheap. The craftsmen aren't necessarily any better, but labor is very cheap. We have tremendous sets which fill an entire soundstage. We've saved millions on the sets alone.

Pier Luigi Basile was hired as production and costume designer to bring the fabulous Hyborian Age to life, and William Stout signed on to take the unavailable Ron Cobb's place as production illustrator. During production, Stout also penned the script for the third *Conan* film.

Returning from the first film was Kiyoshi Yamazaki, the Japanese swordmaster who trained the cast members in the art of the weapon's warfare. (He also appears in the film in a minor role.) But since most of the originals from *Conan the Barbarian* had been hacked to pieces in the first adventure, Raffaella looked around for suitable actors and actresses to play supporting barbarians. Tall, stately Sarah Douglas was cast against type as the evil Queen Taramis. American audiences had first learned of her penchant for villainy when she donned black leather as Ursa in the *Superman* films. She later played a villainess on *Falcon Crest* (1983, CBS) and the battle commander Pamela in *V* (1984, NBC). Los Angeles Lakers basketball star Wilt Chamberlain and recording sensation Grace Jones were both hired for their popular appeal and made their acting debuts in

Conan the Destroyer. Olivia D'Abo, Mako, and Tracey Walter were selected to round out the cast opposite muscleman Schwarzenegger.

Surprisingly, the one person De Laurentiis was unable to secure for the project was writer/director John Milius—of whom Arnold Schwarzenegger had once said, "There *never* would have been a Conan movie without him." Milius, who once said that he

Conan the destroyer defends the virginal princess from an unwelcome kidnapper.

would "be happy to go on directing Conan movies until the day I die," was busy producing *Uncommon Valor* and directing *Red Dawn*. Raffaella was hard pressed to find a substitute and turned to her father for suggestions. He immediately recommended the man who had made *Amityville 3-D* into such a popular success for DEG (De Laurentiis Entertainment Group), Hollywood veteran Richard Fleischer.

Having won an Academy Award in 1947 for his documentary *Design for Death*, Fleischer has seldom been without work, and in the intervening thirty-seven years, he had directed more than his share of action and science-fiction films, including such clas-

(Left) Allied with a fierce warrior-woman named Zula (Grace Jones), Conan faces overwhelming odds.

(Below) Conan and company (left to right, Tracey Walter, Mako, Olivia D'Abo, Grace Jones and Wilt Chamberlain) discover the secret of Dagoth.

sics as Disney's *20,000 Leagues Under the Sea*, *Fantastic Voyage*, and *The Vikings*. (After filming *Conan the Destroyer*, he had time to pause only briefly before traveling to Italy to begin work on *Red Sonja*.)

Fleischer recalled:

> I liked the first *Conan* film very much; in fact, I saw a lot of *The Vikings* in it. It was a very well-made film, and it had many excellent dramatic qualities. Milius gave it a sort of Wagnerian feel. I thought he did an excellent job. It was a heavy picture, but then the theme was very heavy—and it was imaginative in its design. Its problems came because it, for the most part, lacked humor. There were some jokes, but too much of the film was unrelieved drama.
>
> And, of course, Arnold was not the actor that he should have been or could have been. At that time, he was just not capable. He had the wonderful look. He's so right for Conan. But because he wasn't an experienced actor, they didn't give him too many scenes where he had to act, which was wise.

Fleischer was very concerned about being "handicapped" with an actor who was not much more than an amateur and delayed meeting with Schwarzenegger until after he had read most of Robert E. Howard's stories. (Prior to his involvement with *Conan the Destroyer* and *Red Sonja*, Fleischer had never even heard of the "barbarian.") When he finally completed his research, Fleischer approached the former Mr. Olympia and immediately had all his fears put to rest by Arnold's professional demeanor.

Schwarzenegger said:

> The first day Fleischer came to see me work out, he told me, "Arnold, could you put on some more muscles?" I couldn't believe it! It turned out that Fleischer thought that Milius's decision to keep Conan clothed throughout the first film was a mistake. Fleischer believes that people want to see my body much more often then they did the first time around, so they will. I spend most of my time in *Conan the Destroyer* fighting off people while I'm dressed in a loincloth.

Subsequently, at the director's request, Schwarzenegger added ten pounds to his weight, working out five hours a day for a full two months

Dagoth, the sleeping god, turned into a horned demon.

prior to the shoot.

Conan the Destroyer began principal photography on November 1, 1983. Veteran cinematographer and director Jack Cardiff was behind the camera. Ten weeks of filming took place at Churubusco Studios, with four soundstages and three back lots being used for the production. Another four weeks were spent at eleven locations, including Pachuca, Nevado de Toluca (an extinct volcano), and the Samalayucca Desert (near El Paso). During the location shooting, the elements proved to be a major problem, particularly at the extremely high elevations. At times, the weather was unseasonably cold; at others, the scorching hot deserts and sand dunes took their toll of the cast and crew. After a much-needed Christmas break, principal photography was completed in early February. The final sequence to be filmed (and coin-

In tribute to the brawny Cimmerian and his friends, Jehnna awards the positions of captain of the guard to Zula, court counselor to Akiro (Mako), and fool to Malak (Tracey Walter).

cidentally the last major set piece of the motion picture) was Arnold's battle with Carlo Rambaldi's Dreaming God (a cable-controlled, six-and-a-half-foot-tall creation built around British stuntman and wrestler Pat Roach). Optical effects—including an animated smoke bird and a human turning into a column of blood—were supplied by Van Der Veer Photographic Effects under the supervision of Barry Nolan.

While he may have found the entire project very exhausting, Richard Fleischer was extremely satisfied with the one-hour-and-forty-five-minute product he turned in to Raffaella De Laurentiis. The director was also anxious to begin work on *Red Sonja*, even though he readily acknowledges the genre's difficulty. "These action-adventures are a very tough type of motion picture to do," Fleischer admits, adding with a smile, "After all, this is not a 'parlor-bedroom-bath' type of film. This is *Conan the Destroyer*. This is action at its best!"

Critical Commentary

When it was released on July 4, 1984, *Conan the Destroyer* faced stiff summertime competition from several other genre favorites, including *Star Trek III: The Search for Spock*, *Indiana Jones and the Temple of Doom*, *Gremlins*, and *Ghostbusters*. The film debuted with a strong promotional campaign to attract younger viewers and gained a strong return from holiday box-office receipts, but by the second week of business, it had fallen well behind the pace of the other four. Surprisingly, critics who had savaged John Milius's *Conan the Barbarian* for its violent approach were just as quick to jump on *Conan the Destroyer* for being too sophomoric. *People* magazine offered one of the few positive reviews, writing:

> The action is large-scale, the plot suitably fantastic, and the climax, a fight to the death between Conan and a god brought back to life (the monster was designed by *ET* creator Carlo Rambaldi), is slambang.

By the end of the summer, the motion picture had finished well out of the running for box-office champion. (*Conan the Destroyer* fared much better in the international markets, however.)

Although it failed to receive better reviews than its predecessor and grossed a more modest but still respectable $30 million in the United States ($100 million worldwide), its star continued to cement his reputation as a major box-office draw. He also demonstrated how considerably he had grown as an actor with another fine performance as Conan. Arnold seems much more relaxed and confident than he did in the first Conan film, even though one misses the hard edges that were present only in that one. Schwarzenegger adds more sophistication to the way Conan carries himself, and the character also shows a side that never appeared in any of the Howard stories—humor.

Arnold explained his character's transition from barbarian to mercenary:

> Conan's a lot more experienced in this movie. He's more at ease with himself and his position in the world. And he really loves the joy

In a rare publicity photo, Schwarzenegger poses with Olivia D'Abo. (Courtesy Universal Pictures)

of adventure. Since he's much more skilled in fighting now—much more slick about knowing how to break into places and steal things—he just goes in, does it, and has a good time. Let's hope audiences do, too.

Unlike Robert E. Howard's ruthless barbarian, however, the second Conan of Cimmeria to reach the silver screen is portrayed much too sympathetically to be a man of violent action. Whereas John Milius's Conan measured up to the "thief, reiver, slayer with gigantic melancholies and gigantic mirth," Richard Fleischer's Conan seems less extraordinary, in spite of the fact that Arnold has an even bigger physique. When the mighty swordsman and his party first encounter Zula, Conan must be prompted by Jehnna to "do something" in order to free the Nubian from her savage captors. Only then does he become an instrument of action. Howard's Conan (and, by extension, the Conan of the first movie) would not have needed prompting to free Zula; he would have leaped into the fray and begun hacking limbs. Soon after, when Jehnna is kidnapped twice (once by Thoth-Amon and the other by the elite guard) Conan requires little prompting to effect her rescue from their evil clutches. And yet Howard's creation, a keen and highly resourceful individual, would have never fallen into either trap. Not only has Fleischer turned Conan into a charmer who easily ridicules himself with self-parody; he has also made him a bungler. The Cimmerian redeems his rugged image by defeating the god Dagoth; but by then the larger-than-life hero has lost most of his mythic proportions.

Besides the transmutation of the story's central figure, screenwriter Stanley Mann (working from several treatments by Roy Thomas and Gerry Conway) has greatly altered or discarded elements of Milius's bizarre Hyborian Age to favor his strange medieval world of queens and monsters, swords and castles, warriors and fools. Names have been inexplicably changed, and characters—not the least of whom is Conan the Cimmerian—have been totally rewritten. Akiro, for example, is now a traveling wizard instead of the mysterious keeper of the mounds; Subotai the Mongol (played by Gerry Lopez in the original) inexplicably has been dropped as Conan's traveling companion in favor of Malak the Quick. While Malak's appearance may provide the necessary comic relief for a PG rating, the sword-slinging barbarian would have never befriended such a cowardly fool. Thulsa Doom (James Earl Jones) and Valeria (Sandahl Bergman) are sorely missed and have been replaced by carbon-copy caricatures in the personages of Bombaata (Wilt Chamberlain), Zula (Grace Jones), and Jehnna (Olivia D'Abo). Only Sarah Douglas stands out as the wicked Queen Taramis.

Other elements, including the assault on Thoth-Amon's castle, several unspectacular sword battles, and the subterranean quest for the horn of Dagoth, seem borrowed and restaged from the first film. Only Conan's climactic battle with the hideous monster emerges as truly imaginative.

Director Fleischer tries his best to make these disparate elements come together into a cohesive narrative; unfortunately, lacking the skill and vision of a John Milius (who admittedly borrowed from Fleischer's *The Vikings*), his cinematic approach to the material is rather a conventional one. He seems comfortable staging the large, lavish production numbers, but when it comes to creating an atmosphere of terror and menace, he is completely out of his depth. The dark, brooding nature of Conan the Cimmerian is never fully explored by Fleischer. Similarly, the party's journey into Thoth-Amon's ice castle or the subterranean lair lack any real tension or suspense. (They might was well be walking into a mall.) And yet the most formidable problem for the director, bringing the Dreaming God to life in the film's amazing climax, is handled with great finesse.

Conan the Destroyer was a box-office blockbuster when it was later released in Europe (and other international venues) and spawned a Schwarzenegger semisequel (entitled *Red Sonja*), which premiered the following year. Although critics were quick to find fault with the production, particularly in light of *Conan the Barbarian*, the film went on to become one of MCA/Universal Home Video's most popular rentals. When viewed in retrospect on videocassette or cable television, the flawed but still entertaining motion picture causes viewers to yearn for more barbaric adventures of the violent Cimmerian.

Present plans—and Schwarzenegger's contract—provide for four subsequent adventures; but whether those tales will ever be spun remains a question. Just after the release of *Conan the Destroyer*, Universal added a $3 million stunt-and-special-effects attraction, "The Adventures of Conan," to its studio tour. Featuring fierce sword fights, laser-beam sorcery, and a seventeen-foot mechanical dragon, the show is one attraction that sells out every day of the week. The studio also purchased film rights to all the Conan novels and short stories by Howard, L. Sprague de Camp, Lin Carter, and others, and it has been negotiating with Dino De Laurentiis for years.

Arnold Schwarzenegger explained his own involvement with the role:

The cast of *Conan the Destroyer:* (left to right, Tracey Walter, Mako, Grace Jones, Arnold Schwarzenegger, Olivia D'Abo, and Sarah Douglas). (Courtesy Universal Pictures)

There is nothing definite going on right now with another sequel. As long as they keep making Conan movies, I'll be involved. I am really committed to Conan. He is a fun character to play, to bring to people. I could see myself playing him until *Conan X.* I could do a Conan every few years and other projects in between them. But that's not up to me. It was a fact that *Rocky IV* was supposed to be the last Rocky movie, and now they're working on *Rocky V; First Blood* was supposed to be one movie, and now there are two others. So it all depends.

Conan the Destroyer is currently available on videocassette and laserdisc from MCA/Universal Home Video and appears regularly on many cable channels.

FOUR

THE LEAN, MEAN KILLING MACHINE

The Terminator

1984. Orion Pictures in association with Hemdale. *Director:* James Cameron. *Producer:* Gale Anne Hurd. *Executive producers:* John Daly and Derek Gibson. *Screenplay:* Cameron and Hurd. *Photography:* Adam Greenberg. *Music:* Brad Fiedel. *Special Terminator Effects Created by:* Stan Winston. *Editor:* Mark Goldblatt. *Starring:* Arnold Schwarzenegger, Michael Biehn, Linda Hamilton, Lance Henriksen, Rick Rossovich, Bill Paxton, and Paul Winfield. Released on October 26, 1984. [108 minutes]

The Terminator, James Cameron's futuristic retelling of the Frankenstein story, remains the best of Arnold Schwarzenegger's early films. With the modest budget of $6.5 million and doubt on behalf of the Hollywood establishment, the motion picture still managed to transcend its humble origins to best *2010* and *Dune* as the season's biggest box-office feature. The film also broke new thematic ground that would have a long-range influence on science-fiction productions. By making the villain an empathetic character, functioning as both protagonist and antagonist, the adaptation demonstrates considerable insight: the Terminator represents an extension of modern technology gone mad. But the real strength of the production lies in Schwarzenegger's performance as the unstoppable robot from the future. Though the film may appear limited in light of its bigger-budget sequel, *The Terminator* still thrills as both a thought-provoking and action-packed movie.

(Opposite) Arnold Schwarzenegger as the Cyberdyne Systems Model 101 (nicknamed "the Terminator"). This "killing machine" fears no pain and feels no pity or fear. (Courtesy Orion Pictures in association with Hemdale)

The Screen Story

From the nuclear war-torn future of 2029, the Year of Darkness, a cyborg (part man, part machine) has been sent back to present-day Los Angeles. Representing a world that has become dominated by mechanized intelligences, the Cyberdyne Systems Model 101 (nicknamed "the Terminator" by resistance leaders) has been programmed kill a young woman named Sarah Connor (Linda Hamilton),

The lean, mean killing machine from the future arrives in the unsuspecting world of May 12, 1984, programmed to kill a young woman named Sarah Connor.

whose life could alter the course of history. Her unborn son may be the next century's only hope against the computer technology that rebelled, wanting all human life exterminated. This "killing machine" (Schwarzenegger) feels no pity, no pain, and no fear and is capable of leaving behind him a path of unspeakable destruction. A brilliant flash of light and an ear-splitting explosion mark the arrival of this mechanical monster in the unsuspecting world of May 12, 1984.

At the same time, just moments after the machines have dispatched their emissary of death, the human resistance manages to overthrow its enemies and take command of a secret military base. Their victory over the machines is far from complete, however. Skynet (the central machine intelligence)

(Left) Kyle Reese (Michael Biehn), a seasoned young guerrilla fighter from the future, emerges through the same time warp.

(Below) After "terminating" the two other Sarah Connors (from the phone book), the killer robot from the future tracks his final target to the "Tech Noir" nightclub.

has used time-displacement equipment to send a terminator back in time to reshape the future by changing the past, and John Connor knows that his unsuspecting mother is the likely target. Forced to make the difficult decision of sending one of his own men to face certain death, the leader of the resistance looks to them for a volunteer. (Yet secretly, deep down inside, he already knows who the volunteer will be.) Kyle Reese (Michael Biehn), a young but hardened guerrilla fighter from the trenches, steps forward to accept the suicide mission, knowing that, against all odds, he must locate and eliminate the Terminator before it can fulfill its deadly mission.

Reese, too, emerges through the same time warp but finds himself immediately hunted by the police for several murders that his predecessor has committed. Resorting to his unusual combat training, the time traveler manages to temporarily evade the Los Angeles police and arm himself with a shotgun. Once back on the street, he mingles with the other lost souls of the night. Somewhere in this dark city lives the woman he must protect and a relentless murderer that he must stop!

Leaving a double path of destruction in their wake, each of the two future warriors struggles to find the young woman before the other. Meanwhile, a baffled police force is somewhat confounded by two unconnected killings, until they realize the murdered women share the same name and follow each other in the telephone directory. Sergeant Vukovich (Lance Henriksen) and Lieutenant Traxler (Paul Winfield) attempt to warn the third Sarah Connor, but she has just left her apartment to eat dinner. Fearing that Sarah may yet be targeted by the "phone-book killer," Traxler decides to release a statement to the press. His televised speech reaches Connor at a pizza joint but is much too late to save Sarah's roommate, Ginger, and her boyfriend, Matt, from the Terminator, whose superior programming has already led him to her apartment and, subsequently, on to the restaurant where she is hiding.

As the terrified young woman dodges the

Terminator and Kyle pursues him in a deadly game of search and destroy, the cyborg executes a number of the patrons at a dance club called Tech Noir. Reese springs to her rescue, shouting "Come with me if you want to live," and pulls Sarah Connor from the clutches of the mechanized murderer. Stealing a car, Reese and Sarah race away into the night, with the Terminator (and the police) in pursuit.

Confused and frightened out of her mind, Sarah demands to know what's going on and the reason why anyone would want to hurt a simple waitress like herself. Kyle Reese: Sergeant Tech Com

The Terminator (Schwarzenegger) takes careful aim with his laser-sighted weapon.

DN38416 reveals that he has traveled back in time to protect her from the killer cyborg, but she refuses to believe him. "The Terminator is an infiltration unit—part man, part machine," he continues.

> Hyper alloy combat chassis, microprocessor-controlled and fully armored. ...It can't be bargained with. It can't be reasoned with. It doesn't feel pity or remorse or fear. It will not stop, ever, until you are dead!

Reese further explains that a nuclear war, started by the machines, destroyed the world because Skynet (a computer defense system built for

SAC/Norad by Cyberdyne Systems) believed that all humans posed a threat to its basic programming. He grew up in the rubble after the war, while humans were being rounded up for orderly disposal in death camps. The human race was very close to extinction when one man stepped forward to teach others to fight back, to storm the wires, and to smash the

drive truck into the station house and begins to kill everyone in sight. Against a murderous force of such magnitude, the police stand little chance. (Even Traxler and Vukovich are gunned down in the attack.) But Sarah and Reese manage, once again, to slip through the cyborg's destructive fury and steal away into the night.

Reese springs to Sarah Connor's rescue, shouting, "Come with me if you want to live."

Hours later the two fugitives seek sanctuary first at a highway underpass, then at a flea-bitten motel just off the interstate. There Reese completes his tale of the war-torn future and tells her that each person has the responsibility to make a difference. Sarah binds his wounds, and the two people—from vastly different worlds—share an intimate moment of lovemaking (which will ultimately lead to her pregnancy). Kyle Reese is, in fact, John Connor's father.

The Terminator is not far behind them. By making use of Sarah's address book, the cyborg has tracked down her mother to a mountain cabin and subsequently, thanks to an unauthorized call, the fugitives to the motel. But Reese is ready for him with homemade explosives. The two flee the motel, with the Terminator in pursuit, and race through the darkened streets of Los Angeles. While Sarah pilots their vehicle at breakneck speed, Reese hurls several pipe bombs at their pursuer and manages to time one just right to explode in the tail pipe of an oil tanker. Though the warrior from the future is mortally wounded, the massive explosion temporarily stops the Terminator, melting away its human form.

machines into rubble. His name was John Connor— Sarah's son. The young woman is troubled by his story but cannot accept what he is saying without proof. (That she is being pursued by a Terminator is *not* proof enough.) Similarly, when Reese is arrested by the police after a high-speed chase, the court-appointed psychologist dismisses him as insane.

Badly damaged from his various encounters with Reese, the Terminator returns to a rented room for some makeshift surgery, then arms himself for a possible assault on police headquarters. When he is unable to gain access to his target through diplomatic means, the Terminator warns the desk sergeant: "I'll be back!" Moments later, he crashes a four-wheel-

Within a few moments, though, its chrome exoskeleton rises from the flames to continue pursuit, chasing the two lovers into Cyberdyne Systems. Reese sacrifices himself in an attempt to destroy the robot, but his sacrifice is a hollow one. Simply broken in half, the Terminator once again resumes its pursuit of Sarah through the deserted factory. Alone and totally isolated, she turns to face the deadly machine and finally mangles it totally in a hydraulic

Severely damaged from his encounters with Reese, the Terminator performs makeshift surgery, first on his right arm...

...then on his left eye. The motion picture's superb special effects made this sequence most convincing for audiences.

press. When we last see her, months after her deadly struggle, Sarah is headed for the mountains in Mexico to wait out the nuclear war and give birth to her son John.

Production Details

More than two years before, while completing post-production on *Piranha II: The Spawning* for Roger Corman, James Cameron (then twenty-seven years old) wrote a simple screen treatment for *The Terminator*. The treatment, which contained no dialogue or breakdown of special-effects sequences, told the story of a battle-weary soldier from the future who must prevent an unstoppable robot (also from the future) from assassinating a distant relative of the

resistance leader's family. While the story may reflect elements from Harlan Ellison's teleplays for *The Outer Limits* (1964, ABC), including "Demon With the Glass Hand" and "Soldier," it was really a direct descendant of the Michael Rennie low-budgeter *Cyborg 2087*—just the kind of subject matter that a former art director of Corman's New World Pictures would select as a breakaway project. But somewhere between that early screen treatment and the completed motion picture, Cameron's sense of visual action and inferential plot development came together to make *The Terminator* a thoroughly unique film experience.

Both Cameron and coproducer Gale Anne Hurd (only twenty-eight when *The Terminator* was made) learned their film craft from B-movie mastermind

69

Corman, the legendary entrepreneur who produced hundreds of successful low-budget films in the late fifties and sixties from his basement and had opened New World Pictures in the seventies to localize his productions. There Cameron and Hurd learned the pragmatic side of filmmaking, including the importance of efficiency and budgetary control. Cameron developed skills in art direction, special effects, and photography while working on *Planet of Horrors* and *Escape From New York*. Hurd kept pace with him on productions like *The Lady in Red*, *Alligator*, and *Smokey Bites the Dust*. On *Battle Beyond the Stars*, the two worked together for the first time, with Cameron handling the special effects and Hurd serving as production manager. When James Cameron finished *Piranha II* (a sequel to the *Jaws* rip-off), he and Hurd began work on *The Terminator*.

Cameron credits much of the appeal of his simple story treatment to the way in which he first presented the project to Hemdale. He paraphrases his original pitch to the director of development:

> It's fun to fantasize being a guy who can do whatever he wants. This Terminator guy is indestructible. He can be as rude as he wants. He can walk through a door, go through a

plate-glass window and just get up, brush off impacts from bullets. It's like the dark side of Superman, in a sense. I think it has a great cathartic value to people who wish they could just splinter open the door to their boss's office, walk in, break his desk in half, grab him by the throat, and throw him out the window and get away with it. Everybody's got that little demon that wants to be able to do whatever it wants, the bad kid that never gets punished.

Hemdale, in association with Orion Pictures and HBO Entertainment, gave tentative approval to Cameron and Hurd, contingent upon a completed script and final casting approval. James Cameron obliged by turning in a 122-page script; lacking a romantic encounter between Sarah and Reese, it was approved. (HBO insisted that a deep-felt connection between the two central characters was essential to sell the completed film, and Cameron added the scene that would later add almost mythic proportions to the scope of his project.) Several other sequences were dropped during filming, much to the disappointment of the director. Cameron obviously had a vision of a larger film in mind when he said, "We

(Below) In flashback, Kyle Reese tells Sarah (Linda Hamilton) about his terrifying world of the future.

(Opposite) Relentlessly, the killer robot from the future pursues the two fugitives.

Sarah and Reese share a tender moment that will have time-spanning implications.

had to cut scenes I was in love with in order to save money."

With a completed script in hand, Cameron and Hurd began shopping for actors to play their principals—Sarah Connor, Kyle Reese, and the Terminator. The producers first approached Arnold Schwarzenegger with the part of the human hero, but he quickly developed an affinity for the title role. He stated:

> I have read a lot of action-adventure scripts, and this definitely was one of the best. I knew that I wanted to play the part of the Terminator as soon as I started reading.

(Cameron and Hurd had originally considered O. J. Simpson for the role of the Terminator.)

From his earliest screen appearance as Hercules to his roles as Conan, Arnold had routinely been cast as the "good guy." Recognizing the enormous challenge that the role might offer, Schwarzenegger felt that playing a supervillain would be a refreshing change of pace. "In every film I've been in, I always play the hero," he explained. "In this one I finally get to play a real bad guy. It's quite a bit different for me, and I'm enjoying it a lot."

The casting change meant that producers Cameron and Hurd would have a difficult task finding an actor large enough to compete against Schwarzenegger and decided to cast TV and stage actor Michael Biehn against type as the young-but-hardened guerrilla fighter from the future. For the role of Sarah Connor, the shallow coffee-shop waitress who becomes a seasoned warrior, the producers chose Linda Hamilton.

Hamilton, best known up to this point as the lady in distress in *King Kong Lives* and as Catherine Chandler on TV's *Beauty and the Beast*, was somewhat critical of the film's leading star prior to shooting.

> I didn't take Schwarzenegger very seriously as an actor at that time. I said, "Oh Lord, why cast a man who looks like a machine as a machine? Cast somebody who's very thin to do these superhuman acts." And I was wrong. He was used tremendously effectively, and he was served very well by that film.

In interviews Arnold Schwarzenegger dismissed concerns about critics or other actors taking him seriously. He said, smiling broadly:

> I don't care. The important thing to me is that I'm doing work that people enjoy out there, that the movie makes good money, that the studio makes the money back, and that I'm having a great time at what I'm doing. I don't even consider *myself* serious. So how do I expect people to take me serious? I think this whole Hollywood thing has to be taken much looser...it's just entertainment.

Principal shooting in and around Los Angeles began in mid-March 1984 and ran till the end of May. Director Cameron did not have the luxury of multiple cameras and was forced to make each shot count. (For the most part, what audiences see in the final film is what he shot with a single camera.) Postproduction was a mere three months, through August, and Cameron had to fight for every penny to complete his vision. The director said:

> They were extremely hesitant about going over $4 million. We convinced them this movie could not be made for less than $6 million, especially with Arnold Schwarzenegger starring, because he commanded a significant salary; the final shooting budget was actually $6.5 million.

To complete the film "on time and on budget," Cameron and special-effects coordinator Ernie Farino turned to the specialists at Fantasy II. Many of the effects, including the flash-forwards that depicted the war-torn society of the future, were accomplished by Gene Warren, Jr., Leslie Huntley, and Peter Kleinow with cleverly designed miniatures on a shoestring budget. Kleinow also produced the stop-motion effects of the chrome robot skeleton of the Terminator as it fights on even after its outer body has been burned away. Working closely with Stan Winston's designs and Doug Beswick's superior miniatures, the Fantasy II staff produced over ninety different special-effects shots for *The Terminator*. Even though the work was very difficult and the budget extremely limited, most of the effects are superior to those in films costing three or four times as much.

By early September 1984, Cameron and Hurd had completed the final cut, trimming the film to a mere 108 minutes, and were ready to test their motion picture on the public.

Critical Commentary

Even before *The Terminator* was released on October 26, 1984, word of mouth had it that here was a spectacular surprise, a good old B-movie that harkened back to the simpler days of double features. "Thrill-packed." "Fast and Furious." "Astounding." Audience members and critics alike praised Jim Cameron's nightmare vision as the best film of 1984. The *Washington Post* favorably wrote that "Schwarzenegger creates an inimitable villain, an

Linda Hamilton as Sarah Connor.

unstoppable killing machine, part metal, part man." *Variety* termed the film "a cross between *The Road Warrior* and *Blade Runner*"—yet concluded that Cameron had managed to avoid most of the trappings to create a totally original work. By the end of the year, after *The Terminator* had successfully beaten David Lynch's overblown *Dune* and Peter Hyams's belated sequel to Kubrick's *2001: A Space Odyssey* at the box office, it was voted by *Time* magazine as one of the ten best films of 1984. Later, *The Terminator* won the Grand Prix at the Avoriaz Film Festival in France. The film went on to score a respectable $30 million in domestic rentals.

The film owes much of its strength to writer-director James Cameron and its appeal to Arnold Schwarzenegger. Prior to *The Terminator*, Cameron was a struggling filmmaker who had an eye for art direction and special effects. Like Stanley Kubrick and Ridley Scott before him, he sought to prove that motion pictures could provide a narrative approach through its visual medium. His film generates high premium excitement from the opening frame, dispensing with the need for traditional storytelling in favor of explosive action and nerve-jangling adventure. When it is absolutely necessary, his witty and well-written script provides the essential information to keep the pace moving. His direction is superb,

Michael Biehn as Kyle Reese.

course of the film, yet his cold presence permeates every scene. Very carefully written one-liners—like the classic "I'll be back!" or "Faach yu, ahs-hole!"—are delivered with such grimness and precision that the audience is both frightened and amused. He also perfects deadpan expressions that are befitting a robot, and he moves with determined menace. Schwarzenegger told *People* magazine that "it's much more challenging to play a robot than a human," and if that is true, then Arnold certainly deserved an Academy Award for his performance. He's terrific in the fight scenes and both monstrously powerful and charismatic in sequence after sequence. *The Terminator* marks the real turning point in his career.

In a 1990 interview Schwarzenegger confessed:

There were various stepping-stones in my career. One of them was *Conan*, because it was the first time I did a film with that kind of budget and I had the title role. The next big stepping-stone was *The Terminator*. With *The Terminator*, I think people became aware of the fact that I didn't really have to take my shirt off or run around and expose my muscles in order to sell tickets. After I did *The Terminator* and we had seen it be more successful than the Conan films, people then sent a variety of different kinds of scripts—all in the action-adventure genre, but they were not muscle movies or Viking movies or pirate movies or anything like that....

To their credit, both Linda Hamilton and Michael Biehn perform admirably opposite Arnold. In fact, Hamilton gives what may be the performance of her career as Sarah Connor. By turning in a masterful portrayal of a character who changes from a frightened, bewildered waitress to a seasoned warrior, she shakes off many of the lackluster roles that have typecast her. None of them have better displayed her strengths. Michael Biehn delivers such a powerful performance as Kyle Reese that one wishes he would survive to challenge the killer robot in future installments.

Admittedly, the juxtaposition of a war-torn future into our present is not a new idea in science fiction. Writers have been creating alternate futures (as well as imaginary time lines for the present) since H. G. Wells penned *The Time Machine*. Harlan Ellison claimed that the film's story line had been taken from

with a nice eye for sharp detail. But Cameron views the film as more than a basic action-adventure thriller, citing the theme as being "strictly human and personal." Sarah is forced into a situation in which she has to take responsibility for her own fate as well as that of the planet. That represents high drama for the director. Juggling all of these elements at once, Cameron combines plot, characterization, hard-hitting action, and special effects to create a unique film experience.

Part of *The Terminator*'s appeal also comes from watching a slimmed-down Schwarzenegger stomping and crashing his way through almost every scene. His screen persona as a gentle giant has been stripped away to show Arnold as a dark, relentless killer. Any awkwardness in lengthy conversation scenes that he may have shown in the Conan movies has been eliminated, for he has few lines. The Terminator never says more than a few sentences throughout the

74

two scripts he had written for *The Outer Limits**
some twenty years before and successfully sued
Hemdale and Orion Pictures for proper acknowledg-
ment. (Cable-television prints and videocassettes
[from Thorn/EMI] of *The Terminator* give Ellison a
special credit line.) But Ellison's stories bear only a
modest connection to *The Terminator*. The low-budget *Cyborg 2087* actually resembles James
Cameron's motion picture in more details. In that
earlier film, Michael Rennie as the titular cyborg
Garth must locate and persuade the creator of a revolutionary device (which enslaves men's minds) to
cease experimentation, or terminate him, before
robots from the other side can stop his desperate mission. Directed by Franklin Adreon and written by
Arthur C. Pierce, the 1966 film was made for television but released theatrically with an eighty-six-
minute running time. Like Cameron's Terminator,
Garth has traveled back in time from a totalitarian
world run by technocrats; but his mission is essentially a noble one, whereas the Cyberdyne Model 101
desires to continue machine rule by altering past
events. But all comparisons aside, Cameron's film
succeeds on the strength of its hard, fast-paced style
and not its narrative content.

Following the immediate critical and box-office
success of *The Terminator*, Cameron discussed the
possibility of a sequel with the *New York Times*.
"He's a machine," Cameron reasoned, "and
machines are mass-produced, so there might be
another one in the warehouse...." But before he
could undertake another Terminator film, he and his
partner, Hurd, had contracted with 20th Century-
Fox to direct and write a sequel to *Alien*. He would
later helm *The Abyss* for Fox before beginning work
on *Terminator 2: Judgment Day*.

The original version of *The Terminator* is currently available on videocassette from HBO Video and
Hemdale Home Video and appears regularly on many
cable channels. A special laserdisc, featuring a letter-
boxed edition of the motion picture, became available in 1991.

James Cameron, cocreator and director of *The Terminator*.

*In his award-winning script "Soldier," Ellison relates the story
of a twenty-first-century warrior who is inadvertently yanked
from his nuclear war-torn world and thrust into the 1960s. He is
befriended by a scientist and his family but ultimately sacrifices
his life to kill an adversary sent to eliminate him. In "Demon
with the Glass Hand," Trent is sent back from the future with little knowledge of his own origin beyond five days before. While
battling with alien invaders intent on enslaving the earth of the
future, he discovers that he is a robot that contains valuable
knowledge about mankind's salvation.

FIVE

SHE-DEVIL WITH A SWORD

Red Sonja

1985. Metro-Goldwyn-Mayer/United Artists in association with Dino De Laurentiis Productions. *Director:* Richard Fleischer. *Producer:* Christian Ferry. *Executive Producer:* A. Michael Lieberman. *Screenplay:* Clive Exton and George MacDonald Fraser. *Based on characters created by* Robert E. Howard. *Photography:* Giuseppe Rotunno. *Music:* Ennio Morricone. *Editor:* Frank J. Urioste. *Starring:* Arnold Schwarzenegger, Brigitte Nielsen, Sandahl Bergman, Ernie Reyes, Jr., Paul Smith, Janet Agren, Tad Horino, Pat Roach, and Ronald Lacey. Released on July 3, 1985. [89 minutes]

The box-office success of the two Conans generated this semisequel, which is really little more than a remake of the first film with Brigitte Nielsen in the pivotal role as "the she-devil with a sword." Filmed on the same extravagant sets, utilizing the same lavish costumes and production team, and featuring Arnold Schwarzenegger in a thinly disguised version of Conan, *Red Sonja* virtually repeats the condition of conflict in that earlier movie. The motion picture is also the least satisfying of Dino De Laurentiis's Howard adaptations, again directed by Richard Fleischer, and rather than providing a spectacular climax to what had been a visually striking and particularly remarkable film series, it plods along like an inferior low-budget rip-off.

(Opposite) Schwarzenegger agreed to a cameo appearance as Kalidor to satisfy Dino De Laurentiis but was surprised to learn the Italian filmmaker planned to market the epic with Arnold's name above the title. (Courtesy M-G-M/United Artists in association with Dino De Laurentiis Productions)

The Screen Story

The precredits narrative reveals that "her name was Red Sonja" and that "she lived in a savage world in an age of violence...a fierce warrior with flaming red hair. In the Hyborian Kingdom, her quest for justice and vengeance became a legend...." Red Sonja (Brigitte Nielsen) has been beaten and raped, her family murdered, and her village burned to the ground because she has refused the sexual advances of a powerfully wicked queen. Apparently, Queen Gedren (Sandahl Bergman) has spent years searching for the perfect lover; but when Sonja publicly denounces her, then strikes the queen across the face with a baton (which causes a permanent injury), Gedren's rage reduces the young woman's world to cinders. After being violated by a number of savage warriors, Sonja is left for dead. But a white ghostlike figure awakens Sonja and endows her with great strength and a sword arm that has no equal.

Many years pass, and while Sonja perfects her talents as a warrior without peer, Queen Gedren (now wearing a golden mask to hide her disfigurement) plots to take possession of an all-powerful talisman. Accompanied by her cruel henchman Ikol (Ronald Lacey) and an elite army of assassins, she raids a holy temple and massacres all but one of its Amazonian protectors. (The priestesses had been preparing to plunge the glowing green talisman into total darkness to prevent its power from destroying the world, but the queen has other plans for it.) Varna (Janet Agren), the surviving priestess and a long-lost sister of Sonja's, manages to escape Gedren's wrath but is mortally wounded by two of her soldiers. As she struggles to

warn her sister, Varna enlists the aid of a mysterious swordsman, Lord Kalidor (Schwarzenegger). He promises to help her and rides to Sonja with news of the talisman and her dying sister.

Red Sonja has been studying the art of war with an ancient Chinese swordsman (Tad Horino) in a Tibetan monastery and has vowed never to give herself to a man unless he defeats her in a fair fight. When Kalidor arrives with his distressing news, the red-haired warrior realizes she has less than thirteen days to prevent Gedren from destroying the world. Sonja dismisses Kalidor and sets off on a solitary quest in the strange, hostile land to defeat her enemy. Along the way she reluctantly joins forces with the arrogant Prince Tarn (Ernie Reyes, Jr.), who has lost his city to Gedren, and his bumbling protector Falkon (Paul Smith), yet continually refuses the help of Kalidor. The three travelers fight against the elements, rampaging marauders, prehistoric beasts, and master swordsmen, while the mysterious stranger works behind the scenes to protect their safety.

Meanwhile, Queen Gedren has managed to capitalize upon her newfound power. Destroying city after city and vanquishing those who oppose her, she spreads her ruthlessness throughout the entire world. From her castle in the Land of Eternal Night, as she makes preparations to release the full power of the talisman, her priests warn Gedren that Red Sonja is approaching to oppose her. But the evil queen is not at all concerned. She looks upon the redheaded beauty with lustful designs.

When Sonja and her party are saved by Kalidor from a subterranean sea dragon, she reconsiders her position toward the mysterious stranger. Perhaps she has been too hard on him. Red Sonja, Prince Tarn, and Falkon invite Kalidor to join them on their quest to destroy Gedren and the evil talisman, but he quickly reveals that he is not some mercenary for hire. He is, in fact, the high lord of Kalidor—the man responsible for seeing that the talisman is plunged into darkness. He also reveals his attraction to her and challenges Sonja to a duel. If he bests her in combat, she must yield to him. Believing that he is no match for her, she agrees. The two warriors fight, but after several long hours they stop, too exhausted to continue. Kalidor has failed to defeat Red Sonja in battle but has won her heart.

On the thirteenth and final day, the four travelers

Brigitte Nielsen as *Red Sonja*, the she-devil with a sword.

Arnold Schwarzenegger as the mysterious swordsman Lord
Kalidor.

arrive at Queen Gedren's castle and gain access to
the palace through an underground passageway.
They defeat her elite guards and discover that the talisman has become tremendously powerful. Fearful
that he, too, will be consumed by the evil, Ikol
attempts to flee with the palace jewels. But Tarn
blocks his departure and sends the wicked sorcerer
to his death. Before he can rejoin the others, however, the youthful prince is taken hostage by Gedren.
She demands their surrender and forces Sonja to face
her with weapons drawn. The two rivals battle,
sword to sword, to the death, but Gedren is no
match for the powerful might of the red-haired warrior. Red Sonja easily defeats the wicked queen.

During their struggle, Kalidor manages to penetrate the city vaults (with the help of Falkon) and
comes face-to-face with the glowing green evil of the
talisman. Summoning all his power, Kalidor completes the task for Sonja. The talisman is cast into a
bottomless pit, and the evil fortress collapses down
upon it. Later, in the safety of the forest, Prince Tarn
and Falkon, his protector, look on as spectators as
Sonja and Kalidor fight each other for the power of
love.

Production Details

Dino De Laurentiis once again turned to Conan territory and to the fantastic stories of heroes and villains
created by sword-and-sorcery writer Robert E.
Howard. But wanting something more than a retread
of the two earlier films, the Italian producer turned
to Red Sonja as a feminine answer to Conan. This
sexy, statuesque, red-haired warrior had been first
introduced by Howard in several Conan stories back
in the thirties, then popularized in comic-book
adventures loosely adapted by Roy Thomas for
Marvel Comics in the seventies. Recognizing the
appeal of her character to contemporary audiences,
De Laurentiis purchased the rights to the Sonja stories in 1982. The search then began for the right
actress to play the part.

Sandahl Bergman, who had played Valeria in
Conan the Barbarian, was initially cast in the title
role, but she chose instead to appear as the evil
Queen Gedren in order to avoid typecasting. (As the
villain of the piece, Bergman takes top prize. Her
obsession with power and her controlled madness
are handled superbly, and her lesbian queen represents the only believable character in an otherwise
lackluster production. Regrettably, this talented, leggy

Priestesses prepare to plunge the glowing green talisman into total darkness to prevent its power from destroying the world

blonde was unable to find suitable employment outside the sword-and-sorcery genre, with the exception of Bob Fosse's *All That Jazz*.) De Laurentiis acknowledged her decision and concluded that what his picture really needed was a fresh face.

For nearly a year, beginning in the fall of 1983, a search was conducted for the Amazonian actress who would star in his proposed film. Fans of the comic series Wendy Pini (who would later gain fame as the creator of *Elfquest*), Angelique Trouvere, and many others modeled homemade costumes of Red Sonja at various science-fiction and fantasy conventions, hoping to attract De Laurentiis's attention. But he remained irresolute. Traveling the world, he was determined to find a very unique woman of fire and passion who would be capable of re-creating Robert E. Howard's legendary swordswoman. Then, less than eight weeks before production began, he chanced to glance at a fashion magazine with twenty-one-year-old Danish model Brigitte Nielsen gracing the cover. She was tall and long-legged and had the physique of an Olympic athlete. Studying her photograph carefully, De Laurentiis knew that he had found his Sonja.

Nielsen explained how the famed producer contacted her:

I was in Milan for a three-week modeling job when Dino De Laurentiis called from New York to ask if I'd test for *Red Sonja*. Truthfully, I had *no* idea who Dino De Laurentiis was! So I made a few calls—you never know who's a crackpot—and when I said, "De Laurentiis," they said, "Go for it!" So I flew to Rome to meet him and landed *the title role*.

Born and educated in Copenhagen, the lithe and lissome beauty was anxious to follow a long line of charismatic models who had parlayed their looks into cinematic stardom. Brigitte ("Gitte" to her friends) Nielsen possessed all the right looks to be truly a standout sensation, with a mane of rich reddish hair, a trim 36-24-36 figure, and a six-foot-tall frame. As an international queen of high-fashion photography, she had distinguished herself worldwide with dozens of magazine covers. In addition to being fluent in five languages, she projected an extraordinary presence. Prior to filming, she worked with stunt coordinator Vic Armstrong and studied sword fighting with Kiyoshi Yamazaki. She also learned how to ride a horse and spent many hours on the script with a dialogue coach. Direct, charming, and very confident, Nielsen was determined to make the most of her role.

(Above) When the holy temple is invaded by an elite army of assassins, Kalidor springs into action.

(Below) Varna (Janet Agren), a surviving priestess, escapes Gedren's wrath and demands that Kalidor warn her sister Sonja of the imminent danger.

"Brigitte had a lot of sparkle, had an amazing body, and is an incredible girl," director Richard Fleischer recalled years after being first introduced to her by Dino De Laurentiis. But he did express serious concerns about her limited acting range and ability to "carry" the film totally on her own merits.

De Laurentiis allayed the veteran director's fears by persuading Arnold Schwarzenegger to take second billing to her and to do an extended cameo as Prince Kalidor, a mysterious warrior who comes to Sonja's aid. Following his success with the Conan films and

Red Sonja (Brigitte Nielsen) proves to an ancient Chinese swordsman (Tad Horino) that she has mastered the weapon as well.

James Cameron's *Terminator*, Arnold had become a major box-office draw, and the Italian producer was counting on his participation to sell the movie to American audiences. Arnold felt an obligation to De Laurentiis for having given him his start and, despite objections from fiancée Maria Shriver, agreed to a brief appearance. After reading the script and realizing the extent of his part, however, Schwarzenegger attempted to back out, but he was unable to break his contractual obligations.

Arnold remembered bitterly after the shoot:

Dino De Laurentiis said he wanted me to do a cameo and have me work for three weeks—and then he went and sold the picture with my name above the title and that's bad news. I told him it was a big mistake. It wouldn't work—you can't fool people. But he didn't listen.

Martial-arts specialist Ernie Reyes, Jr., who had become a popular cult figure, was hired as the boy-prince Tarn to satisfy a youthful audience. Beefy character actor Paul Smith, who had scored as Bluto opposite Robin Williams in Robert Altman's *Popeye* and the Beast Rabban in David Lunch's *Dune*, was added for comic relief as the bumbling Falkon. The cast was completed by Ronald Lacey (from *Raiders of the Lost Ark*), professional wrestler Pat Roach, and European beauties Janet Agren and Donna Osterbuhr. The screenplay for *Red Sonja* was written by Clive Exton and veteran George MacDonald Fraser. Danilo Donati replaced both Pier Luigi Basile as production and John Bloomfield as costume designer, while talented composer Basil Poledouris (of the first two Conan films) was dropped in favor of longtime De Laurentiis collaborator Ennio Morricone.

The $15 million production began filming on September 24, 1984, on location in Celano and Abruzzi, Italy, not far from Rome. By mid-December 1984, the crew moved onto majestic sets which were constructed at De Laurentiis's newly refurbished Stabilimenti Cinematografici Pontini studios. The formerly Italian-based producer had learned some valuable lessons about cost overruns from operating in Wilmington, North Carolina, and Churubusco Studios, Mexico City, and decided (early in 1984) to reopen his old Dinocitta facility. He reasoned that a motion picture could be made there for about half of what it costs in North America. The studios had once been the home to a number of De Laurentiis productions in the sixties, including John Huston's *The Bible* and Roger

Vadim's *Barbarella*. When hard economic times forced the closure of the studios during the seventies, the producer and film mogul was forced to move to the United States in order to make movies. But he never gave up hope of someday reopening the studio, which boasted five of the biggest soundstages in the world. Production on *Red Sonja* and *Total Recall* (Canadian director David Cronenberg was then involved with that project) gave him the excuse he needed to return to Italy.

Richard Fleischer had projected that the shoot, including location work, would last eleven weeks but later conceded that his estimate was an unrealistic one. The veteran found that the motion picture's emphasis on sorcery and special effects had actually caused the production to run over schedule. Trimming many elaborate and unnecessary sequences, he chose to focus on the elements of action-adventure. "There is more sword than sorcery in *Red Sonja*," he explained. "In fact, there is very little sorcery. It's played very realistically. It has a fantasy feeling in the costumes and in the story." The director managed to shoot most of the film's other effects, including a climactic earthquake that reduces Gedren's palace to rubble, during principal photography.

Red Sonja wrapped production in February 1985 and was scheduled for a summer release in the United States by Metro-Goldwyn-Mayer.

Critical Commentary

Lacking the strong visual imagination and tremendous narrative drive of the two earlier films, *Red Sonja* stumbles through landslides, earthquakes, swordplay, and rubbery monsters on its pathetic quest for an ancient talisman. Admittedly, there's plenty of action sequences, but the wretched acting and contrived plot condemned this film to an early death. If the motion picture had been played for camp (like Mike Hodges's *Flash Gordon*), perhaps it could have survived. But such lines of dialogue as "I have fought 177 men and the only one to survive has no legs" sound more like outtakes from *Monty Python and the Holy Grail* than an action-adventure film. *Red Sonja* isn't campy enough to be funny or strong enough to be taken as a worthy successor to the Conan films. Showing signs of heavy editing, its eighty-nine minutes of length must have seemed overly boring even to its producers.

The fault lies squarely with the film's producer,

Kalidor surprises Sonja in the forest and challenges her to a duel.

Dino De Laurentiis, and his decision to build a $15 million motion picture around a twenty-one-year-old model he glimpsed on the cover of a magazine. Brigitte Nielsen in fact projects very little screen presence. She comes across as just a tough tomboy, displaying the appropriate "butch" quality required for the character but little else. Red Sonja, the she-devil with a sword, should be a fiery warrior who matches Conan deed for deed. Nielsen also fails to project any of Sonja's exotic sexuality. While she may appear especially good with the stunts (thanks to the choreography of Vic Armstrong and Sergio Mioni), Brigitte is totally outclassed by her fellow performers. Her less than adequate performance gives rise to speculation as to what Sandahl Bergman might have done with the part.

Arnold Schwarzenegger, surer, brisker, and more sardonic as Lord Kalidor, delivers a performance that is a pleasure to watch. He seems to personify the meaning of "cool" in this film: totally relaxed but able to take command of any situation. He also retains the tough persona and reveals an even more sophisticated wit than as Conan. This is especially true during his later scenes with Nielsen. Rather than reducing Schwarzenegger to a supporting role (and reinventing his character as the mysterious swordsman), the writers would have been wiser to introduce Red Sonja as a secondary figure in a third Conan film. Then audiences would not have felt cheated by his presence and preeminent billing.

Whereas much has been written in the tabloids about Schwarzenegger's torrid love affair with the

Sandahl Bergman as the evil Queen Gedren who seeks dominion of the world through the power of a sacred talisman.

Danish bombshell, very little documentation exists. Journalist Wendy Leigh, in *Arnold: An Unauthorized Biography*, claims that the two had "sex anywhere, anytime, and anyhow," even though Arnold was practically engaged to Maria Shriver. Others have said that Brigitte tried unsuccessfully to seduce Arnold several times during the production, while others suggest he was so attracted to the female mirror image of himself that he took her without prior consent. Later, after the production wrapped (we're told), he "gave" Ms. Nielsen to rival Sylvester Stallone as a peace offering. Compelling though each of these rumors may be, none of them have any basis in fact. Nielsen and Schwarzenegger's lack of on-screen chemistry together is, in itself, proof of that.

Red Sonja debuted on July 3, 1985, to appalling reviews and disappointing box-office returns. Genre favorites, like *Cocoon*, *Lifeforce*, and *Back to the Future*, easily outpaced its tired, lackluster formula.

Kathleen Carroll of the New York *Daily News* called the movie "shamelessly silly," while Archer Winsten of the *New York Post* described it simply as "bubble-headed." Michael Clark of *USA Today* was probably *Red Sonja*'s harshest critic, referring to the film as "a strong sleeping pill." Several months later, when the motion picture finally opened in Europe, it proved to be a major disappointment there as well. The failure of *Red Sonja* (and *Dune*, earlier that year) spelled the death blow for DEG. Dino De Laurentiis has not been able to mount a major production since, and the balance of Robert E. Howard's properties (including the characters Conan, King Kull, and Red Sonja) would seem to be forever lost in litigation.

Although it was a resounding flop (and received the dubious honor of being named as one of the worst films of the year), *Red Sonja* did not appear to affect Schwarzenegger's career. He was already at work developing other projects, including the big-budget *Commando*, and did not participate in the film's publicity (something he did for all his other

Red Sonja is captured by Gedren's elite guards.

84

motion pictures), nor did he attend the world premiere. Shortly after its release, he confessed:

Red Sonja is really the only film that really went into the toilet. It was a pitiful performance, and I was so happy that it did as bad as it did because people had no chance to see the movie. It was one of those films where I felt I should do a favor to Dino De Laurentiis, to participate and do a cameo, and he ended up using every frame that I did.

When I went to see it with my wife, we looked at the film and we looked at each other afterwards. Maria said if this film doesn't ruin your career in two seconds, then you have tremendous staying power in this town. Sure enough, the movie came out, it had no impact on my career. When *Commando* came out, it went through the roof.

Ironically, while *Red Sonja* was shooting on the stages of Stabilimenti Cinematografici Pontini studios, an early version of *Total Recall* was being readied as De Laurentiis's next production. Production designer Pier Luigi Basile (who had worked on *Conan the Barbarian* and *Dune*) was busily sketching the futuristic sets for Mars, while then director David Cronenberg was preparing for principal photography to begin later in the year. Had *Red Sonja* been even moderately successful, *Total Recall* would have begun filming in 1985 *without Schwarzenegger!* The $22 million production was, in fact, canceled, and both De Laurentiis and Schwarzenegger turned their attention to a modest little thriller (financed by Columbia Pictures) called *Raw Deal*. Years later, the superstar would persuade Carolco to purchase the Ron Shusett–Dan O'Bannon script from DEG.

Red Sonja is currently available on videocassette and laserdisc from M-G-M/UA Home Video.

Arnold Schwarzenegger and Brigitte Nielsen share a rare off-camera moment on the set of *Red Sonja*. (Courtesy M-G-M/United Artists in association with Dino De Laurentis Productions)

Six

THE SAGA OF G.I. JOE

Commando

1985. 20th Century-Fox. *Director:* Mark L. Lester. *Producer:* Joel Silver. *Associate Producers:* Joseph Loeb III and Matthew Weisman. *Screenplay:* Steven E. de Souza. *Based on an original story by* Loeb, Weisman, and de Souza. *Photography:* Matthew F. Leonetti. *Music:* James Horner. *Editors:* Mark Goldblatt, John F. Link, and Glenn Farr. *Starring:* Arnold Schwarzenegger, Rae Dawn Chong, Vernon Wells, Dan Hedaya, James Olson, David Patrick Kelly, Alyssa Milano, Charles Meshack, Carlos Cervantes, and Bill Duke. Released on October 4, 1985. [88 minutes]

Fresh from *The Terminator* and an unfortunate detour into *Red Sonja*, Arnold Schwarzenegger again turned to the action-adventure genre to play another deadly warrior in *Commando*. But what made his Col. John Matrix, a retired commando who is forced to undertake the most desperate mission of his life, different from the others was the finely written character by Steven E. de Souza. Based on a story by Joseph Loeb III, Matthew Weisman, and de Souza, produced by Joel Silver, and directed by Mark. L. Lester (not, of course, the onetime child actor who starred in *Oliver!*), the film offered Schwarzenegger his first real opportunity to demonstrate his skills as an actor. The violent fantasy also allowed Arnold to cement his reputation as a genuine crowd pleaser and box-office force.

He looked upon the film as an important step in his acting career, for the character of Matrix was fully realized and multidimensional. He revealed during a nationwide press junket for the motion picture:

(Opposite) Schwarzenegger portrays Col. John Matrix, the retired leader of a Special Forces commando unit. (Courtesy 20th Century-Fox)

In the beginning of *Commando*, I play a loving, gentle, and understanding father to my daughter Jenny. I educate her and protect her; it's one-hundred-eighty degrees from the life I used to lead. Then she's kidnapped, and I have to immediately snap back into the personality many associate with *The Terminator* and the Conan films. I become a fighting machine that will not stop until my objective is completed.

The Screen Story

After the assassinations of several retired members of a special operations strike force assigned to political hot spots, Gen. Franklin Kirby (James Olson) decides to pay a surprise visit to the former leader at his hillside retreat on Mount Baldy, California. Intelligent, cool under pressure, physically imposing, an expert in martial arts and the use of firearms and combat weaponry, Col. John Matrix (Schwarzenegger) was a commando without peer. But like many soldiers, Matrix had outlived his usefulness and was "retired" by the military. Still armed with the physical skills and knowledge that made him a superb soldier, Matrix lives under a new identity in a rural setting with his eleven-year-old daughter, Jenny (Alyssa Milano).

Kirby arrives and warns Matrix that his former cohorts have turned up missing or dead. Kirby posts several guards to protect him, but they are no match for the hired army of killers that storm Matrix's home.

Years before, Matrix's strike force played a key role in the ouster of General Arius (Dan Hedaya), a vicious dictator of the South American country of Val

Verde, and subsequent installation of a democratically elected president. The deposed Arius harbors resentment toward Matrix and, aided by renegade soldier-for-hire Bennett (Vernon Wells), has tracked him down. Bennett takes Jenny hostage and forces Matrix (if he ever hopes to see his daughter alive again) to take one last mission: return to Val Verde, where he is a "hero of the revolution," and kill President Velasquez so that Arius can return triumphantly to power. "However, if you try anything else," Bennett

Meshack) with a deadly swift karate chop and jumps from the plane while it is taxiing down the runway for takeoff. Back in the airport terminal, he kidnaps a young stewardess named Cindy (Rae Dawn Chong) in order to follow Sully (David Patrick Kelly), one of the general's toughs. Matrix and the reluctant Cindy are not exactly fond of each other, but he needs her help.

When she inquires about the fate of a villain that Matrix has literally just dropped from a precipice, he

(Left) Matrix as the seasoned warrior… and (right) a loving father to Jenny (Alyssa Milano).

warns, "I'll send her to you in pieces."

But John Matrix knows that he faces the classic no-win situation; even if he were to capitulate to Arius's demands, his daughter would be killed, if only for the gratification of Bennett. ("They offered me one hundred grand…but you know something? When I found out I'd be getting my hands on you, I told them I would do it for nothing.") Angered, Matrix decides to follow a dangerous course that might lead to the rescue of his daughter. "I'll be back," he warns Bennett, but the renegade agent is less than bothered by his threat. Once aboard the plane to Val Verde, Matrix kills Arius henchman Henriques (Charles

replies, "I let him go."

Arius has a clandestine army billeted in an island fortress off the coast of Santa Barbara in the Channel Islands. Foremost among them is Bennett, the man in love with war who masterminded the kidnapping of Matrix's daughter. He truly wants the chance to go up against his former commander and prove that he, not Matrix, is the commando without peer. It's only a deadly and brutal game for him.

Matrix casts aside the role of the loving parent and unleashes the ultimate soldier and one-man army. With only eleven hours before the body on the plane to Val Verde will be discovered, he robs an army surplus store and arms himself for combat with an arsenal of weapons—a Valmet full-auto battle rifle, a selective-fire Uzi, a Desert Eagle .357 Magnum auto, a twelve-gauge Remington H70 laser shotgun, a rocket launcher, two sixty-pound M-60 light machine guns, and a Colt M-16, among others. He is momentarily captured by the police, but his stewardess friend Cindy reluctantly agrees to free him with a rocket launcher.

Attempting to help Matrix but always one step behind is General Kirby, the man who trained Matrix and gave him his new identity.

Disregarding the overwhelming odds that face him, Matrix steals an amphibious plane and, with the help of Cindy, sets out for Arius's island fortress. Several hours later, just as the plane with Henriques's body is landing in Val Verde, Matrix wades ashore. Heavily armed, the ultimate warrior takes out the entire garrison and storms the main house, killing Arius. But Bennett is still holding Jenny prisoner, and Matrix is forced to fight for her life.

The "commando" and his renegade friend face off hand to hand, trading deadly blows with knives. Bennett can't resist the challenge of defeating his former commander, and Matrix recognizes that desire as a weakness he can exploit. Momentarily, Bennett gets the upper hand, but he is soon overwhelmed by the superior training of John Matrix.

Reunited with Jenny, Matrix returns to the beach where he left Cindy. Kirby's men have arrived to mop up after Matrix, and the general himself offers Matrix a chance to start up his former unit; but the warrior claims that he is through fighting. Both he and Jenny climb aboard the seaplane and fly off into the sunset with Cindy.

Production Details

The original story treatment for *Commando* had been circulating around Hollywood for several years before Joel Silver acquired it for his newly formed Silver Pictures. Written by Joseph Loeb III and Matthew Weisman while students at Columbia University's film school, the script provided the two with fantasies of

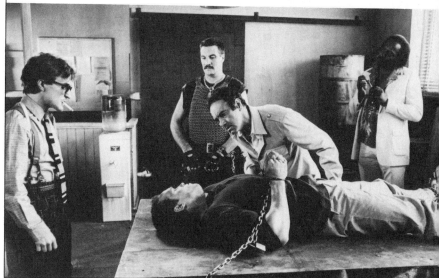

(Top) Forced back into action when his daughter is kidnapped, Matrix finds himself surrounded by hostile forces.

(Bottom) General Arius (Dan Hedaya, below center) and his vicious henchman, (left to right) Sully (David Patrick Kelly), Bennett (Vernon Wells), and Henriques (Charles Meshack), make Matrix an offer that he dare not refuse.

raising the necessary capital and producing the motion picture themselves. They viewed the character as an "American James Bond that people in this country could relate to," according to Weisman, and felt that the time was right to create a series of movies centered around John Matrix. After they wrote the screenplay for *Teen Wolf*, starring Michael J. Fox as a high school student who discovers that he is a werewolf, Silver recognized their talent.

Along with Lawrence Gordon, Silver had produced the box-office smash *48 HRS.*, *Streets of Fire*, and *Brewster's Millions* by the age of thirty. But he

Rae Dawn Chong is Cindy, a stewardess who reluctantly agrees to help Matrix free his daughter.

did not start out as a producer. After attending New York University's film school and making his first film, *Ten Pin Alley*, Silver moved to Los Angeles to break into the movie business. His first job was as an assistant to Gordon, and he eventually worked his way up to the position of president of the motion picture division of Lawrence Gordon Productions. Silver helped develop and market the Burt Reynolds movies *Hooper* and *The End;* he was associate producer of *The Warriors*, coproducer of the musical fantasy *Xanadu*, and sole producer of *Weird Science*. *Commando* represented his fifth film as producer, and he brought it to his former boss (Gordon), who was now the president and chief operating officer of 20th Century-Fox.

Lawrence Gordon felt *Commando* required a major rewrite, including some much-needed comic relief, and instructed Silver to hire one of the best

writers in Hollywood—Steven E. de Souza. A former free-lance writer for the *New York Times*, de Souza had broken into the film industry many years before with a script for Harve Bennett's two-part *Six Million Dollar Man*. He went on to write for many other series before turning producer of *Knight Rider*'s first season and creator of *The Powers of Matthew Star*. At the same time, he began scripting movies. His first effort was the campy superhero musical *The Return of Captain Invincible*, but his collaboration (with Silver) on *48 HRS.* launched his career into hyperdrive. His work on *Commando* would produce a witty, adventure-filled project that Gordon was anxious to green-light.

When Arnold Schwarzenegger was voted the International Star of 1984 by the country's theater owners at their ShoWest Convention in Las Vegas, Joel Silver realized that only one man could play John Matrix. Thus began another long-term relationship of producer and star. "When I deal with a studio, I make what I want clear right at the beginning," Schwarzenegger recalled, not wishing to repeat the past mistakes he made with Dino De Laurentiis. "I muscle my way through it. But as soon as we get to the set, I step back and let the director have his space."

The man Joel Silver had chosen to direct *Commando* was Mark Lester. Lester had been drawing praise for his diverse, imaginative films ever since he won the documentary award at the Venice Film Festival in 1971 for *Twilight of the Mayas*. His other features were low-budget, action-adventure vehicles that generally turned a box-office profit. Both *Class of '84* and *Firestarter* were not very well received by critics or the public, but they demonstrated Lester's singular style and brought him to the attention of Silver. A native of Cleveland, Lester had grown up in the San Fernando Valley and had received a political-science degree from California State University.

Rae Dawn Chong (daughter of Tommy Chong of Cheech and Chong) has amassed an impressive body of films, though none more impressive than her debut in 1982's *Quest for Fire*, and was enlisted as Cindy, the wisecracking stewardess. Dan Hedaya, Carla's slobby ex-husband Nick Tortelli on *Cheers*, came aboard as the deposed dictator Arius, and Vernon Wells, a native of Australia who made his first appearance as the madman with a mohawk in *The Road Warrior* and reprised his madman for Joel Silver's *Weird Science*, was given the role of Bennett. Newcomer Alyssa Milano, from TV's *Who's the Boss?*, was signed on as Jenny.

No matter how much any one of them had been exposed to Arnold Schwarzenegger through his films or his career as a bodybuilder, most of the cast and crew were curious to meet him and begin their work with him. "Who is Arnold?" Chong responded to questions about her costar. "Well, Arnold is a movie star. He's golden. He's smart, beautiful to look at, and more talented than people realize." Wells confessed that he "didn't expect a whole lot from him" at first, "but as it turned out he's an amazing guy to work with, and I was lucky because we developed an unusual chemistry between us that was essential to the finale." Director Lester summed up most of the cast and crew's fear by saying,

> It's easy to fall into a trap about Arnold's abilities when you consider his previous films and his physique. But he has this incredible sense of humor, and it goes all day long. So we brought that element, Arnold's natural humor, into the film.

The company began production on April 22, 1985, at a modern log cabin on Mt. Baldy, California, that served as Matrix's hideaway. Nearly all the crew had worked on previous Joel Silver films and settled

With less than twelve hours to find and free his daughter, Matrix shakes Sully upside down for an important lead.

Stewardess Cindy proves that she is just as lethal as Matrix with a rocket launcher.

into a relaxed, humorous atmosphere. The production then moved to Los Angeles International Airport, followed by three weeks of night shooting in San Pedro and Long Beach. *Commando* spent six days at the Sherman Oaks Galleria, where the sequence of Matrix and Cindy tailing Arius's henchman Sully and the ensuing fight took place. Since the large shopping center normally operates into the evening, work did not begin each night until well after nine.

At the beginning of June, there were eight days of filming at the former Harold Lloyd estate in Beverly Hills, which stood in for the deposed dictator's island fortress. Built in the 1920s by the silent-screen comedian, the Mediterranean-style residence originally consisted of forty-four rooms, twenty-six bathrooms, and forty-eight-thousand square feet of floor space. The seventeen-acre lot, now pared down to seven, had been fully restored to its original splendor for the film and now boasted artwork by Dürer, Raphael,

Rodin, Rubens, Titian, and Whistler. Furniture from the eighteenth and nineteenth centuries, clocks as old as 270 years, and immaculate rose gardens and lawn all supplied the background for Matrix's final assault. The company moved north to the coastline at San Simeon in central California in late June. Permission to film there was granted by the California Department of Parks and Recreation and the Hearst Corporation (who own part of the land). Five army-style barracks and a watchtower were constructed near the water to simulate the outside of the Arius fortress. They were all subsequently blown up in spectacular fireball explosions that rattled windows miles away. Principal photography concluded on July 3, 1985, and the remainder of the second-unit work was completed a short time thereafter under stunt coordinator Bennie Dobbins.

Because it was difficult to find a stunt double for Schwarzenegger, he ended up doing a number of his own stunts (which were generally reserved for stuntmen). He jumped through windows, did all the fight scenes, and even hung on to the landing gear of a plane as it whistled down the runway at over sixty-five miles an hour. In the scene where Matrix exits a plane during takeoff, Arnold remembers having to

> climb down the wheel, but there was no place to step on—if I made a mistake, I would have been crushed by the wheel. The danger was real! But sometimes the emotional strain and the psychological pressure you go through almost equal the physical pain and danger.

"There's nobody else but Arnold who could have done what he did," said director Mark Lester during the production. "I've made fifteen pictures, and he's the only actor who has ever done the kind of action that we've done."

(Opposite) Matrix infiltrates Arius's island fortress, armed with more than a dozen deadly weapons, in search of his daughter.

But he paid the price from time to time, with stitches in his hand and elbow and a dislocated shoulder, but he was never allowed to perform stunts that were literally life threatening. Acknowledging how important it was for him to attempt his own stunts, he recalled:

> I was injured, but it was never more than a few days' layoff. In movies like *Commando*, it is my presence that really stands out. I dominate, and people go to see my films because they know that I'm pushing myself to the limit.

When the production crew finished final shooting, everyone knew they had a winner.

Matrix in action.

Critical Commentary

Released on October 4, 1985, *Commando* quickly dismissed any doubts people may have had about the drawing power of Arnold Schwarzenegger (the poor showing with *Red Sonja* notwithstanding) and went right to the top of the charts. Though many critics were not as enthusiastic about his latest work, some were decidedly split in their reviews. D. J. R. Bruckner of the *New York Times* recognized how

93

(Left) Matrix faces his former friend and comrade in arms, Bennett (Vernon Wells), who (right) holds Matrix's daughter Jenny hostage.

(Below) Matrix and Bennett duel to the death with knives.

much more accomplished Arnold had become since the Conan movies and complimented him for being "more supple and faster in *Commando* than he has ever been." But *USA Today* critic Jack Curry took exception to the film's violent approach, claiming that Matrix's "moral authority" to rescue his daughter had been diminished by his killing of innocent bystanders. Their unfavorable reviews, however, did not bother ticket buyers. By the end of the year, *Commando* had outpaced *The Terminator* by several million dollars in domestic rentals and was gearing up for a worldwide release.

Schwarzenegger is in top form both physically and mentally as John Matrix. Whereas the Conan movies showed him as a barbarian, thief, and seasoned warrior and *The Terminator* demonstrated the dark side of his personality (as the villainous killing machine from the future), *Commando* gives us a gentle father, combat soldier, and master of one-liners. John Matrix is not only a more fully realized character (than the previous entries); he is also more human. He has greater sophistication, and Arnold brings his character to life by relying on charm and good looks that are undercut by a certain cynicism. Audiences can clearly relate to his desperate situation and to the comic quips he uses to keep from going over the edge. Somewhere between his last Conan movie and the debacle over *Red Sonja*, Arnold Schwarzenegger became an actor.

The rewrite by Steven E. de Souza is also very funny. The dialogue is witty, and scenes progress very quickly, from one to the other, on sometimes slender and chance threads of information and coincidence. James Horner's music is incessant, percussive, and loud, with a tense staccato that instantly reminds audiences of John Barry's James Bond theme. Rae Dawn Chong is an important asset to the film and an entertaining foil to Arnold's stoic warrior, and Vernon Wells creates a truly memorable villain (worthy of Schwarzenegger).

Although parallels will inevitably continue to be drawn between Schwarzenegger's *Commando* and Stallone's *Rambo: First Blood Part II*, some cynical (aimed at showing how Fox was attempting to cash in on the Rambo phenomenon or of the country's social unease), both films are, in fact, a curious expression of political emotionalism felt by an America that had lost the Vietnam War and were suffering through Ronald Reagan's presidency. (*Commando* was already in development when Stallone's movie first came out and became a sum-

Triumphant, Matrix emerges from the island fortress carrying his daughter Jenny to safety.

mer box-office champ.) Joel Silver put the connection another way when he said,

> Of course *Rambo* and *Commando* have a lot in common. They are both larger-than-life stories about cartoonlike characters that take on enormous odds and win. I think, because of Arnold's unique presence, *Commando* has a sense of humor that *Rambo* doesn't have.

Unfortunately, the very first rumors of a rivalry between the two box-office champions began shortly after the release of *Commando* and continued (thanks to the tabloid papers) through *Raw Deal*. While publicizing his new action-adventure, Arnold Schwarzenegger came under fire from critics who claimed his film was a rip-off of *Rambo*. In response to their accusations, he told journalist Ian Harmer (*News of the World*):

> I'd be angry at hearing my name mentioned in the same breath as Stallone's. Stallone uses body doubles for some of the close-ups in his movies. I don't....We probably kill more people in *Commando* than Stallone did in *Rambo*, but the difference is that we don't pretend the violence is justified by patriotic pride. All that flag waving is a lot of bull.... I've made a better film than Stallone's, and I'm happy to wait for time to prove me right.

Commando was a box-office bonanza, but it did not come close to eclipsing the success of Stallone's movie. Schwarzenegger's irresistible drive to become a much larger movie star did finally win out in 1987 when he was named Star of the Year. He has since never lost that title to Sylvester Stallone.

Possible Sequels

After completing work on *The Running Man*, Arnold Schwarzenegger told *Starlog* magazine that he enjoyed playing the lead character in *Commando* and that he would like to return to John Matrix someday soon. "I make a point of always leaving my next picture open until I've finished the one I'm doing," he explained to Kim Howard Johnson. "It could be *Commando II* or *Terminator 2*. It could be any of these—whatever I feel [next spring], I will do." Although his name had been attached to such follow-up projects (including *Predator 2* and *Conan III*), as well as such comics-based adaptations as *Watchmen* and *Sgt. Rock*, Schwarzenegger was committed at that time to only one film—*Red Heat*. He remained irresolute for several months, finally agreeing to play opposite Danny DeVito in *Twins*.

At the same time that Arnold was deciding upon his next project, Steven E. de Souza had completed work on a sequel to *Commando* for Joel Silver. "*Commando II* takes place entirely in Los Angeles," the screenwriter told *Starlog*.

> It's a very urban story, it's not going to have huge armies. It'll be more like a thriller than a war movie...like a James Bond movie, an adventure about a guy who is now a highly trained civilian with a military background. The movie begins with Colonel Matrix getting a job running security for a big international conglomerate. My whole feeling is that if we're going to do a sequel, let's *not* have him rejoin the service. He's going to be in the private sector, and it all takes place in a very compressed time frame. Rae Dawn Chong is back, and she's a lawyer this time. Arnold's schedule is so booked that *Commando II* won't be filmed until next spring, so it won't be released until October of 1988.

De Souza's original script for *Commando II* was very exciting, but Joel Silver already had an urban thriller in the development stage. When Schwarzenegger failed to commit to the sequel, de Souza joined forces with J. E. B. Stuart to script *Die Hard*. In fact, many of the key sequences de Souza had written for *Commando II* were refined for Bruce Willis. (Midway through the actioner from Fox, Willis comically remarks, "There's enough explosives here to warp Arnold Schwarzenegger," clearly paying homage to the former bodybuilder and his influence in the action-adventure genre.) *Die Hard* debuted the same summer as *Red Heat* and went on to become the summer's biggest hit. To this day, one wonders what might have happened to *Commando II* if Schwarzenegger had chosen to overlook *Red Heat* (and *Twins*) in order to return to the character of John Matrix.

Commando is currently available on videocassette and laserdisc from CBS/Fox Home Video.

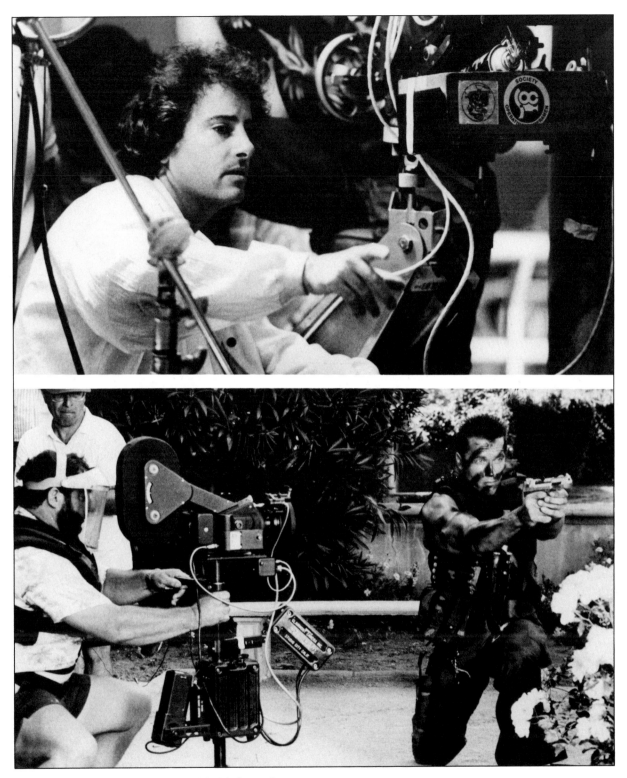

(Top) During the course of *Commando*, Mark L. Lester directs a key sequence.

(Bottom) The Steadicam helped place viewers in the center of the action, along with Schwarzenegger.

SEVEN

MARRIED TO THE MOB

Raw Deal

(a.k.a. Triple Identity), 1986. Columbia Pictures in association with De Laurentiis Entertainment Group. *Director:* John Irvin. *Producer:* Martha Schumacher. *Screenplay:* Gary M. DeVore and Norman Wexler. *Based on a story by* Luciano Vincenzoni and Sergio Donati. *Photography:* Alex Thomson. *Music:* Tom Bahler, Albhy Galuten, and Chris Boardman. *Editor:* Anne V. Coates. *Starring:* Arnold Schwarzenegger, Kathryn Harrold, Darren McGavin, Sam Wanamaker, Paul Shenar, Blanche Baker, Steven Hill, Joe Regalbuto, Robert Davi, and Ed Lauter. Released on June 6, 1986. [97 minutes]

A belated and conspicuously low budget addition to Arnold Schwarzenegger's very short list of box-office failures, the lackluster *Raw Deal* contributed yet another twist to the actor's film career. Freely adapted from a story by Luciano Vincenzoni and Sergio Donati, Dino De Laurentiis's production tried to build upon Arnold's previous successes by copying key sequences from the Conan movies, *The Terminator*, and *Commando*. High on carnage and bloody violence but low on the goodwill that audiences had come to expect from a Schwarzenegger vehicle, this cynical, by-the-numbers approach to moviemaking ultimately failed at the box office. The motion picture also forced the former Mr. Universe to be more selective about his cinematic endeavors.

Schwarzenegger voiced his own concerns about *Raw Deal—*"I want to be bigger in films than I am in

life, not smaller"—but many of those concerns were ignored by a producer more interested in quantity than quality.

The Screen Story

Five years before, a top FBI agent named Mark Kaminsky (Schwarzenegger) was forced to retire his federal badge for excessive violence. (He roughed up a suspect who had raped and mutilated a little girl.) Taking up residence in a small southern town, Kaminsky has been desperately trying to forget his past mistakes, but his alcoholic wife Amy (Blanche Baker) won't let him. She longs for the glitter and prestige that his former position with the bureau afforded her. When the son of a former colleague is murdered by mob enforcers, Kaminsky is enlisted by Harry Shannon (Darren McGavin) to infiltrate the Chicago mob, headed by Luigi Patrovita (Sam Wanamaker), and find the killers. Shannon also wants Kaminsky to uncover the FBI mole who keeps tipping the crime family with bureau secrets and attempt to destroy the organization from within. "Who do I look like? Dirty Harry?" Kaminsky quips before insisting that no one else must know about his cover. If Kaminsky is successful, Shannon promises to see that he is reinstated with the bureau; if the former agent fails, however, no one will save him from being "terminated" by the mob.

After faking his own death in a chemical-factory explosion, Kaminsky assumes the identity of a small-time hood from Miami. With twenty-five thousand in cash and his new identity as Joseph P. Brenner, he heads for Chicago and in no time at all destroys the crooked gambling casino of Patrovita's rival Lamanski

(Opposite) Schwarzenegger is former FBI agent Mark Kaminsky, who goes undercover as Joseph Brenner to destroy the Chicago mob. (Courtesy Dino De Laurentiis Entertainment Group)

Brenner blasts his way into a crooked gambling casino...

(Steven Hill). (By hurting the rival gangleader, Kaminsky hopes to attract the attention of Patrovita.) Later he hijacks Lamanski's limousine and steals thousands of dollars in jewelry from Lamanski's girlfriend. His actions do not go unnoticed by Paulo Rocca (Paul Shenar), Patrovita's lieutenant, and mob enforcer Max Keller (Robert Davi).

By slowly gaining their trust, Kaminsky penetrates Mafia security, and despite objections from Keller, he is rewarded with a job by Rocca. The Patrovita family continues to be suspicious and enlists district attorney Marvin Baxter (Joe Regalbuto)—the FBI mole—to learn everything that he can about the new man. (Baxter is, coincidentally, the same person who forced Kaminsky into retirement for excessive brutality.) For secondary measures, Keller hires Monique (Kathryn Harrold), a pretty but hopelessly poor gambler, to seduce Brenner in order to discover his real reason for seeking out the Patrovita family. Kaminsky's identity holds up to mob scrutiny, but his lack of interest in Monique nearly betrays him. (But since Monique

secretly despises Keller, she helps Kaminsky with his masquerade.)

During the night, special FBI agents raid one of Patrovita's coke houses and seize more than $100 million in cash and drugs. Angered by the loss, Patrovita demands that his people break into police headquarters to steal it back. An elaborate plan is hatched: A fake bomb is planted, and members of the bomb squad (actually Patrovita's men) are called to disarm the device. Once inside police headquarters, the squad detonates the bomb and steals back Patrovita's cash and drugs.

Meanwhile, Kaminsky (as Brenner) has proved his loyalty to the Patrovita family several times by roughing up informants and joining Keller on a hit against the rival gangleader. Along with Monique, he has been beaten and chased by rival mob enforcers. Patrovita is satisfied that Joey Brenner is legitimate and invites him to become a permanent part of the family. But Keller continues to doubt Brenner's authenticity and soon learns (from a Miami cop) that the real Joey Brenner is serving time in prison. This

100

information shakes the core of the organization. Rocca wants Kaminsky and his FBI contact dead and arranges for the undercover cop to take on a hit—to assassinate Harry Shannon.

Kaminsky accepts the assignment, unaware of his target, and drives away with Keller and another hit man. When Kaminsky realizes Shannon is the target of the hit, he is forced to kill the other men. In the ensuing gunfight, Shannon is shot a dozen times. Devastated by the shooting, Kaminsky swears an oath of vengeance to his badly wounded old colleague. Arming himself with as much artillery as he can carry, including a machine gun, a Mac-10 machine pistol, a .38 caliber Smith & Wesson revolver, and a twelve-gauge shotgun, the savage mercenary wages a one-man war against the syndicate.

First, Kaminsky plows through Patrovita's heroin farm, killing everyone in sight; then he rips through the gangster's casino. Single-handedly, to the tune of the Rolling Stones' "(I Can't Get No) Satisfaction," he finishes off the entire gang, including Baxter, the man who cost him his job five years before. Before the police arrive, Kaminsky liberates $250,000 in cash from Patrovita's vault for Monique and sends her packing for a better way of life. She asks him to come with her, but Kaminsky confesses that he already has a wife. Somehow Monique already knew what his answer would be.

A few days later, Kaminsky arrives at the hospital with flowers and greetings for his friend. Shannon has suffered many wounds from the gun battle and may never walk again. But Kaminsky refuses to accept the doctor's somber news and helps Shannon to his feet. After all, the agent remarks, he wants the godfather of the baby he and his wife are expecting to be strong enough to fulfill his duties. Shannon is so overjoyed with the news that he begins to walk.

…and watches Monique (Kathryn Harrold) lose another round of cards while awaiting an audience with mob boss Patrovita.

(Above) In order to cement his cover as a small-time hood, Joseph Brenner begins dating Monique.

(Below) Schwarzenegger, working undercover, is seduced by Kathryn Harrold, a high roller indebted to the mob…

Production Details

Raw Deal originated as a simple story entitled "Triple Identity" (by Luciano Vincenzoni and Sergio Donati) about mob enforcers, FBI moles, and undercover agents, but it soon developed into a project that simply didn't come together. Calculated and cynically designed to capitalize on the success of a rising star, *Raw Deal* is more a lesson in greed than moviemaking.

Preproduction on *Total Recall* had stalled because of financial difficulties, and Dino De Laurentiis was looking for a fast return on several low-budget projects in order to get the film rolling again. Arnold Schwarzenegger still owed him a movie (based on the original contract he had signed for *Conan the Barbarian*), and the Italian producer knew what a box-office draw the star had become with *The Terminator* and *Commando*. On the other hand, Schwarzenegger was very interested in playing the lead in *Total Recall* and tried to convince Dino to give him a shot. De Laurentiis remained adamant, demanding that he play the lead in *Triple Identity* (later changed to *Raw Deal*). (Arnold would eventually convince Tri-Star Pictures to purchase the film rights to *Total Recall* from De Laurentiis for him.) *Raw Deal* was certainly not Arnold's first incursion into the gangster genre. He had played a mob enforcer in Robert Altman's *The Long Goodbye*, but this time he was in command of his involvement in the project. He accepted De Laurentiis's offer in exchange for an agreeable conclusion to their three-year-old contract.

De Laurentiis then hired screenwriters Gary M. DeVore and Norman Wexler to transform the original story into an action-adventure vehicle for Schwarzenegger. Having seen both *The Terminator* and *Commando*, De Laurentiis was determined to transfer the same high-explosive entertainment to his production. To achieve his goal, he insisted that DeVore and Wexler become familiar with Arnold's film persona and the slick but familiar style of his pictures. Several specific scenes and whole action sequences from those other films were then studied item for item, and a script was produced that capitalized on the persona he had created and the short-tempered, violent nature he represented. The simple-minded *Triple Identity* became the larger-than-life *Raw Deal*.

In addition to the familiar action sequences, Schwarzenegger was given his first on-screen romance with not one but two women. When the

...and subsequently prepares to do battle with the mob.

film opens, he is married to an alcoholic wife who both loves and despises him at the same time. Later, after faking his own death to assume the identity of Joe Brenner, Arnold gets to make love to a beautiful seductress. "We don't get into the sex right away," the superstar explained in an interview with the *San Francisco Chronicle*. "That's old stuff. Instead we have a relationship that keeps growing."

De Laurentiis then cast Kathryn Harrold (who is clearly in the same sexy mold as Kathleen Turner and

Lauren Bacall, whom she played in the 1980 TV movie *Bogie*) as Monique. Known for her less than noteworthy appearances in genre films, Harrold played in the television series *Magruder and Loud* (1986, ABC). Blanche Baker (actress daughter of one-time screen sex bomb Carroll Baker) was signed for the role of Amy Kaminsky. Joe Regalbuto played Marvin Baxter; Steven Hill, rival boss Lamanski; and Paul Shenar, Paulo Rocca. For the key role of Luigi Patrovita, De Laurentiis hired the expatriate American stage and screen actor and director Sam Wanamaker. Wanamaker was certainly no stranger to films or film-making. De Laurentiis was counting on his presence in *Raw Deal* to lend the production a certain amount of class, and he was not disappointed.

Darren McGavin, a popular figure with genre fans because of his *Night Stalker* character Carl Kolchak, was also added to the cast. Over the years, McGavin had proven that he could play a wide range of roles, from unpleasant villains to tough guys, in television series like *Crime Photographer* (1953, CBS), *Mike Hammer* (1958, syndicated), and, of course, *The Night Stalker* (1974, ABC) or in dozens of films. Robert Davi, who would later score big with *Die Hard* and as the Bond villain in *Licence to Kill*, rounded out the cast as mob enforcer Max Keller.

With John Irvin at the helm as director, *Raw Deal* began principal photography on November 1, 1985, exactly two years after the start of *Conan the Destroyer*. Eight weeks of filming took place at Earl Owensby Studios in Wilmington, North Carolina, with three soundstages and the only back lot being used for the production. Another four weeks were spent at a dozen locations in and around the Chicago area. During the location lensing, the elements proved to be a major problem because of the Windy City's unpredictable weather. At times, it was very, very cold; at others, the dry cold gave way to a freezing drizzle, which is seen at key spots in the film. After a much-needed Christmas break, principal photography was completed in early February. The final sequence to be filmed (and coincidentally the last major set piece of the motion picture) was Kaminsky's assault on Patrovita's stronghold. Several dozen stuntmen contributed to a sequence that ranks as one of the best in a Schwarzenegger film. Director Irvin called the production a wrap several days before Valentine's Day and sent all the principals packing.

While he may have found the entire project very exhausting, Schwarzenegger was extremely satisfied with his performance. He told the *San Francisco Chronicle* that Irvin, whom he terms "an actor's director," was very professional.

> He works on your neuroses, trying to get the most out of you. I must say, I like that. Acting is like bodybuilding: The more you do it, the better you get—and each time I see myself getting closer to the perfect delivery of a scene.

Looking forward to a few weeks off before beginning work on *Hunter* (later changed to *Predator*), Schwarzenegger confessed how lucky he was to have found such a successful career in film.

> I'm achieving the kind of success I always knew I would; I'm just savoring it, day by day. I want to keep making movies the world loves to see and become the star I rightfully should be.

Little did Schwarzenegger realize, at the time, how much his on-screen persona had been exploited by Dino De Laurentiis. *Raw Deal* would not have been made without the former bodybuilder's name on the billing, and that fact would inspire him to be more selective with future projects.

Critical Commentary

When it was released on June 6, 1986, *Raw Deal* faced incredibly stiff competition from James Cameron's *Aliens*, John Carpenter's *Big Trouble in Little China*, Ridley Scott's *Legend*, David Cronenberg's remake of *The Fly*, and Sylvester Stallone's *Cobra*. Debuting in over a thousand theaters, the film failed to make much of a splash with either critics or moviegoers. By the second week, in fact, business had fallen off so substantially that the industry was calling it a bomb. Following his enormous box-office success in *Commando*, Arnold Schwarzenegger was crushed to learn that he had his first bona-fide motion-picture flop (*Red Sonja* notwithstanding). Vincent Canby, known to be a Schwarzenegger fan, tried cheering him up with his review in the *New York Times*, writing that "the former Mr. Universe wears well as a film personality, partly because there's something comic about the massiveness of his frame and the gentleness of his manners (when in repose)." Jay Maeder of the New York *Daily News* was similarly kind, stating that "Schwarzenegger is a considerably appealing presence in pictures like this. May he make many more."

Single-handedly, Mark Kaminsky infiltrates Patrovita's com-
pound and takes on the entire gang.

But practically all the other reviews were extremely negative. Far from a high point in his career, the motion picture finished well out of the running for ticket receipts.

Although gangster thrillers have long been a staple of Hollywood films, *Raw Deal* was certainly no *Godfather*. In fact, the story line is so weak and predictable that it would have probably been rejected by script editors of TV's *Wiseguy*. The blame rests with Dino De Laurentiis and his scripters Gary DeVore and Norman Wexler. In trying to emulate the formula of Schwarzenegger's earlier successes, they created a motion picture in which the sum of its parts doesn't equal the whole. For example, the revenge plot, in which Arnold not only has a score to settle with a dishonest district attorney but also with the shooters of Shannon (and his son), has been lifted from *Conan the Barbarian*. Mark Kaminsky, like Conan, would probably not be very interesting without the violent edge that drives him; in fact, there would probably not be a story, either. The on-screen romance between Kaminsky (as Joey Brenner) and Monique has been borrowed from the lost scenes in *Commando* in which Matrix falls romantically for the offbeat stewardess after trading insulting barbs. The numerous car chases and Kaminsky's raid on Patrovita resemble scenes of mass destruction precipitated by the Terminator. Even Kaminsky's preparation for the raid seems lifted from both *The Terminator* and *Commando*. All of these sequences, though well staged by director John Irvin, have an air of familiarity about them. And the attempts to humanize Arnold's character by giving him an alcoholic wife and tempting him with a gangster's moll are completely out of character.

After scoring major success with the two Conan movies, *The Terminator*, and *Commando*, it was inevitable that Schwarzenegger would take a misstep. Though ultimately proving not to be a major career setback, *Raw Deal* did inspire him to be more selective in his choice of vehicles. Wearing double-breasted suits and slicked-back hair, he looks more like a caricature of a gangster than someone who might be truly deadly. And while he may appear to be having fun (tearing apart a gambling casino or blowing away hundreds of rival gangsters), his on-screen character is far less compelling than John Matrix or the Terminator. Audiences certainly couldn't get beyond that and registered their complaints by bypassing the film in droves. Clearly, the subsequent *Hunter* (later renamed *Predator*) and *The*

Running Man proved that Arnold's persona as the ideal hero of the eighties and nineties was better suited to fantasy or science-fiction films.

Schwarzenegger responded thusly to critics in 1985:

> I'm being called the new Stallone or the new Clint Eastwood. But I think I'm a combination of the two—only brawnier! The success of *Rambo* proves audiences want a strong man they can look up to. And, basically, I'm the logical choice....

Several fan publications, including Jim Steranko's *Prevue*, attempted to create an imagined rivalry* between Arnold Schwarzenegger and Sylvester Stallone through features entitled "Battle of the Box Office" during the superstar's nationwide publicity tour for *Raw Deal*. But there was, in fact, no rivalry between the two musclemen beyond some good-natured kidding. Though the six-foot-two 230-pound Schwarzenegger had obviously hoped to outmuscle the five-foot-ten, 185-pound "Italian Stallion" at the box office, both *Raw Deal* and Stallone's cops-and-robbers movie *Cobra* suffered a terrible beating from pictures like *Aliens* and *The Fly*. And yet the fan magazines could not leave the rivalry alone, pitting each actor against the other in competitive interviews.

The second blow in the "battle of the titans" came when Stallone was quoted out of context, claiming (that unlike Arnold) "I'm not just a piece of meat that looks good on-screen." His statement sent shock waves throughout the industry and added substance to the tabloid rags that thrived on actors' feuds. Schwarzenegger responded in the New York *Daily News* by first conceding that "Sly is a smart man," then stating:

> I respect the man as an actor, a director, and a human being. Aside from his contributions to the industry, he also does great work in the community and charity, and the last thing I want to do is offend him.

He has since good-naturedly poked fun at Stallone in several of his films, particularly *Twins*. But any serious criticism or feud runs counterproductive to Arnold's desire to have fun making motion pictures.

While both have been labeled as "shrewd manipulators" and "animalistic oxen," they are first and foremost entertainers. *Rambo* and *Commando*, *Cobra* and *Raw Deal* cater—to a greater or lesser degree—to the popular taste. And both men have

Schwarzenegger emerges from the final battle with only minor wounds.

proved how successful they are at guessing what the public wants. Whereas Stallone turned to playing more Rockys and Rambos, Schwarzenegger returned to his roots in science fiction and fantasy with *Predator* and *The Running Man*.

Raw Deal is currently available on videocassette and laserdisc from RCA/Columbia Home Video.

EIGHT

SCHWARZENEGGER VERSUS THE ALIEN

Predator

(a.k.a. *Hunter*), 1987. 20th Century-Fox. *Director:* John McTiernan. *Producers:* Joel Silver, Lawrence Gordon, and John Davis. *Executive Producers:* Laurence Pereira and Jim Thomas. *Screenplay:* Jim Thomas and John Thomas. *Photography:* Donald McAlpine. *Music:* Alan Silvestri. *Editors:* John F. Link and Mark Helfrich. *Starring:* Arnold Schwarzenegger, Carl Weathers, Elpidia Carrillo, Bill Duke, Jesse Ventura, Shane Black, Sonny Landham, Richard Chaves, R. G. Armstrong, and Kevin Peter Hall. Released on June 12, 1987. [107 minutes]

John McTiernan's *Predator* combined elements from *Rambo*, *Commando*, and *Aliens*—which were themselves aggregates of other cinematic productions—to create the perfect hybrid of special effects, science fiction, horror, and action-adventure. Produced by Joel Silver, along with Lawrence Gordon and John Davis, and written by Jim and John Thomas, the motion picture also provided Arnold Schwarzenegger with his best starring vehicle since *The Terminator.* Although many critics were apt to dismiss the feature as simply another retelling of the oft-filmed *Most Dangerous Game*, it does manage to succeed on almost every level. Packed with spectacular effects, gut-wrenching combat scenes, and the best alien biomechanoid since *Alien*, it went on to become one of the box-office champions of the year.

(Opposite) Schwarzenegger stars as Maj. "Dutch" Schaefer, the leader of a military rescue team. (Courtesy 20th Century-Fox)

The Screen Story

In a haunting precredits sequence, an unknown spaceship rockets toward the earth before depositing a small one-man craft. The inhabitant of the interstellar vehicle is an armor-clad reptilian biomechanoid capable of near invisibility through a unique "cloaking device." It is a Predator, a monster that comes from another planet to hunt other predators for sport. It has been returning to earth for centuries (because of the violent species there known as man), but in all the fairness of the hunt, it refuses to attack if its prey is weak or sickly, unarmed, or lacking any harmful intent. It has chosen the jungles of Central America for its latest hunt.

Recruited by General Phillips (R. G. Armstrong) and a devious CIA operative named Dillon (Carl Weathers) to rescue hostages held by guerrilla fighters in the same Central American jungle, Maj. "Dutch" Schaefer (Schwarzenegger) and his men embark on what they believe will be a simple one-day operation. As their gunships penetrate the enemy border, the Special Forces unit readies for action. The group includes Blain (Jesse Ventura), a tobacco-chewing cowboy; Mac (Bill Duke), an African-American whose sanity hangs by a fragile thread; Billy (Sonny Landham), a Native American tracker; Poncho (Richard Chaves), a gung-ho Mexican; and Hawkins (Shane Black), a green recruit. None of them trust Dillon, and once they begin their reconnoiter, the men start to sense real trouble.

Soon Schaefer and his unit come upon a downed helicopter and discover that not only are the pilots dead but the gunship has been taken out by a heat-

"We're a rescue team, not assassins," Schaefer tells CIA operative
Dillon (Carl Weathers), suspecting that his group has been set up.

seeking missile. There is no cabinet minister or aide
aboard; this was a deliberate incursion by CIA opera-
tives. "We're a rescue team, not assassins," Schaefer
tells Dillon, demanding to know the truth. But the
government operative is less than truthful. When the
unit discovers the bodies of another six-man team,
skinned and hanging from the trees like sides of beef,
Schaefer goes ballistic and forces his former friend to
tell them the real reason for their mission. The unit
has been dispatched to eliminate a revolutionary
guerrilla faction (financed by Soviet KGB) before they
can launch their own attack against sympathetic
forces. Schaefer wants no part in the devious operation, but unfortunately he and his men are drawn
into deadly combat with the guerrillas. They are
forced to destroy the guerrilla camp, in a pitched battle, and take a woman named Anna (Elpidia Carrillo)
captive.

Their little war, however, has not gone unnoticed
by the Predator. Through the unique camouflage of
his cloaking device, the alien hunter has watched the
whole battle from his vantage point in the trees. It

now believes that it has found the perfect prey and
begins stalking the group of soldiers.

As Schaefer leads his Special Forces unit and the
captured woman back to civilization, they encounter
an unimaginable enemy more deadly than any on
earth. It turns out that the other unit wasn't skinned
by the revolutionary guerrilla faction but by an alien
looking for some sport. One by one, the members of
the unit are murdered in mysterious and bloody fashion by an unseen killer. With their roles now
reversed—the hunters are now the hunted—the
men (and woman) join forces against their common
enemy and attempt to fortify their position with traps
and land mines. But since the Predator travels invisi-
bly through the trees, their jungle fortress is quickly
penetrated by the foe.

Poncho is unwittingly injured, then killed. Dillon
and Mac remain behind to cover their colleagues'
escape, but they are also cut down. Billy, who has
long sensed this unworldly demon, drops all his
weapons to face the Predator with a singular knife,
and he is killed. Ultimately, after Anna is spared,

Schaefer and members of his team (left to right, Sonny Landham, Carl Weathers, and Richard Chaves) discover they are being stalked by some unearthly creature in the jungles of Central America.

Dutch Schaefer must deal with the alien hunter himself. Stripped of his combat weapons, except a knife and some flares, the career soldier relies on primitive survival skills to fight the creature. By combining brains and brawn, he sets a series of deadly traps to ensnare the Predator. Then he lures it onto his battleground. An action-packed final battle between the two ensues, with Schaefer getting the upper hand on the "one ugly, motherfucking monster."

Fatally wounded, the Predator cynically snarls at Dutch, "I am what you are," and rather than be captured fairly, it sets off a delayed self-destruct weapon. Dutch runs for cover and manages to survive the nuclear explosion that lays waste the jungle. Hours later, the bruised and badly injured warrior is rescued by General Phillips and taken to safety.

Production Details

For a few months following the release of *Rocky IV*, a joke was making the rounds in Hollywood. Since Rocky Balboa (Sylvester Stallone) had run out of earthly opponents (having cut Dolph Lundgren, as the Russian champion, down to size), he would probably have to fight an alien if a fifth installment of his boxing series were to be made. Screenwriters Jim and John Thomas took the joke very seriously and turned out a marvelous screenplay.

The Thomas script for *Predator* (then called *Hunter*) was immediately snapped up by Fox in 1985 and turned over to Joel Silver, who, based on his experience with *Commando*, seemed the right choice to turn the vintage sci-fi story line into a big-budget film. With his former boss Lawrence Gordon as coproducer, Silver approached Arnold Schwarzenegger with the lead role and newcomer John McTiernan (fresh from his directorial debut on *Nomads*) with the task of directing his first studio project. But previous commitments by Schwarzenegger delayed the start of filming by several months. Silver used the time to secure a minor rewrite from David Peoples (the man who had cowritten *Blade Runner* and later would do *Unforgiven*).

"I suppose it had almost reached a point with these

Sensing an alien presence in the trees, Schaefer scans the highly dense vegetation for some concrete sign.

action films where one of the heroes would have to fight a creature from another world," commented Joel Silver. "What other possible terror could Schwarzenegger take on in an action-adventure film?"

Schwarzenegger explained his interest and concerns about the Thomas script:

The first thing I look for in a script is a good idea. A majority of scripts are rip-offs of other movies. People think they can become successful overnight. They sit down one weekend and write a script because they read that Stallone did that with *Rocky*. *Predator* was

one of the scripts I read, and it bothered me in one way. It was just me and the alien. So we redid the whole thing so that it was a team of commandos, and then I liked the idea. I thought it would make a much more effective movie and be much more believable. I liked the idea of starting out with an action-adventure but then coming in with some horror and science fiction.

To play his elite band of mercenaries, both Silver and Gordon (with coproducer John Davis) put out a casting net for men of action. Carl Weathers, who had been memorable as boxer Apollo Creed in the *Rocky* films and would later star in *Action Jackson*, was their choice to play Dillon, while professional wrestler Jesse Ventura was hired for his formidable physique as Blain. Native American Sonny Landham and Afro-American Bill Duke, who were often cast as villains, provided the right ethnic balance. (A sometime film and television director, Duke also played opposite Schwarzenegger in *Commando*). As a favor to the author of Joel Silver's latest megahit *Lethal Weapon*, Shane Black was given a small role as the intellectual Hawkins. Veteran R. G. Armstrong (who had played in *Stay Hungry*), Richard Chaves, Kevin Peter Hall (the giant actor who played the Bigfoot monster in the screen and TV versions of *Harry and the Hendersons*), and Elpidia Carrillo helped round out the cast with their own special talents.

Principal photography began in the jungles of Palenque in Mexico during the second week of April 1986, under John McTiernan's direction. Much of the material dealing with the unit's deployment in the jungle was completed in a few short weeks, and both Silver and Gordon were pleased by the dailies provided by McTiernan. On Friday, April 25, production halted so that Arnold could fly to Hyannis Port in order to attend his own wedding on time. He was married on April 26 to Maria Shriver and honeymooned for two weeks in Antigua while the second unit completed additional shooting. The production resumed filming on May 12 and was about to move to some rough terrain near the border of Guatemala when a design miscalculation on the Predator brought filming to a halt. The creature with the backward-bent legs didn't work in their jungle locale.

Originally the producers at Fox had contracted Richard Edlund's Boss Film Studios to produce the alien design and special monster effects of *Predator*, with the proviso that the final result *not* look like

(Previous page) Schwarzenegger displays his perfectly sculptured body prior to a Mr. Universe competition.

(Above) Schwarzenegger pumps iron in George Butler and Robert Fior's 1977 documentary *Pumping Iron.*

(Right) Schwarzenegger as Robert E. Howard's barbarian warrior Conan.

(Below) Conan becomes victorious as a "pit fighter" in *Conan the Barbarian*, 1982.

(Below) Schwarzenegger as *Conan the Destroyer*, 1984

(Right) As Lord Kalidor in the Dino De Laurentiis production of *Red Sonya*, 1985.

(Left) In a rare publicity shot from *The Terminator*, Schwarzenegger appears, weapon in hand, as the futuristic killing machine.

(Above) Severely damaged, and missing an eye, the Terminator has certainly had better days.

(Below) Detective Kimble (Schwarzenegger) finds his undercover assignment as a "kindergarten cop" difficult when confronted with thirty screaming four- and five-year-olds. *Kindergarten Cop*, 1990.

(Above) The Terminator must preserve the life of young John Connor, who is stalked by T-2's fellow robot in *Terminator Two: Judgment Day,* 1991.

(Above left) Schwarzenegger poses with a replica of his Terminator persona at Planet Hollywood. (Props from several of his most famous films are currently on display there.)

(Left) The Terminator protects his young charge (Edward Furlong) from potential danger in *Terminator Two: Judgment Day,* 1991.

(Above) Arnold Schwarzenegger in a rare shot with the director of *Total Recall*, 1990.

(Left) Schwarzenegger rescues Rachel Ticoton in *Total Recall*, 1990.

(Below) As Quaid, Schwarzenegger opts for a night on the town in Venusville, hoping to meet someone who can tell him who he is. *Total Recall*, 1990.

(Top) Leaving bodies flying in the air, Schwarzenegger, as fictional detective Jack Slater, bounds into a convertible to chase more bad guys. *Last Action Hero*, 1993.

(Anove) The "last action hero."

(Left) Jack Slater, accompanied by Danny Madigan (Austin O'Brien), is bewildered by life in the real world on the streets of Manhattan in *Last Action Hero*, 1993.

(Above) Moments after rescuing Helen (Jamie Lee Curtis) from a burning, out-of-control vehicle, Harry Tasker (Arnold Schwarzenegger) holds his wife in the open bay of a helicopter. *True Lies,* 1994.

Harry Tasker (Arnold Schwarzenegger) and his partner Gib (Tom Arnold) realize that their new mission involves the safety of the free world in James Cameron's *True Lies.* (Courtesy of Twentieth Century-Fox)

When several members of his team are mysteriously murdered, Schaefer orders Mac (far right, Bill Duke), and Dillon (Carl Weathers) to question their female captive Anna (Elpidia Carrillo).

some man in a monster suit. Makeup supervisor Steve Johnson met with the film's director several times and worked out a design that gave the alien a backward-bent satyr-like leg. With Doug Beswick (who had provided some dynamic creature effects in *The Terminator* and *Aliens*) and martial artist Jean-Claude Van Damme (who would perform the creature), Johnson transformed McTiernan's ideas into reality. Unfortunately the final design could not be made to work on the film's jungle locations without a harness and wires to provide the proper balance. "The design was poorly executed," McTiernan complained. Having struggled through nineteen-hour days in hundred-degree heat with foreign crews and difficult terrain, the last thing the director needed was a problem with the film's major showpiece. "We only had a few weeks of preproduction, and they did

a terrible job of creating the monster in that short a period of time. It's that simple!"

After six long weeks of filming, the production had to shut down. The crew had already filmed all the parts of the movie that did not involve the alien, and Joel Silver and Lawrence Gordon were on the line for the $15 million that had already been spent. With very few ideas as to how to complete their troubled project, the producers pleaded for an additional $2.5 million from movie and television mogul Leonard Goldberg. They then gathered together their rough footage and asked James Cameron to provide some input as a consultant. Both Rick Baker (who had just completed *Harry and the Hendersons*) and Stan Winston (who had just won an Academy Award for *Aliens*) were also contacted to share their ideas. Eventually Winston was hired to create the deadly

113

Professional wrestler Jesse
Ventura as Blain, the tobacco-
chewing cowboy.

Predator and decided to build it around seven-foot-
two Kevin Peter Hall. Eight months later, filming
resumed for five weeks at the same locations in the
dead of winter. Optical effects by R/Greenberg and
Associates required several more weeks of filming,
and by the end of February, slightly more than three
months before its release date, *Predator* wrapped
production.

Recalling those last few weeks of filming,
Schwarzenegger said:

> I took more abuse in *Predator* than I did in
> *Conan the Barbarian*. I fell down that water-
> fall [forty feet] and swam in this ice-cold water
> for days and for weeks was covered in mud. It
> was freezing in the Mexican jungle. They had
> these heat lamps on all the time, but they
> were no good. If you stayed in front of the
> lamps, the mud dried. Then you had to take it
> off and put new mud on again. It was a no-
> win situation. The location was tough. Never
> on flat ground. Always on a hill. We stood all
> day long on a hill, one leg down, one leg up.

It was terrible.

Although director McTiernan felt, at the time, as
though he had also been hit by the same physical abuse
that Arnold suffered (because of the many problems), he
had nothing but praise for his star. "The range of things
he can do is expanding daily," McTiernan said several
months after the production had wrapped. "The guy
could be another John Wayne."

Once the project was fully behind him,
Schwarzenegger mustered similar praise for the new
director and a critical word or two for Fox executive
Barry Diller.

> I was pleased we had John McTiernan to
> direct—he was perfect for the job. I was also
> happy that Leonard Goldberg approved the
> extra $2.5 million needed to bring the extra
> class to the movie. Diller *never* liked the
> movie before we made it, and he was quite
> shocked at how well it did. None of his
> "class" movies even came close to those kinds
> of grosses. But he will learn eventually that
> sci-fi movies, futuristic movies, and action

movies are really the way to go and not all this stuff in which he believes. Thinking back, *Predator* came out really wonderful. It was a really good horror and action movie.

Critical Commentary

Released on June 12, 1987, *Predator* quickly shot to the top of the box-office charts in its first weekend and remained there for over a month (until Paul Verhoeven's *Robocop* supplanted it as number one). Critical reaction to the film was generally favorable, with reviewers crediting McTiernan for its breathtaking pace and nonstop action and Arnold with another fine performance. But not everyone found the concept behind the movie plausible. Roger Ebert complained in the *Chicago Sun-Times* that

> the action moves so quickly that we overlook questions such as why would an alien species go to all the effort to send a creature to earth, just so that it could swing from the trees and skin American soldiers? Or why would a creature so technologically advanced need to bother with hand-to-hand combat, when it could just zap Arnold with a ray gun?

Dean Lamanna wrote in *Cinefantastique* that "the militarized monster movie tires under its own derivative weight." The public did not seem concerned by questions of plausibility or derivation. The film grossed a whopping $70 million (more than twice as much as *The Terminator*) and proved that Schwarzenegger's name above the title meant success. (Later in the year, after Arnold had been given the 1987 Star of the Year Award by the National Association of Theater Owners, audiences were proclaiming him a superstar.)

In a role much different from John Matrix and probably more difficult to play, Arnold Schwarzenegger turns in a fine performance as Dutch Schaefer. His character is very much in command of himself and his handpicked band of mercenaries; but in subtle ways he must also show his vulnerability (as his men are stalked and killed by the Predator). Arnold told reporters during his publicity tour for the film:

> The movie was interesting from an acting point of view. In one way, you can try to look vulnerable [to the camera], but you can't show that to the men around you. So if someone

Drawn into a trap set by the Predator, Schaefer must face the alien creature alone.

gets killed, you look at your men and say coldly, "Okay, we'll move on." You want to show vulnerability and that you're scared, but you're also supposed to show how tough you are to your men.

During the climactic showdown, Schwarzenegger must return to the savage beast (which lives inside all of us) in order to defeat the creature. He achieves that jungle primitive while at the same time retaining his dignity despite several precarious opportunities to lose credibility with the audience.

Predator also solves a major dramatic problem that had slowly become more apparent in Schwarzenegger's films since *The Terminator:* finding a villain big enough and strong enough to be a worthy antagonist. Schwarzenegger clearly overpowers, by his singular presence alone, everyone in *Red Sonja* (including the titular character) and the other gangland members in *Raw Deal*. During the climactic fight scene between Matrix and Bennett (Vernon Wells) in *Commando*,

115

Arnold dwarfs his Australian opponent by several dozen pounds and a few feet. The battle with deadly knives is hardly a contest for him. However, in *Predator*, Hollywood had finally produced a worthy opponent—an alien being that stands head and shoulders above him.

Arnold confesses to have had some initial anxiety when first confronted with the creature:

> There was plenty of fear there, believe me. Working with something like this was wild in reality because he [monster Kevin Peter Hall, who stands a foot taller than Schwarzenegger] couldn't really see. Not only in the movie does he have heat-seeking eyes, but in reality the sonuvabitch couldn't see. So when he's supposed to slap me around and stay far from my face, all of a sudden *whap!* There is this hand with claws on it!

The brief opening prologue in space—showing the alien vessel blazing a path through the earth's atmosphere—is highly reminiscent of countless B-movies (including John Carpenter's *The Thing*). However, once that has been established for audiences, John McTiernan wastes little time getting into the main story. He establishes Dutch Schaefer's platoon of mercenaries (in a sequence that is far superior to a similar one James Cameron's *Aliens*), then proceeds to eliminate them one by one suspense-

The Predator, created by makeup artist Stan Winston and articulated by the late actor Kevin Peter Hall.

fully as the unit stalks, and is ultimately stalked, through the harsh Central American jungle. Each sequence is underscored by a haunting, repetitive score by Alan Silvestri that seems to keep the action moving at a rapid pace. Occasionally McTiernan pauses to provide audiences with a brief perspective shot through the Predator's "thermal vision" detector (utilizing special effects) but then wisely cuts back to the main action with intuitive speed. He continues to keep things moving at a brisk pace and makes the jungle setting doubly exciting with tight close-ups and remarkably inventive camera work. The climactic one-on-one between the alien and Schwarzenegger ranks among the most intense action sequences on film. (John McTiernan would use his slick directorial skills to make two subsequent blockbusters, *Die Hard* and *The Hunt for Red October*, as well as the poorly received *Medicine Man* and *Last Action Hero*.)

Stan Winston's intergalactic predator—an armor-clad reptilian humanoid with turquoise eyes, toothy mandibles, and Rastafarian hair—is truly inspired (although the original designs of a creature on stilts from Richard Edlund's Boss Film Studios would have revolutionized alien monsters on the screen). Building upon the success of the exoskeleton of *The Terminator* and the aliens in *Aliens*, Winston again demonstrates his peerless work. But the real showcase of *Predator* is the alien's unique cloaking device under which the creature remains concealed for most of the film. The special-effects work by R/Greenberg and Associates of New York, which allows the predator to glide through the jungle landscape as a rippling, shimmering blemish, invisible to the soldiers, is simply incredible and well worth the price of admission. (The special effects were nominated for a much-deserved Oscar.)

Although the plot is dangerously close to *The Most Dangerous Game*, with elements from *Rambo* and *Aliens* thrown in, the derivative formula does work. Packed with state-of-the-art special effects, plenty of action, a wonderfully realized alien, and a handful of winning performances, *Predator* was the perfect summer movie extravaganza. About the only thing that was missing from the film was a little romance. But Arnold Schwarzenegger was quick to defend this oversight: "You have this Predator monster wiping out all the soldiers around you....You don't have any room for a love scene. My love interest is my gun at this point."

Sequels

While *Predator* may appear to be the perfect Schwarzenegger vehicle, combining science fiction, horror, and nonstop action, Fox was unable to lure the superstar back for a 1990 sequel. Lawrence Gordon and Joel Silver (who had produced *Commando* for Arnold in 1985) took over control of *Predator 2* late in 1988, after a number of attempts to mount a sequel fell apart in the development stages. Several *Predator* movies were envisioned, similar to the *Alien* series, with Arnold squaring off against the creature in different locales. Written by Jim Thomas and John Thomas, the new film would have had Dutch Schaefer working as a consultant for the Los Angeles police force during a gang war between rival drug dealers. Enter the Predator, who is drawn by the heat and conflict, and a mysterious government agent who is searching for extraterrestrials. *Predator 2* was to have had the same electrifying special effects and the climactic confrontation between the creature and Schaefer. But Schwarzenegger had turned a corner with his acting career in *Twins* and was interested in completing only one sequel—*Terminator 2*.

Rather than lose the production and the time spent in development, Gordon and Silver made *Predator 2* without Schwarzenegger. The central character was rewritten as police lieutenant Mike Harrigan for Danny Glover, and the final confrontation was changed to emphasize wit over brawn. Some of Arnold's previous costars, including Maria Conchita Alonso (from *The Running Man*), Bill Paxton (from *The Terminator*), and Robert Davi (from *Raw Deal*), had key roles, and a reference to Schaefer's battle with the Predator in Central America was inserted in the script for continuity. Directed by Stephen Hopkins and released in November 1990 (instead of summer), *Predator 2* did not fare as well as its predecessor. However, the producers were smart enough to leave room for a second (and possible third) follow-up.

The Predator also made several comic-book appearances in which it stalks game in a big city, the Alien (in an "Aliens Versus the Predator" series), and the dark knight himself, Batman, for Dark Horse Comics. The series is imaginatively scripted and beautifully drawn and makes a fine addition to the *Predator* legacy.

Both *Predator* movies are available on videocassette and special wide-screen editions on laserdisc from CBS/Fox Home Video.

NINE

RUN FOR YOUR LIFE

The Running Man

1987. Tri-Star Pictures in association with Taft/Barish Productions and Home Box Office. *Director:* Paul Michael Glaser. *Producers:* Tim Zinnemann and George Linder. *Executive Producers:* Keith Barish and Rob Cohen. *Screenplay:* Steven E. de Souza. *Based on the novel by* Richard Bachman (Stephen King). *Photography:* Thomas Del Ruth. *Music:* Harold Faltermeyer. *Editors:* Mark Roy Warner, Edward A. Warschilka, and John Wright. *Starring:* Arnold Schwarzenegger, Maria Conchita Alonso, Yaphet Kotto, Jim Brown, Jesse Ventura, Prof. Toru Tanaka, Gus Rethwisch, Erland Van Lidth, Mick Fleetwood, Dweezil Zappa, Marvin J. McIntyre, and Richard Dawson. Released on November 13, 1987. [101 minutes]

Combining elements from Norman Jewison's *Rollerball, The Most Dangerous Game*, and the most ludicrous television game shows, *The Running Man* made the perfect starring vehicle for Arnold Schwarzenegger. Even though the troubled project had gone through five directors, a half-dozen scripts, and a budget that ballooned from $15 million to $28 million, the film still managed to transcend its bumpy origins to become one of the biggest box-office features of 1987. It also broke new ground for Schwarzenegger by demonstrating his penchant for comic timing. More important, *The Running Man* consolidated his dominance of the action-adventure genre; he received a $3 million salary, and the box-office take of $70 million justified his worth. Arnold said:

(Opposite) Game-show host Damon Killian (Richard Dawson) introduces Ben Richards (Arnold Schwarzenegger) as the next contestant on "The Running Man." (Courtesy Taft/Barish Productions)

I really enjoy doing pictures like *The Running Man* because they are very sophisticated kinds of films. I like the whole idea of the modern gladiator, the government being in control of the [TV] network and fixing the contest, and the show being organized to prevent people from rioting and protesting by keeping them glued to the television set. But I also like the whole idea and challenge of injecting comedy into the picture to lighten tension.

The Screen Story

Based on a story by Stephen King, writing under the name of Richard Bachman, the futuristic film tells us that

in 2017, the world economy has collapsed. Food, natural resources, and oil are in short supply. A police state, divided into paramilitary zones, rules with an iron hand. Television is controlled by the state, and a sadistic game show called 'The Running Man' has become the most popular program in history. All art, music, and communications are censored. No dissent is tolerated, and yet a small resistance movement has managed to survive underground. When high-tech gladiators are not enough to suppress the people's yearning for freedom...more direct methods become necessary.

High above Bakersfield, California, those "more direct methods" take the form of military helicopters armed with enough firepower to disperse the "food riot" of fifteen hundred people. Ben Richards (Schwarzenegger), the leader of one gunship, refuses to fire on unarmed civilians, so his men are ordered to commandeer the vehicle and continue the mission. For violating the direct order, Richards is framed by the government for the massacre and sentenced to life imprisonment as the "Butcher of Bakersfield." Eighteen months later, Richards, his buddies, William Laughlin (Yaphet Kotto) and Harold Weiss (Marvin

Richards, an ex-cop wrongly imprisoned for mass murder, fights to escape captivity from a worker's death camp

McIntire), and other convicted criminals stage a prison break, penetrating the gulag's sonic deadlock. Once free, they seek help from the underground to have their explosive collars removed, but Richards declines an offer to fight alongside the revolutionaries. He thinks the leader of the resistance, Mic (Mick Fleetwood), and his men don't stand a chance against the totalitarian regime unless they locate the uplink satellite that controls television, and they are not likely to find it. Ben simply wants his freedom; he's not interested in politics.

120

While Richards searches the city for his brother Edward, Damon Killian (Richard Dawson) arrives at the network building. He is very concerned with the ratings on his TV show "The Running Man" and demands that his people find him something special for the next episode. (The Justice Department has been supplying him with convicts who are then given the chance to achieve a full pardon by taking part in the lethal television game show, but recently most of the participants have been rather dull.) Killian wants a killer who would be equal to his heavily armed "stalkers," but no one is available.

Ben Richards discovers that his brother has been "taken away for reeducation" and that his apartment has been leased to a low-level network executive, Amber Mendez (Maria Conchita Alonso). Feeling nothing but contempt for the network, the escaped convict breaks into his brother's former home and takes Amber hostage long enough to get him out of the city. He also tries to tell her that the government, in cooperation with her network, manufactured the evidence that put him behind bars. Richards was not responsible for the massacre. Unfortunately, when the unlikely couple arrives at Los Angeles International Airport, Amber betrays Richards to police. He is again forced to run for his life, scrambling through the departure gate and onto the airport runway. But his speed is no match for several security units in all-terrain vehicles, and he is brought down by a large net. Richards's escape from prison and subsequent recapture at the airport have been documented by ICS cameras and provide Damon Killian with some interesting viewing. "I can get ten rating points alone for each bicep," he boasts, insisting the prisoner be turned over to him.

Before Richards can be returned to the maximum-security prison by the Justice Department, the ruthless host of "The Running Man" offers him a deal. If the "Butcher of Bakersfield" agrees to participate on the show, Killian promises him an opportunity to win his freedom. Like other caged criminals, he has an option—similar to gladiators in the Roman arenas: He must fight in "The Network Games" and either die or win valuable prizes, such as a private cell, conjugal visits, or even a full pardon, or report to the Euthanasia Office. Richards is contemptuous of Killian and the network but reluctantly submits to the former's terms in exchange for the lives of Laughlin and Weiss. What he does not know is that Damon Killian plans to use his prison buddies as a handicap to slow him down. (When Amber is caught trying to verify Richards's innocence of the Bakersfield massacre, she, too, is thrown into the game as a dangerous handicap.)

Later that night, as the games are about to begin, Richards learns of Killian's treachery and warns him, "I'll be back" to seek vengeance. The host of "The Running Man" is momentarily startled by his words but then dispatches Richards and his buddies in rocket sleds. Forced into the "Game Zone," four hundred square blocks condemned after the Great Earthquake of 1994, the "running men" are allowed a five-minute head start and awarded points for every one of four quadrants they enter alive. Richards and his men have to run not just for their freedom but also for their lives, pursued by heavily armed stalkers. The stalkers are a four-member team whose names and gimmicks match their colorful costumes. Subzero (Prof. Toru Tanaka) makes use of a razor-sharp hockey stick and exploding pucks to eliminate his victims; Dynamo (Erland Van Lidth) operates high-powered chain saws, and Fireball (Jim Brown) fires a deadly flamethrower. Apparently, only three others have survived the challenge, but that, too, is a lie advanced by the network.

Members of the audience choose Subzero as the first stalker of the evening, but when his friends become endangered, Richards makes mincemeat of the demented hockey player. His death sends ripples

of a shock wave through the network—never before has a stalker been killed! (During the ensuing chaos, Weiss realizes the uplink satellite for the network has been hidden in the game zone and, with Amber's help, attempts to decipher the access code.) Two other stalkers are dispatched to deal with the criminals. Even though they are a well-armed and athletically superior group of killers, Richards proves to be more than their match. He cuts Buzzsaw down to

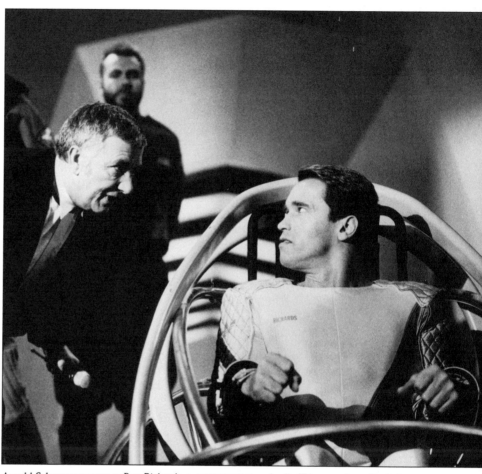

Arnold Schwarzenegger as Ben Richards, a contestant on a deadly TV game show (hosted by Richard Dawson) known as "The Running Man."

size and short-circuits Dynamo, but not before Laughlin and Weiss are brutally murdered. With his last dying breath, Weiss repeats the access code (18-24-61-B-17-7-4) to Amber, while Laughlin forces Richards to promise he will take the code to the revolutionary underground.

During the halftime show, in an attempt to appease his bloodthirsty audience, Damon Killian offers Richards (by way of a private television hookup) a three-year contract to be a stalker. Richards tells him to go to hell and, with Amber, runs

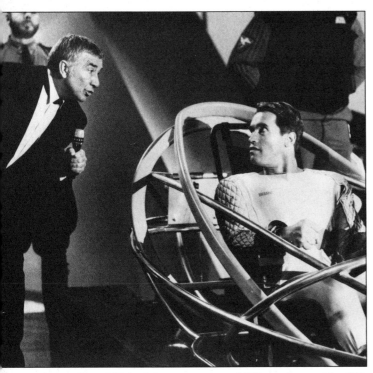

(Above) Richards is contemptuous of Killian and warns him, "I'll be back...."

(Below) Forced into the Game Zone, four hundred square blocks condemned after the Great Earthquake of 1994, Richards and his two companions, William Laughlin (Yaphet Kotto), and left, Harold Weiss (Marvin McIntyre) have less than five minutes' head start.

into the final quadrant pursued by Fireball. Meanwhile, audience sympathy seems to be changing in Richards's favor; most believe that "the next kill will be made" by him.

Ben Richards and Amber Mendez accidentally stumble upon the bodies of the three men whom the network claims to have survived the challenge. Of course, Richards has always been contemptuous of the network, and this only adds proof to his claims. Their discovery of the bodies is cut short by the appearance of Fireball. The two are again forced to flee for their lives, but Richards manages to circle back upon him. With cunning imagination and quick reflexes, Richards forces the stalker into his own deadly firetrap and starts his liquid flame. Fireball is destroyed in a titanic explosion.

Only one stalker now remains—the retired Captain Freedom (Jesse Ventura)—but he wants nothing to do with fancy props or weapons. He insists upon challenging Richards to a hand-to-hand contest. Damon Killian disapproves of this antiquated approach, knowing full well that the "Butcher of Bakersfield" would probably crush the aging stalker. Instead, the host of "The Running Man" decides to fake Richards's death with a televised computer sim-

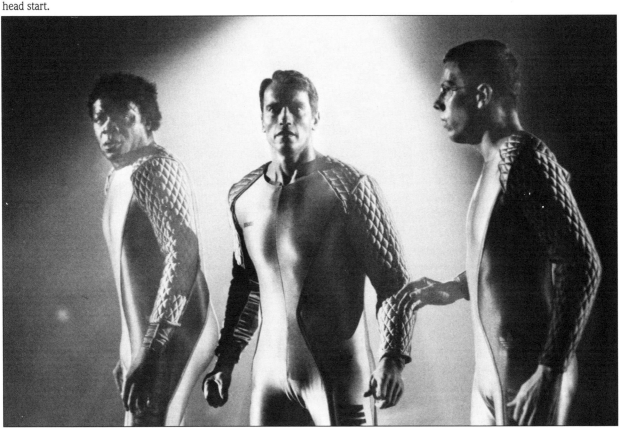

ulation, then later, off-camera, hunt the two criminals down with crack Justice Department troops. His devious plan almost works.

Richards and Mendez continue working their way through the fourth quadrant and eventually fall into the hands of the resistance. With the uplink code, Mic and Stevie (Dweezil Zappa) plan to disrupt the network's signal and cut in with their own. They also intend to broadcast the truth about the government's totalitarian hold, but Amber supplies them with much more damning information. She gives them enough information to clear Richards's name and expose the lies of "The Network Games." Of course, the resistance can only continue broadcasting as long as the satellite link remains in place, and Ben Richards volunteers to lead an armed assault group against the ICS building.

Richards overpowers Subzero (Prof. Toru Tanaka), the first of four deadly stalkers.

Chaos erupts when Richards and his group arrive at the network and take control of the television cameras. Members of the audience have just watched Richards die in the finale to "The Running Man," and yet he is still alive! Further confusion regarding the truth in the Bakersfield massacre sends the audience into a panic. Damon Killian tries to get away in the commotion, but Richards has a special treat for him. He offers the host his own roller-coaster ride of thrills and chills and sends him off into the unknown in a high-speed rocket sled. Amber arrives with news that the resistance has struck its first blow for freedom, and the two warriors depart amid cheers from the audience.

Production Details

The Running Man began in the early seventies as a modest science-fiction novel, about the ultimate game show of the future, by Stephen King/Richard Bachman. In the novel, which is a cross between Phillip K. Dick's *Do Androids Dream of Electric Sheep?* (which became *Blade Runner*), Ray Bradbury's *Fahrenheit 451*, and George Orwell's *1984*, participants are given thirty days to hide anywhere in the United States and survive the onslaught of game-show heavies, known as hunters. The world is heavily polluted, and the lead character must risk his life for an ailing daughter and a prostitute wife. The book skips around details as to how the game show is covered on television, but the end result finds all the principals dying in the dystopian society. Hardly the basis of an upbeat action-adventure film but containing enough raw material that Taft/Barish Productions purchased the rights in 1985 and hired Steven E. de Souza (who had written *Commando*) to formulate a screenplay.

De Souza explained in a 1987 interview:

I felt that the novel had all the earmarkings of being written in the late 1960s. It was a depressing and dark piece. America was being run by corporations that aren't even on the blue chip stocks anymore. The hero had a daughter who was fatally ill, his wife's a prostitute, he dies, his wife dies, everybody dies.... Ultimately, we came down to the old Hollywood cliché—that they would buy the book, keep the title, and throw everything else away. We kept the premise, but that was about it.

De Souza began working on his first draft after completing the sequel to *Commando* and fashioned a story that was highly original. In his version, which some consider a cross between *Rollerball* and *Blade Runner*, an escaped convict, wrongfully imprisoned for a crime he didn't commit, must participate as a contestant on a futuristic game show. The object: to elude flamboyant assassins through a dilapidated sec-

Once "The Running Man" has begun, Amber Mendez (Maria Conchita Alonso) is sent into the Game Zone as a handicap for Richards.

tion of Los Angeles in a limited amount of time. By giving Ben Richards (the lead character) a different, more heroic background and introducing four cartoonish supervillains (now known as stalkers), Steven E. de Souza had broadened the concept of *The Running Man* for contemporary audiences. De Souza commented:

A better title [for the original] might have been *The Hiding Man*, because the book had very few confrontations. One of the things I had to do was create a whole game show which had to be more sophisticated and more outrageous than the game shows on the air now. I also had to eliminate the volunteer aspect; it's now a place where they send condemned criminals. It's like the Roman arena all over again.

While a first draft of the script was being written, executive producer Rob Cohen and producer Tim Zinnemann signed George Pan Cosmatos as director and Christopher Reeve as star. Cosmatos, who had scored big with *Rambo: First Blood Part II*, had definite ideas about what he wanted to put into the picture. He also felt that the film couldn't be made with a modest budget of $15 million and started making demands for $20 million and $25 million from Taft/Barish. Reeve agreed with Cosmatos and tried unsuccessfully to use his Superman muscle to sway the production company. Cosmatos was eventually replaced by two other directors, leading finally to Andrew Davis, and Reeve left to reprise his role as the last son of Krypton in *Superman IV*. Ironically, when Schwarzenegger was brought in to replace Reeve, Tri-Star Pictures helped raise the film's budget to $24 million by advancing Taft/Barish $9 million for the distribution rights. (*The Running Man*'s final budget, however, was closer to $28 million.)

Schwarzenegger discussed his early interest in the novel and subsequent involvement in the film version:

After I had finished reading *The Running Man*, I said to myself, "That would be an interesting part to play." It stuck in my mind, which happens every so often when I read such books. When I heard that Christopher Reeve had been signed for the part in the beginning, I didn't bother to inquire about it—I just felt, "God, that would have been a job I would have liked to do," and dropped it. Then, after their director had a falling out with the company, they contacted me, without even knowing I was interested in the first place.

Arnold was busy filming *Raw Deal* for Dino De Laurentiis when the producers first offered him *The Running Man* role, and after some negotiating, he agreed to begin work immediately after *Predator*.

Plus, Schwarzenegger, as he demonstrated in Commando, can be very funny. Christopher Reeve can't.

One of the biggest tasks facing de Souza was creating a formidable adversary for Schwarzenegger, who in his preceding film had just traded blows with a creature from another world. Working against type, the screenwriter combined two characters from the novel—Dan Killian (the head of the Games Authority) and Bobby Thompson (the show's host)—into one megamythic person, Damon Killian, for the movie. Cast fittingly enough as the brash, ruthless Killian was the onetime *Family Feud* host Richard Dawson. The hunters of the novel were also rewritten to be imposing villains. Then the producers cast some of the sports world's most colorful and ruthless personalities as stalkers. Football great turned star Jim Brown was one of the first choices when casting began for *The Running*

Following Schwarzenegger's signing, de Souza was contacted to write another draft of the screenplay tailored specifically for the muscleman. Steven E. de Souza had already written five different versions of the story for each of the principals who had been involved. His final screenplay for *The Running Man* differed substantially from the original. De Souza remembered some months later:

The roles were very different. When writing it for Reeve, the character could be much more talkative because he's a stage actor. He could have a philosophy. You want Arnold to be a man of action and not of words. It's the difference between casting Gregory Peck or John Wayne, to go back to an earlier era. I think Arnold is much closer to John Wayne than he is to Gregory Peck, who made his share of action films. Arnold is unique among action-adventure guys. He projects a great deal of intelligence and cunning.

Richards takes on Buzzsaw (Gus Rethwisch), one of the four stalkers.

125

Richards runs for his life.

Man. Brown had made a number of popular action-adventure films during the sixties, after his debut in Robert Aldrich's *The Dirty Dozen*, and turned to "blaxploitation" movies in the early seventies, including the popular *Slaughter* films. His acting career faltered during the eighties, but Keith Barish and Rob Cohen had confidence that he could stage a comeback with the right role. The character of Fireball was the first major role he had had in nearly fifteen years. Jesse ("The Body") Ventura, who had played Blain opposite Schwarzenegger's Dutch Schaefer in *Predator*, was cast as the aging Captain Freedom, while pro wrestler Prof. Toru Tanaka and champion weightlifter Gus Rethwisch were hired as Subzero and Buzzsaw, respectively. Erland Van Lidth helped round out the field of stalkers as the opera-singing Dynamo. Maria Conchita Alonso, Yaphet Kotto, Mick Fleetwood, and rock icon Frank Zappa's son Dweezil also contributed their talents.

De Souza said:

This movie's world is the near future. These characters may seem like they've stepped right out of the pages of a comic book. They're colorful, they're glitzy, they're bizarre, and that's what the show within the movie is. Like wrestlers who wear ridiculous costumes and scream, the stalkers know that they're acting. And maybe when these villains go home, they have a beer and take off their costume. That's implied in the movie, anyway.... There are elements in *The Running Man* that are definitely comic book, but Arnold is certainly very human, with very real problems.

During his eight-month sojourn from *Predator*, while Silver and Gordon searched for a new monster maker, Arnold Schwarzenegger worked out and rehearsed for his role as Ben Richards. Because the film called for plenty of physical action, he bulked up to 220 formidable pounds. (Schwarzenegger lost much of that bulk in the final difficult weeks of

126

shooting on *Predator*.) When principal photography began on March 2, 1987, he looked more like the lean, mean killing machine from *The Terminator* than the Cimmerian from *Conan The Destroyer*. Schwarzenegger told reporters during his publicity tour:

> I had to be physically fit because the actual battle scenes between Richards and the stalkers are very unique. I'm fighting these guys with my bare hands, while they use all kinds of vicious equipment, like flamethrowers. There's one guy with a chain saw; Dynamo shoots electric current at people to kill them. One stalker has this very ugly vehicle, with spikes sticking out in front, that is meant to run people down and kill them. Each of the stalkers is an interesting character, with a machine designed to kill people in seconds.

Two weeks into the production, however, the stalking came to an abrupt halt when director Andrew Davis was replaced by Paul Michael Glaser.

(Above) Matching muscle with steel, Richards ultimately defeats the deadly Buzzsaw with his own weapon.

(Below) Amber Mendez tries to escape a deadly pursuit.

127

Richards and Mendez decide to team up for survival.

(Cohen and Zinnemann cited "creative differences" as their reason for dropping Davis from their production.) Glaser, the brunet half of the TV cop team of *Starsky and Hutch*, who had switched from acting to directing, took over as director of the troubled shoot with less than two days' preparation and filmed sixty-nine days without missing a beat. For contractual reasons involving Arnold Schwarzenegger's publicity tour for *Predator*, Glaser was forced to work very quickly, but he found his work with the big star challenging.

Glaser explained in a 1987 interview:

I tried to get in touch with Arnold as a person and as an actor. I felt there was more there than people had used or taken advantage of in the past. Other directors have been exploiting Schwarzenegger's physicality and people's perceptions of that physicality for a long time. But they hadn't been getting in touch with his human side, the warm side, the intelligent side.

Seven weeks of filming on the Schwarzenegger vehicle took place at the Kaiser Steel Mill in Fontana, followed by two weeks of shooting in Los Angeles and other Southern California locations. Three addi-

tional weeks of principal photography, involving some work on soundstages at Warners' Hollywood Studios, miniatures, and special effects were completed near the end of the shoot. Larry Cavanaugh, who had provided the effects for Francis Ford Coppola's *Apocalypse Now*, and his special-effects crew produced a number of elaborate visuals and matte shots during postproduction. Despite its staggering $28 million budget, *The Running Man* wrapped production during the first week of June 1987.

Schwarzenegger confessed:

I'm extremely delighted. This movie started out with problems and ended up being so classy, so I'm extremely happy—I've gone through all these ups and downs with the film. Some movies start out perfectly and continue all the way to the end; others start out perfectly and end up shitty. This one started out with some negativism because of the change of leadership and budget, but the crew all stuck together. We all believed in it. I always felt *The Running Man* would be the final crescendo for my career this year, because I thought *Predator* would be a great warm-up, and that's the way it looks right now. *The Running Man* is going to be a smash.

Tri-Star Pictures also believed that it had a major hit and scheduled the release of *The Running Man* during the lucrative summer months. But the distribution was delayed because Arnold didn't want another of his films competing with his other summer hit. He said:

> When the studio saw some of the dailies, they got all excited and said the summer would be the best time to come out. But my deal with them was quite different. It had to come out in the fall or early winter. They wanted to go back on their word for a while.

But the film's distributor reconsidered when Arnold flexed his contractual muscles. A date in November was chosen by mutual consent.

Critical Commentary

The Running Man sent its competition running for cover when it first hit the theaters on November 13, 1987. In its initial week of American release the movie knocked *Fatal Attraction* off the top of the charts, and later, while grossing an incredible $34.9 million in its first three weeks, it inflicted serious box-office damage on John Carpenter's *Prince of Darkness*, Clive Barker's *Hellraiser*, Rob Reiner's *The Princess Bride*, Emile Ardolino's *Dirty Dancing*, and an *Alien* rip-off entitled *The Hidden*. Audiences and critics alike praised the inventive nature of *The Running Man* and its inspired casting (notably Schwarzenegger and Richard Dawson), but some reviewers did find fault with its exploitative violence. Dennis Fischer of *Cinefantastique* called the film "as contemptible as the wrestling and game shows it is satirizing," further stating that it was "contemptuous of its audience" and "though it starts well," it was not as good as the Stephen King novel. Similarly, Ralph Novak, writing in *People* magazine, could not determine "where the film stops lampooning TV audiences' thirst for vicarious violence and starts exploiting it." Regardless of the criticism, *The Running Man* continued to perform well and netted more than $70 million in receipts. In honor of his success with *Predator* and *The Running Man*, the National Association of Theatre Owners awarded Arnold Schwarzenegger the 1987 Star of the Year Award.

Schwarzenegger once again proved in *The Running Man* that he could carry a big-budget action-adventure film and that he was well worth the $3 million salary he received for the picture. No

Amber Mendez, armed and determined to overthrow the totalitarian government.

Dweezil Zappa, son of Frank Zappa, as Stevie, a member of the resistance movement of 2019.

other action star—not Sylvester Stallone or Clint Eastwood or even John Wayne—had ever come close to maintaining his consistency, bankability, or audience appeal. And yet Arnold appeared to be drifting slowly away from the macho ideal he had created for the Conan films, and with his characteristic vision, he seemed to be searching for a more multidimensional image. His one-liners had already become a Schwarzenegger trademark that audiences relied upon from picture to picture. His portrayal of the underdog—the man who turns the tables on his oppressors—had been first introduced in *Commando* and so refined in the three subsequent films that people believed that Arnold was actually one of them (and not a superhero). Schwarzenegger is in top form as Ben Richards both from a physical standpoint and from an emotional one. Arnold confessed, "It's hard to do heroic films and bring out vulnerability," but he demonstrates a compelling urge to bridge an emotional gap with his audience. He is also very charming, cunning, imaginative, violent, and *funny* in moments of light relief. All of these attributes are significant because they help establish his versatility as an actor and not simply a movie star. When he interrupts

Killian's telecast and intones, "I'll be back," Arnold is also reminding audiences that he will return (with their help) with even greater entertainment.

The Running Man, as with *Predator*, solves the singular dramatic problem in Schwarzenegger films by creating not one but four formidable adversaries. The stalkers might, at first glance, seem like simple comic-book characters, with their flamboyant names, costumes, and gadgets, but they are very deadly. During his first encounter with Subzero, Arnold is bloodied and sent sprawling from his strike. While the audience has little doubt who will win, the hard-fought battle is staged very realistically. Much later, Schwarzenegger takes his lumps from Buzzsaw before ripping his antagonist in two with his own weapon, and he permits Dynamo to live after being nearly run over by this spiked vehicle. Even Fireball is a formidable opponent, with his state-of-the-art flamethrower and jet pack. Arnold manages to survive each confrontation with an equal amount of brawn and intellect, only to face an equally ruthless host.

Credit for *The Running Man*'s success belongs not only to Arnold Schwarzenegger but also to the superior work of the entire production company. By casting TV's Richard Dawson as the sleazy Damon Killian, Keith Barish and Rob Cohen hit upon a winning personality. Dawson's witty line readings in front of the camera and ruthless machinations behind help create one of the more offbeat screen villians. Yaphet Kotto and Maria Conchita Alonso provide a perfect balance, with their acting talents, to Schwarzenegger's on-screen persona, in much the same way the stalkers (Jim Brown, Toru Tanaka, Erland Van Lidth, and Gus Rethwisch) counterbalance the muscleman's physical presence. Steven E. de Souza's script is both witty and imaginative,* far outpacing Stephen King's original novel, and Paul Michael Glaser proves his adeptness as an action director.

The Running Man is available on both videocassette and laserdisc from Tri-Star Pictures. (The motion picture should not be confused with Carol Reed's 1963 British film of the same name.)

---

*Science-fiction fans might recognize the name Ben Richards from the television character played by Christopher George on *The Immortal* (1969, ABC) or the televised capture and execution (of Richards) from the original novel and film version of Ray Bradbury's *Farenheit 451*.

Director Paul Michael Glaser (of *Starsky and Hutch* fame) confers with Schwarzenegger on a difficult action sequence.

TEN

GUMBY AND POKEY

Red Heat

(a.k.a. Dimitri), 1988. Tri-Star Pictures/Carolco. *Director:* Walter Hill. *Producers:* Hill and Gordon Carroll. *Executive Producers:* Mario Kassar and Andrew Vajna. *Screenplay:* Harry Kleiner, Hill, and Troy Kennedy Martin. *Based on a story by* Hill. *Photography:* Matthew F. Leonetti. *Music:* James Horner. *Editors:* Freeman Davies, Carmel Davies, and Donn Aron. *Starring:* Arnold Schwarzenegger, James Belushi, Peter Boyle, Ed O'Ross, Larry Fishburne, Gina Gershon, Brent Jennings, and Richard Bright. Released on June 17, 1988. [106 minutes]

Considering the amount of talent and advance publicity that it had, *Red Heat* should have been another *Commando*, *Predator*, or *The Running Man* for Schwarzenegger; instead it became his least successful vehicle to the time, ranking with *Red Sonja* and *Raw Deal* as the worst films of his later career. (Perhaps he should avoid films whose titles begin with the letter "R.") Cowritten, coproduced and directed by Walter Hill and costarring James Belushi, the motion picture had all the right elements. Tri-Star tub-thumped the film long before its release by claiming that "people are dying to see it." And yet in a summer that introduced a cartoon legend named Roger Rabbit and propelled Bruce Willis into big-screen stardom with *Die Hard*, audiences were less than enthused with Arnold's latest offering. The momentum gained from his two previous entries was wasted on yet another buddy movie.

The Screen Story

Capt. Ivan Danko (Schwarzenegger), a strong, silent, and ruthless Russian homicide cop known by his

comrades in Moscow as "Iron Jaw," has spent many months searching through the seedy underworld of all-male health spas and noisy cafés for a notorious drug dealer. When his partner Yuri is gunned down by Viktor Rostavili (Ed O'Ross) during a routine drug raid, Danko is permitted by Soviet officials to track the dealer to his connection in Chicago. Upon his arrival in the Windy City, the Russian policeman learns that Viktor has been arrested for a minor traffic violation and counts his blessings. Unfortunately, the locals are not aware that their captive is wanted back home for murdering a detective. Their sloppy police work allows Viktor to break for freedom when several detectives are ambushed (and one is killed) by the Soviet criminal's associates. The slain police officer, Detective Gallagher (Richard Bright), has been on the force for years, and many want his murder avenged, including his wisecracking partner Art Ridzik (James Belushi).

Suddenly Ridzik is thrown together with Danko on the same case, and they are forced into a reluctant partnership. Ridzik is the type of cop who cuts corners on police procedure and has the reprimands to prove it. Danko works strictly by the book, even when he is in a foreign country. The two do not like each other very much, in spite of attempts by Cmdr. Lou Donnelly (Peter Boyle) to help them find a common ground. Ridzik contemptuously nicknames Captain Danko "Gumby" because of his lime-green suit, and Danko has very little to say beyond making fun of Ridzik's hero "Dirty Harry."

Their contentious investigation leads them to an international drug-trafficking operation controlled from within the walls of a state prison. There the unlikely duo learns from a black godfather that a key

(Opposite) Schwarzenegger stars as Capt. Ivan "Iron Jaw" Danko in *Red Heat*.

133

Militia officer Ivan Danko searches the Russian druzhba for a notorious drug smuggler.

that Danko carries from an earlier encounter represents the secret to Viktor's whole drug-dealing business. However, before they are able to find out what the key unlocks, Katherine Manzetti (Gina Gershon)—Viktor's American wife—attempts to steal it from the two unsuspecting detectives. Captain Danko's simple one-room apartment is raided by the black Mafia, and he is forced to kill several unknown assailants. During the shoot-out, Manzetti is killed by her own husband, Danko is wounded, and Viktor escapes with the key.

When news of the gun battle reaches Donnelly's office, the police commander is furious. He suspends Ridzik from duty, pending a full investigation, takes away Danko's firearm, and turns him over to Soviet officials. They, too, are upset by the botched operation, but that does not prevent the Russian cop from resuming his vendetta against Rostavili. Allied with Ridzik, whom he has come to trust in a curious relationship, Ivan Danko traces the lost key to a bus station. There Viktor waits for his drug delivery from El Paso.

Tracking the notorious drug dealer to the station,

When his partner is killed in the line of duty during a drug bust, Danko is forced to follow his killer to America...

...where he is introduced to Commander Donnelly (Peter Boyle, right) by Sergeant Gallagher (Richard Bright).

Danko forces Viktor into a showdown. The Soviet criminal grabs an incoming bus and tries to get away. But both Ridzik and Danko follow in a companion bus and eventually force him off the road after smashing through assorted cars and buildings. At Chicago's Central Station, among the passing trains, Danko shoots it out with his criminal counterpart. Viktor Rostavili is no match for the tough Russian policeman and ultimately dies in the confrontation. Several hours later, Ridzik escorts Danko to the airport, and as a symbol of their friendship, they exchange watches and farewells.

No-nonsense Danko is reluctantly teamed up with Art Ridzik (James Belushi), a brash, wisecracking Chicago cop.

Production Details

The explosive, high-action premise of *Red Heat* (a.k.a. *Dimitri*) began as an attempt by Walter Hill to duplicate the success of his *48 HRS*. It then developed into a very special opportunity for the director. Hill told reporters in a 1988 press junket:

> I had always wanted to work with Arnold Schwarzenegger. I was impressed by his screen presence, started thinking about what we could do together, and came up with the possibility of a Moscow cop on assignment in

Danko comes face-to-face with his partner's killer, Viktor Rostavili (Ed O'Ross).

the States—the approach seemed fairly unique.

That several previous films, notably *Coogan's Bluff* and *Gorky Park*, had already dealt with transplanted police detectives in big-city settings did not prevent Hill from pitching Schwarzenegger the idea over lunch.

Hill continued:

We have a Russian commenting on America and its perceptions of Soviet society, so there's an attempt at a comedic element running throughout. The film questions certain American values in juxtaposition with a very theatrical Russian sensibility. The characters come together for a common objective; while not liking each other, they grow to respect one another on the way to becoming friends. Arnold hesitated for fifteen minutes, but he's a smart fellow, so he came around....

"We spent a lot of time talking about my character," Schwarzenegger added, "and were very clear what he was before I agreed to play him." He was determined that his character be a fully realized, multidimensional being.

Ivan Danko is a very intelligent guy; he studied languages in Kiev and has risen to the top of his profession. But when he goes to the States to extradite a Soviet drug dealer against

When Viktor escapes, Danko is forced to trail him into the Chicago underworld.

whom he has a personal vendetta, it's like he's wearing blinders. Because of the policeman assigned to help him, he gradually learns many things about the American Way which he takes home with him.

With a tentative agreement from the star, Hill began working on the script (with screenwriters Harry Kleiner and Troy Kennedy Martin) and scouting possible locations for the shoot. He had already decided on Chicago (having ruled out New York and Los Angeles for financial reasons) and was prepared to film in Helsinki (as Michael Apted had before him for *Gorky Park*) when he was granted permission to shoot in Moscow. The forty-six-year-old filmmaker

Ridzik nicknames Danko "Gumby" because of his lime-green suit and strange appearance.

was surprised to learn that Soviet officials had been following his work with great interest for many years. Walter Hill had begun his career in the late sixties as an assistant director on several low-budget thrillers and soon turned to writing such seventies screenplays as *Hickey and Boggs* for Robert Culp and Bill Cosby and *The Drowning Pool* for Paul Newman. When the original director left *Hard Times*, Hill was given the chance to make his directorial debut. Subsequent turns at *The Driver*, *The Warriors*, *48 HRS.*, *Streets of Fire*, and *Extreme Prejudice* helped establish his reputation for white-knuckle thrillers and pulsating violence. He also coproduced the original *Alien*. Hill believed that *Red Heat* would be the perfect vehicle for exploring East and West relations and knew that Schwarzenegger would make the perfect Russian policeman.

But in order to counterbalance the Schwarzenegger persona, Hill needed the right group of costars. For the role of the wisecracking detective Art Ridzik, he hired James Belushi. The versatile younger brother of John Belushi had been one of the original Second City Players when he burst onto the scene in the early eighties with a string of critical successes. Although he preferred to work with off-the-cuff comedy, Belushi had proved that he was equally adept with drama. For drug dealer Viktor Rostavili, Hill

Danko cautiously pursues a killer.

137

Danko (Schwarzenegger) claims that he has never heard of "Dirty Harry" when Ridzik begins boasting about the firepower of the .357 Magnum.

came to Ed O'Ross by way of producer Joel Silver, who had used him in *Lethal Weapon*. Veteran character actor Peter Boyle was signed to play the overworked watch commander Lou Donnelly. Larry Fishburne, Gina Gershon, and Richard Bright helped round out the cast.

To prepare for filming, both Schwarzenegger and Belushi were required to undergo a rigorous training schedule. Arnold explored various aspects of Soviet police work, Russian culture and history, and classic Russian movies while studying the language. "I worked for three months on it," he revealed, admitting that his European accent provided somewhat of a handicap.

> It was not enough to learn English with a Russian accent; I had to learn it from scratch because the vocal sounds are quite different. Besides, the first twenty pages of the script are totally in Russian.

Schwarzenegger also worked out with weights to prepare for the physical regimen and, at Hill's request, lost an additional ten pounds to look leaner, tougher, like a Russian policeman. "Actually, it's easy for me to add or lose twenty pounds; all it takes is discipline."

Discipline was something that James Belushi had to learn during preproduction. In addition to gaining ten pounds, he was required to train with the bodybuilder for the film's more physically challenging sequences. He also did his homework by hanging around with police detectives from the 18th District in his hometown of Chicago. "They taught me a lot," Belushi admitted to reporters in 1988.

> I got ideas, attitudes, even lines from them; clothes and jewelry, too—pinkie rings, for instance. I learned they always carry two pens, because there's a lot of writing in their jobs. They taught me about different weapons and how to search a car— safely. They're brave, strong men, besides being very funny guys as well.

Ridzik and Danko follow Viktor's trail to the state penitentiary.

and on Wacker Drive. Using two steel-reinforced thirty-four-thousand-pound buses (with eighteen-thousand-pound rear-mounted engines that made high-speed maneuvering difficult), the stunt crews roared through the downtown streets, shearing off parking meters, demolishing cars, and crashing into a fountain (built especially for the film). Additional filming at the Stateville Correctional Center, a maximum-security prison sixty miles from the city, was completed during the first week in February, and while the production company packed for Russia, the second unit finished the remaining pickup shots.

Regrettably, the company suffered a fatality on February 6 when stunt coordinator Bennie Dobbins died of a sudden heart attack. At only fifty-four,

Principal shooting in and around Chicago began during the first week of January 1988. On the first day of location lensing however, director Hill was forced to suspend work early in order to bail his chief villain out of jail. Ed O'Ross, who had been hired to play the drug-dealing Russian, was arrested by two undercover narcotics agents shortly after landing at O'Hare Airport. Apprehended because he fit the description of a notorious drug courier, O'Ross had been reluctant to offer the detectives proper identification. (He thought he was the victim of an elaborate practical joke played by Schwarzenegger.) But when the police persisted with their interrogation, O'Ross produced a Screen Actors Guild card and called Hill on location.

"It must have been my five-day growth of beard, the silk shirt, and lizard cowboy boots which did it," the actor said with a nervous laugh. "And I always thought drug dealers wore three-piece suits!"

On the next day, principal photography continued at various locations, including North River, Maxwell Street and Wicker Park districts, the Flat-Iron building, Trailways bus station, and the Wallace Computer Company offices. The climactic chase sequence, which was choreographed by stunt coordinator Bennie Dobbins, was filmed in and around the Loop

Danko questions Katherine Manzetti (Gina Gershon) as to the whereabouts of the Russian drug dealer.

139

Ridzik and Danko fight over the wheel of a bus as they race through the streets of Chicago.

Dobbins (who also worked with Schwarzenegger on *Commando*) had lived two lifetimes, working first as a professional ballplayer for the Boston Red Sox, then becoming a professional stuntman.

On February 11, the crew moved to Moscow, where they became the first American production company ever permitted to film in Red Square. Ironically, they began shooting on the day that Gorbachev announced the Soviet pullout from Afghanistan. Eight days later, the company completed its location photography in Budapest and moved to soundstage interiors in Los Angeles. During each phase of filming, an impressed Walter Hill got a chance to direct Schwarzenegger through various sequences.

> Arnold is a force of nature. He was as friendly as Will Rogers, with a real sense of humor about himself, and he would go out there and fight in the snow with no clothes on and never complain.

Hill completed his twelve-week shoot by mid-March and wrapped *Red Heat* on time and on budget. With the production finally behind him, Schwarzenegger had nothing but praise for his direc-

tor and costar.

> Walter is one of the true geniuses of our time, and Jim is terrific. He took it upon himself to ad-lib often; it was good to work in that kind of atmosphere.

Arnold further explained his admiration of the young actor and hoped that he would get an opportunity to play a comic role.

> Comedy comes naturally to me. Even competing in sports, when everyone else was very intense, I'd always joke around. I look forward to doing straight comedy, perhaps even producing and directing a film project. Those are my goals, not something I'm planning for tomorrow, but you never know....

Critical Commentary

Originally scheduled by Tri-Star for release on June 24, 1988, *Red Heat* opened one week earlier (on June 17) in fifteen hundred theaters in an effort to get a crucial jump on the summer box-office sweeps. (The same company's *Rambo III*, with Sylvester

Stallone, had opened to megabusiness on May 25, opposite *"Crocodile" Dundee II* and Ron Howard's *Willow*.) Unfortunately, *Red Heat* could only manage a small percentage of receipts opposite Penny Marshall's *Big*, which premiered the same day with glowing reviews and good word of mouth. When *Who Framed Roger Rabbit* opened one week later, the Arnold Schwarzenegger actioner was doomed. Although audiences found plenty of fault with *Red Heat*, several critics were impressed by the film's technical brilliance and with Arnold's performance as a Russian cop. *New York Times* reviewer Vincent Canby said, "Though Mr. Belushi is the comedian of the film, the most consistently comic performance is given by Mr. Schwarzenegger." Richard Corliss wrote in *Time* magazine: "Arnold, starched tongue in cheek, is a doll: G.I. Joe in Soviet mufti. He could beat the stuffing out of a toy Rambo." By the end of the summer, *Red Heat* had finished well behind

Bruce Willis's *Die Hard*, Kevin Costner's *Bull Durham*, and even Eddie Murphy's *Coming to America*. It emerged as Schwarzenegger's biggest box-office failure to date.

Part of the blame for the film's lackluster performance rests with Tri-Star Pictures. While the producers may have thought they had another *48 HRS.*, they should have been much more careful with the movie's release date. Their *Rambo III* had already gobbled up most of the money people spend on action-adventure films, and with an enormous glut of other superior products, the best that *Red Heat* could have fared, Schwarzenegger notwithstanding, was a modest take. The superstar's two previous blockbusters had been science-fiction films, and with the poor showing of fantasy offerings in the summer of 1988, the studio could have scored big with another farfetched tale. The buddy formula (borrowed from *48 HRS.*) was also used in five other movies. Finally, there was enormous

Ridzik is angered over the fact that Danko put his life in danger in a wild bus chase with Viktor.

Danko takes careful aim with his deadly weapon as Viktor steps into view.

themselves. (Schwarzenegger had already proved his penchant for comedy in *Commando* and *The Running Man*.)

Hill's formula for creating unlikely crime-fighting teams may have worked once before with Nick Nolte and Eddie Murphy in both *48 HRS.* and *Another 48 HRS.*; it simply doesn't work here. There is very little chemistry between James Belushi and Arnold Schwarzenegger, and what little there is was wasted by the trivial, foul-mouthed banter between the two men. Talented as he may be, Belushi lacks the physical presence or persona to play in an action-adventure film. His cynical one-liners belong in comedies, such as *About Last Night...*, *Mr. Destiny*, or *Taking Care of Business*, and he is miscast against the persona of Schwarzenegger. The two actors appear more like the cartoon characters "Gumby" and "Pokey" than detectives in an action-adventure movie. Besides, Arnold simply functions better as a leader or a loner; he is not really the type to rely on a partner unless it's strictly for fun.

Defending his film against negative criticism, the director said:

> I tell stories for a living, and they're usually very simple, with just enough narrative logic to keep an audience from going out of its collective mind. The important thing is character logic, which I'm most interested in. Beyond that, I try not to get too analytical. Certainly people don't want to see the same exact movie again, but they don't mind seeing the same *type* of movie.

The plot line involving drug pushers and distributors had been already used again and again on TV's *Miami Vice*. Here it does nothing but bridge the action sequences. Hill's direction is less than inspiring and relies totally on fast-paced editing for effect. He also fails to provide a worthy adversary for Schwarzenegger. Viktor Rostavili (Ed O'Ross), as pho-

confusion with the motion picture's title. Two other films, including a horror movie entitled *Dead Heat* and a science fictioner called *Outer Heat* (later changed to *Alien Nation*), were also scheduled for release that summer. *Red Heat* was hardly an original title, and ticket buyers may have thought the titles were interchangeable (as they were).

Though many critics praised his performance, Schwarzenegger's appearance in *Red Heat* as an "iron-jawed" detective was, regrettably, a step backward creatively for the superstar. His hard-as-nails performance is also at the heart of the film's other central flaw—its use of stereotypes. Arnold sleepwalks through the movie looking so stern and stoic because that's how Americans view their Soviet counterparts. He appears to be a one-dimensional cardboard cutout of a Russian police officer with little real identity of his own. That's exactly the kind of character he had been trying to shake for years. Why hire a man who "looks" stern, stoic, and physically awesome to portray the strong but silent type? Walter Hill would have demonstrated much more insight if he had cast Belushi as the Russian cop and Arnold as the wise-cracking guy with the cynical sense of humor. That way, both men could have shown some genuine acting talent instead of walking through the script as

142

At the airport, Ridzik and Danko share a private moment as they exchange farewell gifts.

tographed by Hill, appears to be a two-bit punk rather than some criminal mastermind. After an alien predator and four deadly stalkers, this simple drug smuggler is hardly a match for the muscle power of the former Mr. Universe.

While there is very little that is truly unique about the film, *Red Heat* is available on videocassette and laserdisc from International Video Entertainment (IVE).

ELEVEN

THE BOYS FROM LOS ALAMOS

Twins

1988. Universal Pictures. *Producer-Director:* Ivan Reitman. *Executive Producers:* Joe Medjuck and Michael C. Gross. *Screenplay:* William Davies, William Osborne, Timothy Harris, and Herschel Weingrod. *Photography:* Andrzej Bartkowiak. *Music:* Georges Delerue and Randy Edelman. *Editors:* Sheldon Kahn and Donn Cambern. *Starring:* Arnold Schwarzenegger, Danny DeVito, Kelly Preston, Chloe Webb, Bonnie Bartlett, Marshall Bell, Trey Wilson, Hugh O'Brian, Nehemiah Persoff, and Tony Jay. Released on December 9, 1988. [115 minutes]

If *Commando*, *Predator*, and *The Running Man* had solidified Arnold Schwarzenegger's career as *the* number-one box-office draw in the world for action-adventure films, *Twins* further demonstrated his considerable skills as a comedic actor. Directed by Ivan Reitman and featuring Danny DeVito as Arnold's unlikely fraternal twin, the madcap comedy provided Schwarzenegger with an important breakthrough role. He would not soon again be dismissed simply as a muscle-bound action star. Although critics rejected the film as a one-joke affair, audiences responded with a whopping $110 million in box-office receipts, more than that of any of Schwarzenegger's previous endeavors. The enormity of his success with *Twins* sent his career skyrocketing.

The star looked upon the romp as an important step in his acting career. Schwarzenegger explained in a 1988 interview:

> It made everyone feel uncomfortable with the idea of me doing a film that deals with come-

dy and humor. One thing I realized [a long time ago] was that I really enjoyed doing comedy, but there would always be confrontations with the directors, with the studios. "Naw, naw, naw. What we want you to do is be a tough guy." I was trying to figure out how I could do a comedy from beginning to end, and *Twins* represented the next stepping-stone in my career.

The Screen Story

On his thirty-fifth birthday, Julius Benedict (Schwarzenegger) learns the truth about his birth from a kindly mad scientist (Tony Jay). He already knew that he was the product of a scientific experiment funded by the U. S. government, a top-secret project designed to create a physically, spiritually, and mentally superior being—a superman. He had had six fathers (including a physicist and a world-renowned athlete), chosen for their genetic excellence, and his mother was a remarkable woman named Mary Anne Benedict who had died during childbirth. But he did not know that his mother had given birth to a second baby boy moments after the first. Because the second child, Vincent (Danny DeVito), had none of the superior breeding (of the first) and actually contained most of the genetic "garbage," he was shipped to an orphanage in Los Angeles. Julius remained on the scientist's isolated island, helping with the scientist's research and excelling in math, science, literature, and languages. Pure in body, mind, and spirit, he wasn't equipped to deal with the outside world. However, on learning

(Opposite) Schwarzenegger as Julius Benedict, the product of a unique genetic experiment. (Courtesy Universal Pictures)

145

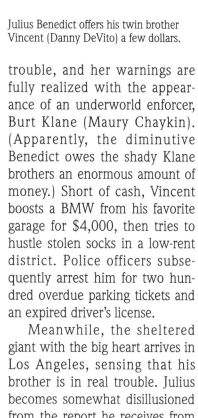

Julius Benedict offers his twin brother Vincent (Danny DeVito) a few dollars.

trouble, and her warnings are fully realized with the appearance of an underworld enforcer, Burt Klane (Maury Chaykin). (Apparently, the diminutive Benedict owes the shady Klane brothers an enormous amount of money.) Short of cash, Vincent boosts a BMW from his favorite garage for $4,000, then tries to hustle stolen socks in a low-rent district. Police officers subsequently arrest him for two hundred overdue parking tickets and an expired driver's license.

Meanwhile, the sheltered giant with the big heart arrives in Los Angeles, sensing that his brother is in real trouble. Julius becomes somewhat disillusioned from the report he receives from the nuns at St. Charlotte's Orphanage and tracks Vincent to the county jail. While the "perfect" brother wants to help his little lesser half, Vincent regards him as a dope. Julius pays Vincent's bail and later rescues him from an angry mob enforcer, after being ditched on the street in Beverly Hills. Vincent quickly recognizes how helpful Julius might be as a bodyguard and allows him to return home for some "nuked food." On the way home the twins encounter Linda and Marnie, who is very attracted to the muscular giant, and invite them to share some birthday cake. The day also happens to be Vincent's birthday, his thirty-fifth!

At the garage where Vincent usually steals cars, two uptight businessmen leave a Cadillac with a high-tech engine in the trunk. (Their instructions reveal a desire to sell the expensive hardware to a competitor for $5 million through a professional hit man.) Vincent unwittingly boosts the Cadillac for some additional cash but soon changes his mind when he realizes that he can earn millions by deliver-

that he has a twin brother, who he believes might be just like him, Julius leaves his tropical paradise and travels to California.

Vincent, who is a pushy, obnoxious pint-sized hustler with an insatiable lust for women and money, has neither the brains nor the brawn of Julius. When we first see him, he is escaping out the window of a married woman's apartment and borrowing money from his girlfriend Linda (Chloe Webb). Her sister Marnie (Kelly Preston) warns Linda that he is real

Twins Vincent and Julius Benedict—only their mother can tell the boys apart.

ing the contraband to a Texas entrepreneur. Julius has desires to locate their long-lost mother, when he learns that she is not dead, and enlists his brother to drive him to the secret lab in Los Alamos, New Mexico. After being joined by the two sexy sisters, the boys hit the road in their stolen car. However, when the industrial assassin Webster (Marshall Bell) is unable to locate the Cadillac, he traces the car to Vincent and follows behind with two bullets—one for each of the Benedict twins.

During the course of their journey, the two men learn valuable lessons from each other. Julius helps Vincent walk the straight-and-narrow path to honesty and fair play, while he himself learns to dress, dance, drink beer, and romance Marnie. At the genetics research facility in Los Alamos, the twins discover the truth about their birth from Dr. Traven (Nehemiah Persoff) and begin to come together as brothers. When the scientist is reluctant to tell them about their mother's whereabouts, Julius explodes and forces him to reveal her location. "I'll be back [if you're lying to me]," the muscle-bound giant intones once he learns that she has retired to an artist's colony outside Santa Fe. Unfortunately, soon after they arrive at Whispering Pines, the twins are told by the groundskeeper (Bonnie Bartlett) that Mary Anne Benedict has died, leaving her fortune to the colony. (In truth, the groundskeeper is Mary Anne Benedict, but she fears the men have been sent by a real-estate developer to cheat her.)

Disappointed, Vincent drives away without his brother or the two ladies and heads for Houston. He is anxious to claim the $5 million, but Julius, fearing for his safety, boards a plane for Texas in order to stop his brother from doing something totally brainless. Unfortunately, Webster is waiting for the two of them. At a deserted factory in a suburb of Houston, Julius and Vincent are forced into a showdown with the industrial assassin. Thanks to his genetic superiority, Julius outthinks Webster and rescues his brother.

Weeks later, Mary Anne Benedict reads of their confrontation in Houston—and their decision to return the high-tech engine to its rightful owners—and decides to seek them out. Julius and Vincent have founded a philanthropic organization (entitled the Benedict Corporation) with the reward money and plan to settle into a simple life with Marnie and Linda. Their mother arrives with a teddy bear in

hand, and the boys welcome her into their family. Years later, in a wonderful epilogue, Marnie and Linda have indeed married Julius and Vincent, and each couple has a set of twins.

Production Details

Three years before, in the spring of 1984, Arnold Schwarzenegger had a chance encounter with Ivan Reitman during a screening of *Ghostbusters*. Arnold had yet to strike the big time with *The Terminator*, but he remembered pulling aside the director and saying, "I would love to do a movie with you sometime." Reitman thought about Schwarzenegger's offer and within a few months (following the premiere of the sci-fi comedy) charged a team of screenwriters to develop a series of high-concept ideas. The most promising scenario had to do with a set of twins produced during a genetics experiment, separated at birth, with one being given all the best that humanity has to offer and the other being placed in an orphanage. Thirty-five years later, the genetically superior brother seeks out the misfit in order to establish a home and family.

"Halfway into my pitch," director Reitman reflected back over the years to his lunch with Schwarzenegger, "he said, 'When do we start?' All of a sudden our picture was a go, and it was [as if he were] producing it."

Reitman still had two hurdles to overcome before

Twins could get off the ground: hiring an actor to play opposite Arnold and finding the right studio to bankroll his project. Since Reitman had a production deal with Universal Pictures, he had little difficulty selling the executives at its parent company, MCA, with the idea. (Universal had profited not only from Reitman's smash *Ghostbusters* but also from Schwarzenegger's two Conan movies.) Next was the task of locating a diminutive actor who could be loud, obnoxious, and slightly brain-dead. He needed someone like Danny DeVito.

Although most people often associate Danny DeVito with his role as the sleazy, immoral dispatcher Louie DePalma on TV's *Taxi* in the late seventies, he is also a talented movie actor, director, and producer. DeVito made his motion-picture debut as one of the emotionally disturbed inmates in *One Flew Over the Cuckoo's Nest*, one of the seventies' most influential films, and later starred with Michael Douglas and Kathleen Turner in *Romancing the Stone* and its sequel *The Jewel of the Nile*.

When first approached by Ivan Reitman, DeVito hesitated because there wasn't a completed script. "Arnold was much easier. He loved the concept so strongly, he believed it would work out," Reitman later commented. In the end, however, DeVito came aboard, and all three agreed to swap their usual up-front fees for a larger percentage of the gross. (Shortly thereafter, Reitman hired Chloe Webb and Kelly Preston as the two sexy sisters and character actor Marshall Bell as the assassin.)

The $15 million production began principal photography during the last week of April 1988 on locations in and around the Los Angeles area (including Mann's famous Chinese Theater). By mid-

Arnold Schwarzenegger and Danny DeVito keep right in step as *Twins*.

Julius dances and
falls in love with
Marnie (Kelly
Preston).

May, the production crew had moved onto the Universal back lot for several key scenes involving Vincent's home and office, a parking garage, the scientific lab at Los Alamos, and an artist's community. Exteriors for Whispering Pines were filmed outside a colony in Santa Fe. The final confrontation between the assassin and the Benedict boys was shot at an abandoned factory in Long Beach. Additional footage in Texas and on the road was provided by the second unit. Since Reitman was obligated to complete the shoot before Schwarzenegger left on his nationwide *Red Heat* publicity tour, the director made certain that every scene was "meticulously choreographed."

"Arnold has extraordinary physical control, and it extends to his face," Reitman noted. "The key in most scenes was to let him be absolutely open—to strip all the acting away and let the real person come through."

During the filming at Universal, numerous luminaries stopped by the open set. In fact, on the day when Arnold was scheduled to sing "Yakety Yak," his old pal Clint Eastwood appeared long enough to deadpan, "I didn't know you had so much talent."

Maria Shriver and other Kennedy family members also visited the *Twins* set, creating quite a stir. (Reitman even assigned Maria a bit part as a woman buying flowers, but her big scene ended up on the cutting-room floor.)

Schwarzenegger proclaimed once production had finally wrapped:

I think *Twins* is going to have a surprising impact. And it's gonna be good for my career, because I can then do more of the movies I would like to do. Which is to do more comedies like that and then do movies like *California Suite*.

After campaigning for George Bush, Schwarzenegger went on to make *Total Recall* with director Paul Verhoeven, but he never forgot his experience with Ivan Reitman. Arnold had begun to relish his moments of light relief in movies so much that he claimed that he would soon make another comedy. Less than two years later, Schwarzenegger made *Kindergarten Cop* with Reitman.

149

Critical Commentary

Dubious of its final product, Universal conducted several *Twins* test screenings in the suburbs beyond Los Angeles and Hollywood. The "real hard-core Arnold audience"—as Schwarzenegger is apt to refer to his loyal fans—felt that *Twins* was the best movie that he had done since *The Terminator*. Many of them were pleased to see their hero with real emotions and frustrations, ups and downs, and a great deal of love and caring. The studio quickly dreamed up a brilliant ad campaign, with the tag line "Only their mother can tell them apart," and scheduled the comedy for the Christmas season. When the film was finally released on December 9, 1988, *Twins* easily trounced Dan Aykroyd's *My Stepmother Is an Alien* and Bill Murray's *Scrooged*, as well as *Cocoon: The Return* and the big-budget historical epic *Dangerous Liaisons*. By year's end, *Twins* had grossed a whopping $110 million in box-office receipts.

The real strength behind the film is that it allows Schwarzenegger to demonstrate a far sweeter and more vulnerable side of his on-screen persona. He is able to indulge himself with self-deprecating humor that the audience just loves and yet, at the same time, maintain a strong screen presence. Arnold not only is given a wonderfully written character; he is rewarded with his first fully realized love affair (since *Raw Deal*), with sexy Kelly Preston. He confessed to *Marquee:*

> In my last five or six movies, my love relationship was basically with guns, with explosives, with grenades and missiles. *Twins* was for me a learning experience all the way through.

In fact, one of the funniest sequences requires Julius, who has just lost his virginity, to react with an expression of beatific shock. This scene is impeccably staged by Ivan Reitman and provides the star with one of those rare cinematic moments. Clearly, Arnold Schwarzenegger delivers his best performance since *The Terminator*.

David Ansen, in *Newsweek,* agreed with that assessment: "He's so endearingly, incongruously sweet. For the first time since *Stay Hungry* he's recognizable as a member of our species." Robert Strauss, in *Movieline*, also praised Arnold's acting, commenting that "he captures the character's built-in naïveté and never makes him seem stupid. Hard stuff." Nearly every other reviewer, while dismissing the film's one-joke approach, recognized Schwarzenegger's sense of comic timing and good-natured humor. (They also praised Ivan Reitman's creative filming and Danny DeVito's turn as Vincent Benedict.)

And unlike Arnold's recent *Red Heat* disaster, *Twins* did have an element of science fiction that helped establish its plot. (While the U. S. government may have conducted genetics research during the fifties and sixties to produce a "superman," no offspring have yet come forward to betray their secretive birth.) By reviewing his film successes of the past decade, one indisputable fact becomes clear. Arnold Schwarzenegger delivers a greater wallop at the box office in movies that have an element of science fiction or fantasy. Even though *Red Sonja* was a resounding failure, both Conan movies took place in the faraway Hyborian Age and featured evil wizards, forgotten talismans, swords, and sorcery. Their combined take internationally was well over $200 million. *The Terminator*, *Predator*, *The Running Man*, and *Twins* easily outdistanced *Raw Deal* and *Red Heat*, with a combined total of $280 million. Only *Commando*, with a respectable $35 million, had done as well as a nongenre favorite. With the films' total box-office gross (in the United States alone) of $415,541,764 to that time, Schwarzenegger was again scheduled to appear in two other science-fiction vehicles—Paul Verhoeven's *Total Recall* and James Cameron's *Terminator* sequel.

Twins is currently available on videocassette and laserdisc through MCA/Universal Home Video and should not be confused with David Cronenberg's *Twins* (which was later retitled *Dead Ringers*), also released in 1988.

(Opposite) Taking a moment from the hectic shoot, Schwarzenegger and DeVito pose for publicity photographs. (Courtesy Universal Pictures)

TWELVE

TOTAL ARNOLD

Total Recall

1990. Tri-Star Pictures in association with Carolco. *Director:* Paul Verhoeven. *Producers:* Buzz Feitshans and Ronald Shusett. *Executive Producers:* Mario Kassar and Andrew Vajna. *Screenplay:* Ronald Shusett, Dan O'Bannon, and Gary Goldman. *Based on a screen story by* Shusett, O'Bannon, and Jon Povill. *Inspired by the short story* "We Can Remember It for You Wholesale" *by* Philip K. Dick. *Photography:* Jost Vacano. *Music:* Jerry Goldsmith. *Editor:* Frank J. Urioste. *Starring:* Arnold Schwarzenegger, Rachel Ticotin, Sharon Stone, Michael Ironside, Marshall Bell, Robert Costanzo, and Ronny Cox. Released on June 1, 1990. [109 minutes]

A masterpiece of special effects, set design, and non-stop action, *Total Recall* is also a haunting psychological mystery that propels viewers on a hallucinogenic, and sometimes violent exploration into the nature of reality. Though the film was tailored to project Arnold Schwarzenegger as the king of the action-adventure genre, it also provided him with his most provocative and challenging role to date by casting him in the role of a high-tech Jekyll and Hyde. Based on a short story by Philip K. Dick, who had written the source novel for *Blade Runner*, the motion picture suffered through a fifteen-year struggle, seven directors, five studios, and nearly fifty different rewrites on its way to completion. But the end result is a tour de force that remains one of the most important science-fiction films of the early nineties.

Schwarzenegger said in explaining his reasons for taking charge of *Total Recall*:

(Opposite) Arnold Schwarzenegger stars as Douglas Quaid in the futuristic thriller *Total Recall*. (Courtesy Tri-Star Pictures/Carolco Home Video)

When you're alone and you stick your neck out for a particular cause, that's heroic. A lot of people want to do that in real life, which is why my movies are such a great escape. I acted pretty much in the position of executive producer [except without taking all that responsibility]. I knew the script was a good one, and I pushed Carolco to buy it for me.

The Screen Story

The motion picture opens in the year 2084 in a world dominated by two warring totalitarian governments. Mars, already colonized and supplying valuable resources to the opposing factions, is in the throes of its own internal problems and political unrest. Douglas Quaid (Schwarzenegger), a simple construction worker on Earth, has been haunted by dreams of a former life on the red planet with a sultry brunet—and yet his beautiful wife Lori (Sharon Stone) and his coworker Harry (Robert Costanzo) continue to assure him that he has never been to Mars. Again awakened by a startling dream in which he has broken his space helmet and is suffocating on the Martian surface, Quaid begins to question his grasp of reality. Perhaps everything he thinks he knows and has experienced is some sort of fabrication. Perhaps he is really someone else entirely.

Totally obsessed with Mars, Quaid visits ReKall, Inc., a travel service that specializes in placing artificial "memories" of the ideal vacation into the minds of its customers. The troubled construction worker chooses a fantasy in which he is a secret agent assigned under deep cover to penetrate enemy forces, seduce a beautiful guerrilla fighter, unlock hid-

153

Awakened from another dream about Mars, Quaid tries to tell the details to his beautiful wife Lori (Sharon Stone).

den Martian artifacts, and save the whole planet. However, when the brain implant is being applied, it triggers a memory cap. Apparently, he *was* a secret agent on Mars, and all his dreams have been a long-suppressed facet of his life that the Agency tried but failed to erase. Or perhaps the triggered memory cap is all part of the ReKall trip? In either event, Quaid suddenly wakes up, shouting "My name is not Quaid!," and is instantly sedated by employees of the travel service. They dump him unconscious in a "Johnny" cab and send him home to his wife.

His coworker Harry, accompanied by several large men, intercepts the cab after learning Quaid has been to ReKall and tries to escort him to an Agency cell. But Quaid breaks free and eliminates all of them in a deadly scuffle. Returning home with a story

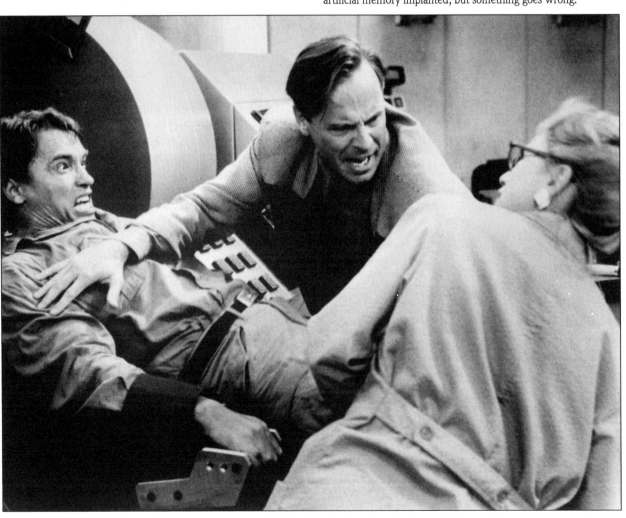

Totally obsessed with Mars, Quaid visits ReKall, Inc., to have an artificial memory implanted, but something goes wrong.

Later, Quaid awakens in a "Johnny" cab, unable to remember what has happened to him at ReKall, Inc.

about men trying to kill him, he sounds like a raving lunatic to Lori. First she tries to calm him down by reasoning with him. Then, realizing that he has begun to have "total recall" of his past life, she summons one of the men responsible for his memory loss, Richter (Michael Ironside), who by chance is her lover. Quaid learns that his devoted wife is, in fact, a deadly spy with the Agency, assigned to keep an eye on him, and that his memories of their life together are nothing but implants. He smashes through the fantasy world that has been created for him and eludes numerous attempts by Richter and his men to capture and suppress him.

Later, contacted by a former confederate and secret agent who fled the Agency, Quaid discovers that his name is really Hauser. He was once a spy in the employ of the ruthless Martian dictator Vilos Cohaagen (Ronny Cox), but Hauser's memory was erased to prevent him from becoming a dangerous liability. He must return to the red planet and use his valuable knowledge to put an end to Cohaagen's rule.

When he finally arrives on Mars, he learns that mutant terrorists, loyal to a mysterious Kuato (Marshall Bell), have been fighting against the iron fist of Cohaagen. Mars was colonized by the Northern Bloc at enormous expense in order to mine tribinium for the war effort, but the hit-and-run tactics of the guerrilla forces have cost the dictator dearly. And rumors of a discovery of ancient Martian artifacts in the sealed-off Pyramid Mines continue to disrupt the normal flow of commerce. Cohaagen has decided to tighten his grip on the Martian colony and force the conspirators out into the open. Quaid's arrival on Mars coincides with Cohaagen's latest crackdown, as security is at a premium all over the planet. But he cleverly manages to elude Richter and government soldiers at Emigration and takes a room at the Hilton. Once there, a mysterious note left in the hotel's safe by Hauser leads Quaid to the "Last Resort," a whorehouse in Venusville.

At the Last Resort, Quaid meets Melina (Rachel Ticotin), the brunet of his dreams and the one programmed for his fantasy vacation at ReKall. Melina has had a long-term relationship with Hauser, which she fears has ended, but Quaid simply doesn't remember her or the affair. She doesn't believe his story about amnesia, dismissing him as some sort of government plant. (Cohaagen wants to see all the mutants destroyed because of the cheap domes he built, and many believe that he will stop at nothing—including the sacrifice of one of his own men— to kill their leader.) Melina still loves Hauser and warns him to go back to Earth before either side exploits him.

Thoroughly confused, Quaid returns to the hotel, driven by an ambitious cab attendant named Benny (Mel Johnson, Jr.), and tries to piece together what has happened to him. But his wife Lori and a specialist for ReKall, Dr. Edgewater (Roy Brocksmith), are waiting for him in his room. Edgewater attempts to convince Quaid that he is suffering from a schizoid embolism and that all the events on Mars are part of a dream gone haywire. Quaid easily sees through the doctor's facade and kills him; then all hell breaks loose as assassins from Martian Intelligence blow open the hotel door and capture him. On his way to the service elevator, and eventual reprogramming,

155

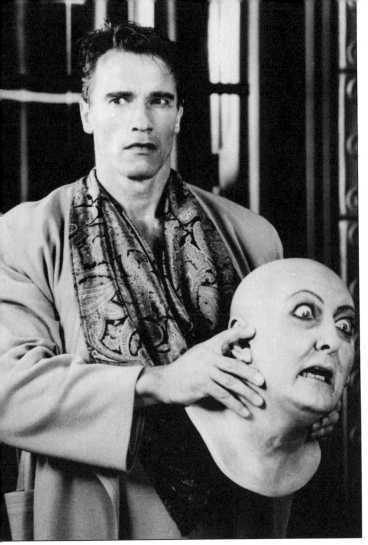

Quaid travels to Mars, disguised as an overweight woman, in a desperate attempt to find out why strangers are trying to murder him.

Melina appears with a deadly weapon and guns his captors down. Moments later, Quaid is forced to fatally shoot the treacherous Lori as she is about to kill Melina. Realizing that more of Cohaagen's assassins will be arriving, the two former lovers, with the help of Benny, escape into the Martian underground to meet with the revolutionary leader Kuato.

Richter is too late to save Lori and demands equal justice. But Cohaagen has a much more dangerous plan to exact vengeance. First he seals the air ducts leading to Venusville, thus cutting off the supply of oxygen to the mutants. He then orders his men to attack the rebel hideout (the location of which he has just learned from his spy Benny). With Kuato dead, Cohaagen expects to rule Mars again with an iron fist. But before the rebel leader is killed, he helps Quaid remember the truth about the Pyramid Mines. (Millions of years ago, the former inhabitants of Mars

built a gigantic nuclear reactor underground to produce oxygen for their dying world. For some reason, they were never able to start the machine, and the atmosphere turned into a nearly airless void. Cohaagen has known about the reactor, but he believes his dictatorial power will become threatened if Mars achieves a breathable atmosphere.) Quaid must start the machine and free Mars from Cohaagen's rule.

Quaid and Melina are captured during the raid on the rebel hideout and taken to the Martian dictator for questioning. Cohaagen subsequently congratulates Hauser/Quaid on his successful mission. Apparently, the secret agent volunteered to have his memory erased and a new one planted, in order to infiltrate the guerrilla forces and destroy Kuato. While Melina feels totally betrayed, Quaid dismisses Cohaagen's story as fantasy. But through a previously recorded message by Hauser, he learns that the dictator was telling the truth. Quaid as Hauser was a ruthless killer working for the Martian Federal Colonies and Cohaagen. The two are taken by Richter and armed troops for reprogramming but escape with only one purpose in mind—activating the nuclear reactor. (The mutants in Venusville have very little time left before they suffer asphyxiation.)

Forced into a showdown with Richter and ultimately Cohaagen himself, Quaid must forget that evil part of himself (known as Hauser) and fight for the good of Mars. Against all odds, and with Melina's help, he manages to turn on the big air-making machine. Within moments, the planet begins to shudder and explode with oxygen pouring from every volcanic fissure. They'd won! "I can't believe it. It's like a dream," Melina exclaims, taking hold of Quaid. "I just had a terrible thought," he returns. "What if this is a dream...."

Production Details

Total Recall faced a fifteen-year-long battle before becoming the high-powered, action-adventure film from Carolco Productions that many regard as Arnold Schwarzenegger's best vehicle. The futuristic thriller began its life in a story conference between the two men responsible for another of science fiction's most successful films. Producer Ron Shusett first met with screenwriter Dan O'Bannon in 1974

(Opposite) When seals on the Martian dome are broken, Quaid is nearly sucked out into the void.

At the "Last Resort" in Venusville, Quaid meets Melina (Rachel Ticotin), the brunet of his dreams and the one programmed for his fantasy vacation at ReKall.

to discuss several story ideas they might turn into films. Shusett had already read Philip K. Dick's short story "We Can Remember It for You Wholesale" and had expanded the concept into his idea for *Total Recall*. O'Bannon, who was fond of B-movies from the fifties and sixties, had dreamed up *Alien*. While O'Bannon liked his collaborator's idea, Shusett dismissed the simple monster movie for its "lack of vision." But after struggling unsuccessfully for months with the third act for *Total Recall*, Shusett and O'Bannon turned their attention back to *Alien*, which, directed by Ridley Scott, made motion-picture history in 1979 and spawned two successful sequels.

Ron Shusett and Dan O'Bannon returned to their work on *Total Recall* but were never able to agree how to end the third act. O'Bannon thought the movie's climax should relate to the title, with the hero having a final, stunning revelation about his

identity, while Shusett wanted something grander. O'Bannon told Carl Brandon of *Cinefantastique*:

> That wasn't supposed to have been a three-fingered Martian handprint. That was supposed to have been a print of Quaid's hand which matched only his hand. Quaid, Earth's top secret agent, went to Mars and entered this compound. The machine killed him and created a synthetic duplicate. He is that synthetic duplicate. At the end of the picture, Quaid puts his hand on the device, and it all comes back to him, who he really is. His total recall of his identity is that he is a creation of a Martian machine. He is, in effect, a resurrection of the Martian race in a synthetic body. He turns and says to all the other characters, "It's going to be fun to play God."

Quaid is accosted by a mutant after meeting Melina.

Lori and a specialist from ReKall try to convince Quaid that he is experiencing a paranoid delusion.

Shusett disagreed with an approach that seemed too much like Harlan Ellison's revelation at the end of "Demon With a Glass Hand," that Trent is really a robot, and rewrote his own climax. Unable to come to terms with his collaborator, O'Bannon dropped out to begin work on other projects.

The success of *Alien*, however, garnered Ron Shusett a development deal for *Total Recall* at Disney in 1981, but chairman Thomas Wilhite and other studio executives were similarly concerned with the film's weak third act. After writing dozens of scenarios, which were each rejected for one reason or another, Shusett watched as the project was placed in turnaround (Hollywoodese for being put on the backburner or shelved completely). Fortunately, producer Dino De Laurentiis picked up Shusett's option to make the film, took it to M-G-M, and turned the project over to David Cronenberg in 1984. Cronenberg subsequently brought in Richard

Dreyfuss for the role of Quaid and wrote several versions of the third act himself, emphasizing a more human, intellectual discovery than a large-scale one. (In Cronenberg's version, Quaid discovers that he is actually chairman Mandrell, the dictator of Earth, and with Melina as a cabdriver at his side, he defeats Cohaagen and assumes control.) "This change gave the third act an interesting twist," conceded Shusett, but not interesting enough to attract a distributor. M-G-M wanted a more heroic and visually exciting script and withdrew its support of the De Laurentiis project.

Over the next several years, Ron Shusett wrote close to fifty different drafts as the project moved from director Cronenberg to Fred Schepisi, Richard Rush, Russell Mulcahy, Lewis Teague, and Bruce Beresford, and from M-G-M to Universal to Avco Embassy. Finally, in 1987, after nearly ten years in development, *Total Recall* looked as if filming would

Melina blasts her way into Quaid's room and fights hand-to-hand with Lori.

begin, in Australia with Bruce Beresford directing and Patrick Swayze starring as Douglas Quaid, when the De Laurentiis Entertainment Group (DEG) folded due to financial difficulties. (Shusett had written an adaptation with Steve Pressfield that Beresford found "challenging.") "It was like an Egyptian curse," the writer and producer explained. "Every time a start date was announced, someone or something would screw it up."

After De Laurentiis's DEG collapsed, it seemed that *Total Recall* was again stalled. But Schwarzenegger, who had often been associated with the project and remained very much interested, convinced longtime friend Andrew Vajna, one of the founding partners of Carolco, to buy it. Even though the script had accumulated more than $6 million in development fees, Vajna was able to acquire the rights for Carolco fairly cheaply at $3 million. (De Laurentiis was having a fire sale on properties.) At Schwarzenegger's request,

Quaid and Melina are captured during a raid and taken to the Martian dictator Cohaagen (Ronny Cox).

Carolco brought in writer Gary Goldman (who had written *Big Trouble in Little China* for John Carpenter) to revise the script with new dialogue for the star, who was determined to make *Total Recall* his ultimate action-adventure vehicle.

For a role that many critics contend is "the most challenging of his career," Arnold Schwarzenegger is very much aware how fortunate he was to have snatched up the project for himself. Jeff Bridges, Richard Dreyfuss, Christopher Reeve, and Patrick Swayze had all been linked with the film at one time or another to play Douglas Quaid. For years De Laurentiis had talked about having Schwarzenegger play the lead role. De Laurentiis used *Total Recall* to lure him to other projects, but he never really intended to give him the plum assignment. (In the original story, Quaid was a Walter Mitty character who desperately wanted to go to Mars and turned out to be a secret agent.) Arnold recalled:

> When I first read the script during the days when I was doing *Red Sonja* for Dino De

The treacherous Cohaagen tries to convince Quaid that he is actually someone else.

161

Arnold Schwarzenegger as his alter ego Hauser, a ruthless killer who works for Cohaagen.

Laurentiis, it just stayed with me... I could not put it down. I thought there was a lot I could do with the movie.

Pier Luigi Basile, who worked as a production designer on *Conan the Destroyer*, didn't think the Italian producer was serious when he announced the selection of Schwarzenegger as Quaid. Basile explained:

I worked with Arnold on two Conan films. When Dino said Arnold would be the actor, I thought, well, that's a very strange choice, because I couldn't see Arnold in the part at all. The script was very serious. I didn't think Arnold was a good enough actor for that.

Gary Goldman's rewrite not only introduced a stronger, more heroic image for Quaid but also resolved the climax of the third act in a way that O'Bannon, Shusett, and the others had never really considered. By placing the emphasis on plenty of action, Shusett (and Pressfield) had practically elimi-

Cohaagen decides to have Quaid reprogrammed as Hauser.

Quaid escapes Cohaagen's trap and sets out for the Pyramid Mines with Melina.

nated the psychological level. What Goldman did with his rewrite was to restore the element of surprise (that O'Bannon had been striving to create). The climax of the third act now reveals a twist in Quaid's persona by creating the alter ego of Hauser. Douglas Quaid is, in fact, a ruthless double agent commanded by Vilos Cohaagen. With that final element in place, Schwarzenegger sent a copy of the *Total Recall* script to director Paul Verhoeven, whom he had met in 1987.

The fifty-one-year-old Dutch-born director was intrigued by the Hitchcockian plot contrivances and readily accepted Schwarzenegger's offer. Having been pro-

Michael Ironside as Cohaagen's villainous right-hand man Richter.

Armed and dangerous, Quaid and Melina penetrate Cohaagen's heavily armored fortress.

pelled into Hollywood's elite directorial
group (which includes James Cameron
and John McTiernan) by the phenomenal success of *Robocop* in 1987, Paul
Verhoeven now had his choice of big-
budget projects. But the opportunity to
work with Schwarzenegger was one that
he simply could not pass up. "I liked him
so much in real life," said Verhoeven,
"that I wanted to use Arnold as he is—a
nice, charming, normal, vulnerable
man." Like many other foreign directors,
Verhoeven was lured to this country not
only by money but also the opportunity
to work with some of the world's best
talent. His earlier features, including
Turkish Delights and Soldier of Orange
(both with Rutger Hauer), *The Fourth
Man*, *Spetters*, and *Flesh + Blood* (also
with Hauer), had helped him develop a
unique style—which some have called
outrageous and violent—but he'd never
had much of a budget or crew. (His five
films combined cost a mere fraction of
the special-effects budget on *Total
Recall.*) Upon his arrival in America,
Orion Pictures gave him $14 million and

Quaid battles one-on-one with the deadly Richter.

the services of Rob Bottin and Peter Weller, and the Dutch director came through with the stylish thriller about a slain policeman who is reborn as Robocop. The film was critically well received and grossed an impressive $55 million.

Paul Verhoeven's agreement to direct *Total Recall* was precisely the type of luck Schwarzenegger needed to break Shusett's "Egyptian curse." With the internationally renowned director aboard, coproducer Buzz Feitshans approved a $43 million budget. That $43 million soon blossomed into $49 million, then $60 million, and finally settled at $73 million (thanks in large part to Shusett, who fought to maintain the film's integrity). The next step was finding the right cast and crew.

While Arnold Schwarzenegger was being paid a reported $10 million plus a percentage of the profits for acting (as well as serving as an uncredited executive producer), Carolco was aware that *Total Recall* needed an especially talented group of actors for star support. For the key role of Vilos Cohaagen, Arnold's chief nemesis, Verhoeven did not have to look beyond his *Robocop*. Ronny Cox had more or less made a career out of portraying salt-of-the-earth good guys, but Paul Verhoeven was much more interested in exploiting his dark side.

For the role of Richter, Cohaagen's right-hand man, Verhoeven tested a number of actors, but he kept coming back to Michael Ironside, whom he had once considered for the role of Clarence (eventually played by Kurtwood Smith) in *Robocop*. Ironside had specialized in playing screen nasties, from the renegade agent in David Cronenberg's *Scanners* to the "Overdog" in *Spacehunter: Adventures in the Forbidden Zone*, or from more familiar roles in Walter Hill's *Extreme Prejudice* to Hamilton Tyler in *V: The Final Battle* (1983, NBC) and *V: The Series* (1984, NBC). Verhoeven thought Ironside's intensity and movie villainy would make an appropriate balance to his star's physical presence.

Sharon Stone, who would find stardom later in Verhoeven's *Basic Instinct*, was the perfect choice for the film's ice goddess. From an early guest role in *Magnum, P.I.* (1980, CBS) as disturbed twins to a featured role as the widowed wife of a navy pilot in *War and Remembrance* (1988, ABC), Stone had been working for years to shed the image of the beautiful but dumb blonde. Her subsequent roles in *King Solomon's Mines* and *Allan Quatermain and the Lost City of Gold* with Richard Chamberlain brought her to the attention of the Dutch director.

Because the script called for Schwarzenegger to have not one but two love interests, Rachel Ticotin was hired as his Martian lover Melina. Ticotin first came to notice opposite Paul Newman in *Fort Apache: The Bronx*. Michael Champion, Mel Johnson, Jr., Ray Brocksmith, Robert Costanzo, and Dean Norris helped round out the *Total Recall* cast. Vic Armstrong, Harrison Ford's double and the action unit supervisor for the Indiana Jones movies and *Red Sonja*, was brought in to choreograph the difficult

Melina insists Quaid kiss her just in case it's only some dream.

action scenes, while Rob Bottin, a veteran of *Robocop*, came aboard to handle the makeup effects. (Dream Quest Images, which won an Academy Award for *The Abyss*, had already been contracted for the visuals.)

The oft-scheduled production finally began principal photography during the first week of April 1989. Six months of filming (which required a shooting schedule of one hundred thirty days) took place at Churubusco Studios, just outside Mexico City, on forty-five sets spread across eight soundstages. The production, which involved nearly three hundred people, was the biggest ever mounted at the studio, easily dwarfing Dino De Laurentiis's large-scale *Dune*. (Incredibly, there were sixteen full pages of

Sharon Stone as Lori, the double-crossing wife.

technical credits in the press material for the film.) Paul Verhoeven had originally wanted to shoot in Houston, utilizing the city's futuristic look of glass and steel, but there were no adequate soundstages to hold the bulk of the production. Additionally, the cost of shooting in the United States was much higher than in the Central American country. Unfortunately, public-health conditions in Mexico City, with its overcrowded population, overwhelming pollution and dying vegetation, and lack of sanitary drinking water, were terrible. The company's full-time doctor saw an average of twenty-two people a day, and very few kept healthy throughout the entire shoot, including Verhoeven and Schwarzenegger. (Even though Schwarzenegger had learned his lesson during the filming of *Predator* and brought his own chef, the cook eventually took ill himself, and Arnold followed suit.)

Additional filming, on production designer William Sandell's advice, took place at a military academy just outside Mexico City, saving the company both time and money as well as the need to build exterior sets to represent the city Quaid lives in on Earth. Location shooting in the lobby and penthouse

of Mexico City's posh Nikko Hotel also cut valuable corners. Allegedly, toward the end of the shoot, coproducer Ron Shusett was dismissed because of the skyrocketing budget. Shusett later told reporters:

> I was trying so hard to get the movie I wanted on the screen that they had to throw me off. I was influencing Paul and Arnold not to cut costs. The financiers wanted us to cut two or three things....

Verhoeven and Schwarzenegger came to his rescue and agreed to several cost-saving measures. (The location work is hardly noticeable in the final film.) Principal photography wrapped toward the end of August, and the balance of its special effects were completed during the remaining months of the year. (Dream Quest Images had not finished the one hundred movie opticals required by the script when production wrapped and moved to Simi Valley, northwest of Los Angeles, for the remainder of its shots.)

Even after his grueling experience on *Total Recall*, Paul Verhoeven had nothing but praise for his star. He said:

> Arnold is great. He's one of the few people in my life that I really admire. He's so much in control of everything. He can accept so much endurance, suffering, whatever. He's also done a really good job acting. He has no ego. You can say whatever you want to the guy. You can say, "Oh, Arnold, don't open your eyes. Don't walk like this. Don't talk like that." And he says, "Oh, sure."

Though the filming was difficult at Mexico's Churubusco Studios, Arnold Schwarzenegger had similar praise for his director.

> Paul Verhoeven is a genius with tremendous energy. He works from six A.M. to twelve midnight and never stops. It's hard to keep up with that kind of energy and enthusiasm. Every time we shot, he demanded the ultimate performance. But we all had a good time.

The first tantalizing look at their collaboration on *Total Recall* was greeted with great enthusiasm by sci-fi fans in Boston at the 1989 World Science Fiction Convention. While the slides and commentary were very vague at the now-annual Labor Day get-together, fans recognized the film's true brilliance. Several months later, Schwarzenegger got another

166

early indication of the motion picture's potential when he screened the "work-in-progress" for its distributor, Tri-Star Pictures.

> I wanted to draw them in and make them really feel that it is also their movie. Although it's a Carolco picture, it's they [Tri-Star] who really have to feel it is their movie. Then they will go all out in the promotion and marketing.

Both Jon Peters and Peter Guber, then studio heads for Columbia (Tri-Star's parent company), were also very impressed, proclaiming that *Total Recall* would be "better than *Batman*." Their only fears centered on the film's ultraviolence; also, it turns out, a concern of the MPAA, which thought it too excessive.

Several cuts were suggested in order for the film to avoid an X rating. (Verhoeven had been forced to make similar trims in *Robocop* in order to receive the R rating he had agreed to deliver to Orion Pictures.) The director explained:

> I'm always violent in my movies. I like violent effects. When I get to the violent scenes, I get carried away. I grew up in Amsterdam during the war, and violence was so much a part of my real world. So I have to restrict myself a little bit, especially in a movie like this, where the tone is a little bit lighter.

Several trims were made, including one scene in which an assailant is stabbed with the spike on the end of a ReKall chair armrest and another in which Benny is drilled by Quaid and spurts blood. The cuts amounted to very little loss for the film as a whole and allowed *Total Recall* to garner an R rating.

With the film finally complete, Tri-Star scheduled *Total Recall* for release on June 15, 1990. That date was later moved up two weeks to take advantage of the number of weak releases scheduled before it. The fifteen-year saga to make *Total Recall* had finally ended.

Critical Commentary

On its release *Total Recall* quickly rocketed to the top of the box-office charts, grossing $33 million in its first weekend. In the weeks that followed—thanks to the positive response of critics and general audiences to its unusual mix of science fiction, action-adventure, and a haunting psychological mystery—the film easily dispatched *Die Hard 2*, *Back to the Future Part III*, *Gremlins 2...*, *Dick Tracy*, *Days of Thunder*, and

Rachel Ticotin as Melina, the hooker turned rebel leader.

other warm-weather blockbusters. (The only film that fared any better, because of its mid-summer release, was *Ghost*.) Gene Siskel of the *Chicago Tribune* called the motion picture "visually stunning," and Roger Ebert of the *Chicago Sun-Times* ranked Schwarzenegger's performance as "the best of his career." *Variety* wrote: "Standing head and shoulders above his competition, [Arnold] richly deserves the title of the thinking man's behemoth." By the end of the summer, the film had passed the $110 million mark on its way to becoming one of the all-time box-office leaders. On March 25, 1991, the Academy of Motion Picture Arts and Sciences honored *Total Recall* with a special award for its visual effects. Even though Kevin Costner's *Dances With Wolves* was the big winner with seven Oscars, the special recognition paid to a genre (science fiction, to which the Academy seems to have an aversion) made the night clearly an important one. (One year later, *Terminator 2: Judgment Day* would dominate in seven categories and emerge as a winner in all of the Academy's technical categories.)

To date, *Total Recall* represents the pinnacle of Arnold's career as an action-adventure star, for the role allowed him to demonstrate his talents as both hero and villain. Douglas Quaid is an incredibly complex character whose slowly developing memory links him with an evil twin named Hauser (who is, in fact, himself). For the role of Quaid, Arnold must be not only fearless but also slightly vulnerable, confused, and uncertain of the person that he really is. In one sequence, he is called upon to perform a pretty elaborate love scene with Sharon Stone, who is masquerading as his wife. Less than an hour into the film, he must shoot her in a kill-or-be-killed situation. This grim moment, somewhat lightened by Quaid's responding to Lori's plea "But I am your wife" with "Consider that a divorce," places the actor squarely in a difficult confrontation that other, lesser talents would not have played convincingly. Quaid is not really certain what he's supposed to be doing, as if his actions are, in fact, reactions to others, and Arnold manages to convey his confusion and uncertainty with some skill.

And though Hauser is only briefly glimpsed in two key scenes, his presence dominates most of the film as Quaid begins to learn more and more about his violent other half. Schwarzenegger combines the subtleties of his killer robot from *The Terminator* with his characters from *Raw Deal* and *The Running Man* to create a memorable villain in Hauser. Ironically, Arnold has at last found the perfect adversary in this darker side of himself. In fact, on one level, the film plays like a gladiatorial contest for Quaid's soul between John Matrix, Dutch Schaefer, and Ben Richards *and* the Terminator. This takes considerable acting talent to play the good and evil parts of one character! But Schwarzenegger was completely overlooked for consideration as Best Actor at Oscar time, probably because of the film's violent, futuristic nature. The problem is that after *Total Recall* there was nothing new that could be done with Schwarzenegger as an action hero. From then on, the Arnold formula would be repeated again and again, only making it more elaborate each time. (Schwarzenegger's subsequent role in *Kindergarten Cop* would again demonstrate his range as an actor by placing him in contrasting roles as a ruthless police detective and a lovable though reluctant schoolteacher.)

Total Recall is also the most perfectly realized of all of Schwarzenegger's films, with hardly a wrong step made throughout its length. It moves at an incredibly fast and furious pace, but the plot holds together logically enough (more so, in fact, than the original short story or subsequent novel), with its unique blend of the real and the fantastic. The film is also the most visually striking of the star's projects; thanks to William Sandell's production design, the central theme pervades every scene with a distinctive motif. *Total Recall* also has two of the best villains, two of the most attractive women, one of composer Jerry Goldsmith's best scores, and a very witty and clever script (principally) by Ronald Shusett.* (Sharon Stone is particularly engaging as the loving wife and deadly assassin.)

Director Paul Verhoeven's contribution included a smoother and more sophisticated visual style than that of his contemporary American counterparts and a brilliance of imagery and skillfully controlled rhythm that is all-absorbing. While some have criticized the motion picture for its violence, Verhoeven's penchant for gritty realism actually makes this rough, tough form of entertainment that much more interesting. His vision of nightmarish reality easily lived up to the promotional campaign that advertised "Get ready for the ride of your life!" Similarly, Verhoeven's inconclusive ending, which suggests that most of the film's narrative was a dream, adds an element of unease and uncertainty that is unique in contemporary motion pictures.

Total Recall was released to home video in December 1990, and sales of videocassettes and laserdiscs by Live Home Video, Image Entertainment, and International Video Entertainment (IVE) went through the roof, making it one of the all-time winners.

---

*Science-fiction fans will no doubt recognize similarities between the 1970 television movie *Hauser's Memory* and *Total Recall*. In the former, which was released theatrically overseas and directed by Boris Sagal, David McCallum plays a young scientist who boldly takes an injection in order to transplant the memory of another person into his. As he works his way through this Cold War espionage thriller, he begins to remember the truth about who he really is. O'Bannon and Shusett were obviously impressed enough with the little-known film to name their villain Hauser.

Director Paul Verhoeven prepares a difficult scene with Arnold Schwarzenegger. (Courtesy Tri-Star Pictures/Carolco Home Video)

THIRTEEN

BACK TO SCHOOL

Kindergarten Cop

1990. Universal Pictures. *Director:* Ivan Reitman. *Producers:* Reitman and Brian Grazer. *Executive Producers:* Joe Medjuck and Michael C. Gross. *Screenplay:* Murray Salem, Herschel Weingrod, and Timothy Harris. *Based on an original story by* Salem. *Photography:* Michael Chapman. *Music:* Randy Edelman. *Editors:* Sheldon Kahn and Wendy Greene Bricmont. *Starring:* Arnold Schwarzenegger, Pamela Reed, Penelope Ann Miller, Linda Hunt, Richard Tyson, and Carroll Baker. Released on December 21, 1990. [111 minutes]

Kindergarten Cop marked Arnold Schwarzenegger's second collaborative project with director Ivan Reitman, and while it was not nearly as successful as *Twins*, the film proved that the star's first outing with comedy was not a fluke. Combining elements from *Dirty Harry*, *The Champ*, and *To Sir, With Love*, it placed Arnold's tough-guy persona (as a cop with a bad attitude) into an elementary school with thirty screaming tots. His attempts to provide less muscle and more laughs won him the gentle praise of critics and the film a respectable $85 million in box-office receipts.

"This was one of the few times when I could look at a movie of mine and say, I think my performance was good," he told *Interview*.

The Screen Story

Sporting a beard, sunglasses, and sawed-off shotgun, Detective John Kimble (Schwarzenegger) looks like a

(O pposite) Schwarzenegger stars as John Kimble, a detective who goes undercover as a kindergarten teacher. (Courtesy Universal Pictures.)

Dirty Harry figure from hell. He has been trailing the notorious drug dealer Cullen Crisp (Richard Tyson) for months and is just about to make a bust when his chief witness Danny (Tom Kurlander) is murdered— by Crisp—and Danny's sister Cindy (Alix Koromzay) refuses to identity the killer. Frustrated and angry, Kimble arrests Crisp anyway, hoping the woman will change her mind. When she still refuses to talk, he follows her to a drug palace and tears the place apart. He then warns her that this is just a sample of what he intends to inflict on her if she remains silent. Ultimately she cooperates, and Crisp is formally charged with murder.

While Crisp is being arraigned, Kimble learns that he has been searching not only for $3 million in drug money that Crisp's ex-wife stole but also for the son he hasn't seen in five years. To force him to reveal his contacts, Kimble decides to go undercover to Astoria, Oregon, with his reluctant new partner Phoebe O'Hara (Pamela Reed) in order to locate Crisp's estranged wife. Since there are no recent photographs of her and her child, they decide to search the only kindergarten in town. Unfortunately, Crisp's mother Eleanor (Carroll Baker) has also learned the whereabouts of her grandson and will stop at nothing short of murder to claim the youngster. She even arranges to have an assassin kill the state's only witness so that her jailed son can go free.

Prior to reaching Astoria, O'Hara becomes violently ill and is unable to go undercover as a kindergarten teacher. Ill suited for the job but with the attitude "They're six-year-olds, how much trouble can they be?" Kimble reports to school. The diminutive but formidable school principal, Miss Schlowski (Linda Hunt), suspects there's something wrong with

(Left) Sporting a wig, beard, sunglasses, and sawed-off shotgun, Kimble looks like a Dirty Harry figure from hell.

(Below) Kimble and his new partner Phoebe O'Hara (Pamela Reed).

him and warns him that she will be watching his every move. The hard-edged cop is then given his first lesson in kindergarten as thirty small children terrorize him, throwing toys, painting on walls, screaming, crying, and demanding to make bathroom visits. By the end of the first day, little Dominick (twins Joseph and Christian Cousins)—the five-year-

Paulmarie (Penelope Ann Miller), who invites him to dinner. Without realizing that she is the woman he is looking for, Kimble gradually falls for her and her son.

Meanwhile, back in Los Angeles, Cindy is murdered with a stash of poisoned drugs, and Eleanor arranges to have her son released from jail. With

Kimble awaits his turn to speak with the principal, Miss Schlowski.

old son of a teacher at the school—assesses his performance as pitiful.

John Kimble returns to Astoria Elementary School on the next day, armed with his pet ferret and an iron will, to teach the children discipline. Like a drill sergeant, he forces the four- and five-year-olds to learn respect, obedience, and physical fitness. He also manages to narrow his list of suspects down to three by questioning the children about their fathers. The undercover cop's new regimen in the classroom impresses the principal and Dominick's mother Joyce

knowledge of the whereabouts of his son, Crisp is determined to be reunited with his money and child.

As Detective Kimble grows fonder of Joyce and young Dominick, he learns from the boy that they have been forced to move around from city to city in order to keep one step ahead of the "bad people." Working on a hunch, he checks into her background and learns the truth about her first marriage. But he's not the only one who's been checking backgrounds. Miss Schlowski has learned that Kimble has no teaching credentials at all or background in higher

173

After a very difficult first day, Kimble teaches the kindergarten children discipline.

education and demands to know what he's doing there. The cop is reluctant to tell her the whole story, fearing that his cover as a kindergarten teacher will be blown, and reveals enough to stay employed. Later, at the Astoria Fair, the principal is forced to admit before the community gathering that Kimble has done a good job teaching his group of children.

Crisp suddenly arrives in town with his equally demented mother, and John Kimble must finally reveal his identity to Joyce. At first she feels betrayed by his deception and again tries to run. But then she realizes that Kimble is all that stands between her son and his nasty father. She reluctantly accepts his help, and together with O'Hara, they plan a way to force Crisp out into the open. Their plan works, and although both Kimble and O'Hara are wounded in the showdown with Crisp and his mother, the rambunctious tots are saved from the fire that the drug dealer has set.

Weeks later, after his wounds have healed, John

Kimble returns to his kindergarten class, loudly proclaiming, "I'm back...." The veteran cop has decided to give up police work in favor of education and is welcomed to his new life by Joyce and Dominick, Miss Schlowski, and his class of four- and five-year-olds.

Production Details

While completing work on *Twins*, director Ivan Reitman had told Arnold Schwarzenegger about an original screen treatment (by Murray Salem) he had read in which a hard-boiled police detective is forced to go undercover as a kindergarten teacher in order to capture a notorious drug dealer. The notion suggested "What if Dirty Harry was suddenly forced to deal with four- and five-year-olds?" Perhaps the two could again team up for another comedy.

Soon after finishing *Ghostbusters II*, Reitman remembered Schwarzenegger's tentative interest in what would eventually become *Kindergarten Cop* and, assembling in part the team of screenwriters he had worked with on *Twins* (Herschel Weingrod and Timothy Harris), began the long process of turning the comedic idea into a workable script. Universal had already agreed to finance the picture *if* Schwarzenegger was aboard as its star. Unfortunately, Arnold had already committed to producing and starring in a film based on the all-American comic-book hero Sergeant Rock. But when the project was temporarily shelved, he gained renewed interest in the story.

> For ten years I have been telling writers, producers, directors, and studio executives that I would love to do a film where a kid or children are a very important part. Something like Jon Voight did in this boxing movie [*The Champ*]....

With the star signed to the project, Reitman had little difficulty zeroing in on the adults to hire as Arnold's costars. He had seen Richard Tyson in several smaller roles and thought his presence as the villain Cullen Crisp would provide a nice counterbalance to Arnold's persona. For his cop partner there would be Pamela Reed, and Penelope Ann Miller was cast as his love interest. Carroll Baker, not often seen on-screen in recent years, was brought in as Crisp's diabolical mother, and Oscar-winner Linda Hunt added plenty of class as the tiny but tough school principal, Miss Schlowski. The most difficult

Detective Kimble returns to Astoria Elementary School armed
with a whistle and a little bit of willpower.

part of the casting, according to Reitman, was locating thirty four- and five-year-olds who could act in front of a camera. The director and father of three children said:

> Right from the beginning, I spoke to them as intelligent young people and tried not to condescend. I told them that acting was not about memorizing lines and saying them by rote. The closer you get to the real thing, as though it were really happening and not "the movies," the more truthful it would look.

While accompanying Reitman to the various schools for the casting process, Schwarzenegger learned that his films were very popular among the younger set. He seemed to be the favorite on most of the kids' top-ten list, and many could name his films from memory.

Schwarzenegger was flabbergasted by their knowledge of his work.

> I was in a state of shock. Ivan would ask the kids, "Does anyone know who this is?" And they would all go, "Yeah! *Predator! Terminator! Twins!* He's Danny DeVito's twin brother! Whatever happened to your twin brother?"

His rapport instantly established with the children,

Like a drill sergeant, Kimble forces the thirty four- and five-year-olds to learn respect, obedience, and physical fitness.

176

Kimble falls in love with Joyce Paulmarie (Penelope Ann Miller), the woman he has been sent to find.

Arnold began drilling his lines with Reed, who would play his partner Phoebe O'Hara, and Miller, the mystery woman. Kimble's relationship with Joyce Paulmarie gave Schwarzenegger yet another opportunity to display his skills as a romantic leading man. He told reporters during his publicity tour for the movie:

> The character I play in this movie goes through a complete transformation. At first he's a cop who knows only one thing—his job. And the way he goes about it sometimes rubs even the police department the wrong way. And then all of a sudden he goes undercover and has the painful experience of facing thirty children in the classroom with absolutely no idea how to communicate with them.

He meets a beautiful woman and has no idea how to communicate with her. The experiences change him completely.

The modest little production began its principal filming during the third week of June 1990 on locations in and around the Los Angeles area (including Hollywood Boulevard's famous Walk of Fame). On July 2, the production crew moved into the Sherman Oaks Galleria, where John Kimble first learns of Cullen Crisp's treacherous murder, for an eight-day shoot. By mid-month they had moved onto the Universal back lot for most of the scenes inside the school, at Joyce's home, and in the drug dealer's den. Exteriors for the Astoria Elementary School were filmed on location in Oregon. Additional shots in the city of Astoria and on the road were completed by

In two rare publicity photos, Arnold Schwarzenegger poses with his pint-sized costars. (Courtesy Universal Pictures)

Ivan Reitman toward the end of the shoot.

On July 30, while filming a critical scene at the elementary school, the cast and crew paused for a moment to throw a surprise party in celebration of Schwarzenegger's forty-third birthday. The well-wishers included Arnold's wife, Maria Shriver, and their seven-month-old daughter, Katherine Eunice, comedian Milton Berle, and a dozen of his bodybuilding pals. The thirty kindergarten children sang him "Happy Birthday" and, to the tune of "A Bicycle Built for Two": "Arnold, Arnold, you are the best to us / Arnold, Arnold, we don't want to make a fuss / But somebody's got to tell ya / Our hearts are yours forever /So thanks a lot / For all you do / And happy birthday to you." That one day typified the fun and goodwill that he experienced during the production.

Schwarzenegger confessed:

Once the filming was complete, *Kindergarten Cop* was one of the few times when I could look back and say I had a very pleasurable experience making this movie. Those children were incredible. They would make drawings for you and give you little photographs. They brought you little gifts, and they cut out hearts and wrote on them. You really looked forward to going to the set and seeing all these kids and having laughs. Now, all of a sudden, boom! They're not here anymore. Then the mood takes a dive.

Critical Commentary

Debuting on December 21, 1990, and quickly ascending to the top of the box-office charts, *Kindergarten Cop* easily defeated Kevin Costner's *Dances With Wolves*, Francis Ford Coppola's *The*

Godfather, Part III, and Martin Scorsese's *GoodFellas*. The only film that faired any better was the about-to-be megahit from John Hughes entitled *Home Alone*. In its first few weeks, *Kindergarten Cop* grossed $25 million and won the hearts of even the most severe critics. Ralph Novak of *People* magazine called the movie "One of the year's ten best! Totally enjoyable." Joel Siegel of *Good Morning America* declared that "*Kindergarten Cop* gets straight A's!" Even Roger Ebert of the *Chicago Sun-Times* had nothing but praise for Arnold's work:

> When Schwarzenegger plays a love scene …he is touchingly sincere. He uses gentleness, not machismo; he behaves toward a woman as a protector, not an aggressor. John Wayne often used that same approach.

By the end of the season, the film had not only grossed an impressive (for a nonaction film) $85 million; it had firmly established Schwarzenegger as a comic actor.

During the spring of 1991, a *Hollywood Reporter* survey of the world's most bankable stars concluded that Arnold Schwarzenegger was number one in virtually every country in which his films play. With a perfect score of one hundred—straight A-pluses from all pollees—the actor was considered more bankable than Tom Cruise, Sean Connery, Harrison Ford, Jack Nicholson, and Sylvester Stallone. (The only other actor who scored one hundred was Mel Gibson.) Arnold's success in managing different types of roles, from comedy to action-adventure, was the key reason given by most pollees for their vote of confidence. "The man has really proven he can work in genres besides just straight action-adventure," CAA Management agent Jonathan Weisgal explained of Arnold's success. Jean-Louis Rubin, president of Largo International, agreed with Weisgal, adding, "Arnold Schwarzenegger has run his professional career brilliantly."

With *Kindergarten Cop*, Schwarzenegger continued an exciting new phase in his career that began with *Twins*. Gone was the self-conscious, formidable muscleman, and in its place was the vulnerable, irresistible giant whose growing sophistication and uncanny penchant for comedy firmly established him as a "leading man." Even though John Kimble is a crude, violent man, a veteran of the mean streets of Los Angeles, ready and able to kill anyone who crosses the line, he eventually changes into a loving, protective, and humane role model. By the same token,

Arnold makes a similar decision, changing from a man of violent action (as represented by the Conan movies, *The Terminator*, *Raw Deal*, and *Red Heat*) into a loving father (*Commando*), a protector (*Predator* and, to a lesser degree, *The Running Man*), and an example of humanity at its best (*Twins*). The success of *Kindergarten Cop* brought him closer to the ideal he had set for himself in film, paving the way for more mainstream roles and superstardom.

Pamela Reed and Penelope Ann Miller provide perfect examples of strength and tenderness with their portrayal of multidimensional women of the nineties. Richard Tyson and Carroll Baker help to balance the dark side of John Kimble with eye-catching performances as a twisted mother-and-son team of villains. Linda Hunt once again proves that good things come in small packages with a fine turn as the principal. But the film's real discoveries are twins Joseph and Christian Cousins. While so much praise was being heaped on Macaulay Culkin for his overrated performance in *Home Alone*, the Cousins duo was turning in a much more understated and earnest acting job. Having started in tandem in the business as young Bobby Ewing in the long-running *Knots Landing* on television, Joseph and Christian had graduated to making commercials and being featured in other roles. *Kindergarten Cop* was their big-screen debut and was followed by another starring turn in the 1992 TV movie *Intruders*. Audiences can certainly look forward to seeing them perform again in other motion pictures.

While much has been written criticizing the film's darker side (including its focus on child abuse, drugs, divorce, and children in danger), both Reitman and Schwarzenegger felt that the negative press was "totally unjustified." Insightful is a word that more aptly describes *Kindergarten Cop* ; for although the film is by turns charming, funny, cruel, sad, and occasionally quite terrifying, it does provide a rich and complex portrait of the people, events, and images that make up today's world. It grows in the mind the way only movies of exceptional insight do.

Kindergarten Cop is currently available on videocassette and laserdisc from MCA/Universal Home Video and has made several direct-to-network appearances on NBC television.

Director Ivan Reitman goes through a scene with Arnold
Schwarzenegger and his costars. (Courtesy Universal Pictures)

FOURTEEN

"I'LL BE BACK..."

Terminator 2: Judgment Day

1991. Tri-Star Pictures in association with Carolco Pictures. *Producer/Director:* James Cameron. *Executive Producers:* Mario Kassar and Gale Anne Hurd. *Screenplay:* Cameron and William Wisher. *Based on characters created by* Cameron and Hurd. *Photography:* Adam Greenberg. *Music:* Brad Fiedel. *Editors:* Richard A. Harris, Mark Goldblatt, and Conrad Buff. *Starring:* Arnold Schwarzenegger, Linda Hamilton, Edward Furlong, Joe Morton, Robert Patrick, Xander Berkeley, and Earl Boen. Released on July 3, 1991. [135 minutes]

For years, Arnold Schwarzenegger had reminded audiences in *Commando*, *The Running Man*, and *Twins* that he would "be back," and with *Terminator 2: Judgment Day*, he reprised the role that had turned his career around. Costing more than any other motion picture in cinema history (a whopping $94 million), the film not only reunited him with director James Cameron but also helped secure his status as the most popular movie star in the world, with record-breaking box-office returns and popular critical appeal. The astounding special effects, non-stop action, and humorous throwaways were simply a bonus to moviegoers.

Schwarzenegger explained in *US* magazine:

I've been offered a lot of money to do sequels to my other films, like *Predator* and *Commando*, but the only one I really wanted to do was *Terminator*. I also made it clear that I wouldn't do it without Jim.

(Opposite) With *Terminator 2*, Arnold Schwarzenegger returns to the role that made him famous. (Courtesy Tri-Star Pictures/Carolco Home Video)

The Screen Story

The motion picture opens in the nuclear war-town future with a simple off-screen narrative by Sarah Connor (Linda Hamilton):

Three billion human lives ended on August 29, 1997. The survivors of the nuclear fire called the war Judgment Day. They lived only to face a new nightmare—the war against the machines. The computer which controlled the machines, Skynet, sent two Terminators back through time. Their mission was to destroy the leader of the human resistance, John Connor, my son. The first Terminator was programmed to strike at me in the year before John was born, 1984; it failed. The second was sent to strike at John himself when he was still a child. As before, the resistance was able to send a lone warrior—a protector—for John. It was only a question of which one of them would reach him first....

In the year 1994, two futuristic time travelers arrive in Los Angeles; only it is not quite certain which of these two has been sent to protect John Connor and which has been sent to kill him. The T-800 (Schwarzenegger), an exact duplicate of the lean, mean, killing machine from the first film, arrives buck-naked outside a motorcycle hangout in Venice known as "The Corral." To the wide-eyed appreciation of several females, the Terminator strides into the bar and demands the leather attire—and motorcycle—from a biker who roughly matches his size. At first the bruising cyclist just laughs at him, while his friends attempt to subdue the "muscu-

The Terminator must preserve the life of a young boy stalked by a fellow robot.

lar nude." Then, fearing that he will be beaten like his buddies, he quickly undresses. Moments later, the Terminator emerges from the bar with leather jacket and pants, boots, T-shirt, shades, and a fearsome assault rifle. Fearing no one or nothing, he climbs aboard the biker's "wheels" and drives off into the night.

Meanwhile, in the parking lot of an abandoned factory, the second time traveler appears. The T-1000 (Robert Patrick) is a much leaner version of the Terminator series, with many hidden specifications. He easily overwhelms a police officer, takes his clothes, and steals the cop's squad car. With access to the onboard computer, he has little difficulty locating young John Connor (Edward Furlong) and his foster parents, Todd and Janelle Voight (Xander Berkeley

and Jenette Goldstein). But the T-1000 is moments too late to prevent the boy from breaking into the automatic teller at a Federal Security bank (in order to steal $300) and heading toward the mall with a friend.

A patient at Pescadero State Hospital for the criminally insane, Sarah Connor doesn't take the news well when her request to see John is denied by Dr. Silberman (Earl Boen), so the orderlies are forced to sedate her. She has stabbed her doctor with a pen and made repeated attempts to escape. Even though Sarah continues to have recurring dreams about August 29, 1997, Judgment Day, no one seems to believe her stories about the world being devastated by a nuclear war. The doctors are even more skeptical about her delusion of "terminator machines" from 2029 and her reasons for attempting to destroy several computer factories. They simply dismiss Sarah as being insane and order six more months of isolation.

At Cyberdyne Systems, Dr. Miles Bennett Dyson (Joe Morton) continues to run tests on the computer chip and mechanical arm of the first Terminator. He has no idea where his company discovered the highly sophisticated pieces of equipment, and he is unaware that his work will ultimately lead to a revolutionary type of microprocessor and the creation of Skynet. (Skynet is the supercomputer of the future that will actually gain self-awareness on August 29, 1997, and launch a nuclear war to destroy the humans it views as a threat.)

At the Sherman Oaks Galleria, both the T-800 and the T-1000 search for John Connor. (At this point, it is still unclear as to which Terminator is a killer and which is a protector.) When John learns from his friend that the police are looking for him, he escapes through the rear of the arcade and runs into the waiting arms of the T-800. Following a brief scuffle at the mall between the two titanic machines and a high-speed chase through the flood-control channels in and around the mall, the T-800 helps John elude the T-1000's deadly tow truck. John then learns that "his" Terminator has been programmed by the resistance to protect him with all the ruthlessness and brute strength that his predecessor used to try to "terminate" Sarah (in the first film) and that the T-1000—the next generational design of the Terminator series, capable of imitating anything that it touches—has been programmed to eliminate the future leader. The boy insists on calling his foster parents to warn them, but the T-1000 has already beaten him to their home and has killed them both by assuming Janelle's shape.

Realizing his mother Sarah is the T-1000's next logical target, John and the T-800 head for the hospital to help her. The shape-changing Terminator has once again anticipated their actions and is searching

learns about the T-800's mission to protect John, and she accepts the Terminator as a surrogate father for her son. John continues to teach the Terminator new things, including phrases such as *No problemo* and how to give a thumbs-up sign. Gradually the "old model" Terminator turns from being a killing machine, inhuman and unthinking, to a caring, humanized protector, while Sarah, who is obsessed

Robots of the future try to wipe out the final survivors of "Judgment Day."

the institution for Sarah Connor, who has already engineered an escape from her cell. After an intensive interrogation by cops (still looking for the assassin who destroyed a police barracks in the first film), she follows through with her plan. The desperate woman takes Dr. Silberman hostage and forces her way to the entrance. John arrives with the T-800 (who has sworn an oath to the boy not to kill anyone), and the three fugitives narrowly escape the hospital and the deadly metallic clutches of the T-1000.

Later, at an abandoned service station, Sarah

with Dyson and the creation of Skynet, becomes a cold, unfeeling "terminator." The former inmate decides that the only way to alter the future is to change the present, so she plans to kill Dyson. The unlikely trio drives to a small survivalist camp in the desert, where Sarah arms herself for her mission.

Hours later, with Miles Bennett Dyson in the cross hairs of her automatic weapon, Sarah cannot pull the trigger; she is simply not a Terminator. Intercepting John's mother at the inventor's home, the T-800 graphically explains to Dyson why he shouldn't continue his current experiments. He is

shocked to learn "the history of things to come" and decides to help the trio break into the main complex of Cyberdyne Systems.

At the computer facility, a silent alarm is tripped, and the efforts of the three to destroy all the computer files are eventually discovered by a massive police action. (Meanwhile, the T-1000 has arrived at Dyson's home and followed the leads to Cyberdyne.) As Sarah Connor and Miles Dyson wire explosives to the computer systems and John breaks into the vault to steal the important computer chip and mechanical arm, the T-800 fights a one-sided battle against the police SWAT team. Dyson is mortally wounded in the conflict but manages to buy the others time to retreat by holding on to the detonator. However escape from the Cyberdyne complex proves to be futile, as the SWAT team's gunfire pins down Sarah and her son. The T-800 promises, "I'll be back," and strides directly into the conflict, taking numerous bullet hits on its human tissue. The Terminator steals a SWAT van in order to free John and his mother, and the trio escapes moments before the building explodes.

Commandeering a police helicopter, the T-1000

Upon his arrival in the present, the T-800 demands the leather attire of a biker and commandeers his motorcycle.

A second Terminator (Robert Patrick), much more sophisticated than the T-800, also arrives from the future and takes on the appearance of a policeman.

pieces, saying "*Hasta la vista ...baby.*"

Within moments, even though the machine has exploded into several thousand shards of frozen polyalloy, the heat from the molten steel permits the deadly Terminator to re-form, and Sarah and her son are again forced to flee for their lives. The good Terminator tries to prevent the shape changer's advance, but he has been too damaged by gunfire and explosions. The two titanic machines trade massive, punishing blows, and eventually the T-1000 gets the upper hand. Then, disguising itself as Sarah to capture John, the bad Terminator confronts the real, heavily armed Sarah. She fires round after round at him, but the gunfire seems to have no effect. Sarah will be the T-1000's next victim.

Although the "old model" Terminator has been almost completely destroyed, the broken machine staggers to its feet to save John and Sarah. The T-800 blasts its evil counterpart into a vat of molten steel, and the cyborg's unique transmutating capabilities are totally consumed by the liquid. Unable to re-form, the T-1000 finally sinks down into the vat and melts away. Victorious, the good Terminator moves forward to embrace Sarah and John, claiming "I need a vacation."

Then, recognizing that his continued existence might still result in a nuclear-war-torn future, the Terminator decides that it, too, must be destroyed in the vat of molten steel. John, who has become very attached to him, is devastated by the T-800's decision but accepts his decision like a man. After saying his farewells, the machine is lowered into the vat and destroyed forever. In a voice-over epilogue, traveling down a darkened road, Sarah explains, "The

takes off in pursuit. The chase takes all down a major section of freeway, into the path of innocent pedestrians and other travelers. Eventually the T-1000 attempts a suicide drop on the SWAT van with his helicopter, but his crash is not successful. The T-1000 grabs a passing tanker truck (filled with liquid nitrogen) and continues the pursuit into a steel factory. His counterpart, the T-800, forces the truck to jackknife on the road and rides it into the mill. Neither Terminator is injured, but when the escaping liquid nitrogen freezes the T-1000, the T-800 blows him to

Teenager John Connor (Edward Furlong) is a resourceful young man who finds himself the target of a killer cyborg.

unknown future rolls toward us, and I face it for the first time with a sense of hope. If a computer can learn the value of human life, maybe we can, too...."

Production Details

In the intervening years since the original *Terminator*, not only had Schwarzenegger become the world's most popular actor but James Cameron had also worked exceptionally hard to establish himself as one of Hollywood's top directors. After *The Terminator*, he went on to cowrite *Rambo: First Blood Part II* for Sylvester Stallone, write and direct *Aliens* with Sigourney Weaver, and write and direct the brilliant but largely undervalued *The Abyss*. Discussions about a sequel had begun almost immediately after the release of the first film, but because of various legal and creative differences with Hemdale Films, which owned the rights, Cameron became involved in other things. The director recalled:

In a rare still from a scene cut from the final print of the film, Sarah Connor (Linda Hamilton) fantasizes a meeting with Reese.

The ending of the first *Terminator* wasn't structured with a sequel in mind. Sarah Connor was going toward a known future, and the audience knew what she was heading into. I felt everything about that story was there and that there wasn't much left to say.

Schwarzenegger remembered his attempts to change the director's mind.

I told Jim Cameron we should have an ongoing story line because it was such an interesting subject, but I realized as long as Hemdale Films was involved it would never happen, because it was not a company that was capable of making a classy movie that demanded a big budget—they would want to make it cheap.

Throughout their various productions, the *Terminator* sequel was always the topic of conversation whenever Schwarzenegger and Cameron got together. "He was much more enthusiastic about doing a sequel than I was," Cameron explained. "But as the years went by, I began to take the idea more seriously." The director sought out his friend William Wisher, who had written the novelization for the first film, and began throwing ideas around, never really believing the project would get off the ground.

When Hemdale faced finan-

Sarah has fashioned herself into a tough warrior to protect her son and herself from the impending war between man and machines.

tracts were finalized, and James Cameron had less than fourteen months to deliver a finished project in exchange for a $5 million salary. Carolco was determined to release the movie on July 3, 1991. (For his efforts, Schwarzenegger received a $12 million Gulfstream G-III jet and a percentage of the film's profits.)

The morning after the *Terminator 2* project was given a green light, Cameron and Wisher began work on a screenplay based solely on a single incomplete sentence the director had written years before: "Young John Connor and the Terminator who comes back to befriend him." Their first draft, which focused on a confrontation between two Terminators, one good and one bad, but both played by Arnold, turned out to be somewhat "gimmicky" and "visually unappealing." Cameron knew that he would have a difficult time selling his audience on the concept, and since Schwarzenegger had just played a "Jekyll and Hyde" role in *Total Recall*, the notion would have seemed repetitive. A second draft provided Sarah Connor with an interesting way to get back together with Kyle Reese, but relied too heavily on time travel and not enough on the Terminator. After

cial difficulties and possible bankruptcy, Schwarzenegger urged Mario Kassar, the president of Carolco, to make a bid for the project. "I reminded Mario that this is something that we've been looking for for years," he said, in much the same posture he demonstrated with Andrew Vajna prior to the purchase of *Total Recall*, "and that it should be him that should go all-out, no matter what it takes to make a deal." Carolco paid $5 million to Hemdale and a similar amount to Gale Anne Hurd, Cameron's ex-wife and producer of the first film. By May 1990, the con-

reviewing John Carpenter's *The Thing*, they labored for several weeks on another draft that featured a shape changer. Even though Stan Winston, who had been hired again to provide the prosthetic makeup, dismissed the concept as being not "frightful enough" for modern audiences, Cameron settled for the concept. A revised script helped fine-tune the shape changer and introduced Sarah as a "terminator" as well, at least from a psychological point of view. Several scenes, which involved the resistance locating the timetravel equipment and an alternate

(Right) The T-800 reveals his endo-skeleton in order to convince Dyson that his work is much too deadly to proceed.

(Below) The Terminator, scientist Miles Dyson, and Sarah Connor break into the Cyberdyne building.

191

ending, with Sarah Connor as an old woman in Washington, D.C., were later trimmed from the film but remain in the novelization.

Based on his final shooting script, Carolco guaranteed Cameron $88 million, but that figure eventually climbed to $94 million, making *Terminator 2: Judgment Day* the most expensive film in cinema history. Many of the special effects (involving the shape changer) that were called for in the script had to be invented, and Cameron turned to Dennis Muren and the technicians at George Lucas's Industrial Light and Magic to make them happen. Other effects were contracted out to Fantasy II and Stan Winston, both of whom had been involved in the first film.

Schwarzenegger was surprised to learn that his Terminator had been cast in the role of the underdog this time around and that he would be taking lots of battle damage from the T-1000, but he remained good-natured about Winston's prosthetics.

> The new Terminator with all these new capabilities is much more threatening, and I'm much too handsome—no camera can take all these good looks—so what they do is put appliances and terrible makeup on my face to tone my good looks down.

Opposite Schwarzenegger were his costar from the first film and several newcomers. Linda Hamilton had also spent the intervening years, between the first film and its sequel, develop-

Robert Patrick as the T-1000, the much leaner version of the Terminator series.

ing her talents as an actress in television's *Beauty and the Beast*. When she left to have a baby in the show's third season, the series literally fell apart and was canceled by the network. For her part in *Terminator 2: Judgment Day*, Hamilton spent three months before shooting began working with a trainer and learning how to handle weapons from an Israeli commando. Her appearance had to be substantially altered so that she could be Schwarzenegger's equal as a lean, mean fighting machine.

Robert Patrick, who looks like a cross between David Bowie and James Dean, was cast over favorite Billy Idol and many other actors as the new Terminator. Unable to find someone who was bigger or badder than Schwarzenegger, director Cameron felt Patrick's diminutive size was complemented in the film by his amazing ability to change into different shapes. The Georgia-born actor had already played in a never-released-theatrically 1986 science-fiction rip-off of *The Terminator* entitled *Future Hunters* as well as *Warlords From Hell*, *Another 48 HRS.*, and *Die Hard 2*. His performance in *Terminator 2: Judgment Day* was one of the most important in the film because he had to provide counterbalance as the evil cyborg T-1000 to Arnold's Terminator.

The most difficult role in the film to cast was that of John Connor, who had to have a strong presence opposite the other heavyweights. "It was the single scariest creative decision of the film," James Cameron confessed, but casting director Mali

Linda Hamilton as the hard-driven Sarah Connor.

Commandeering a police helicopter, the T-1000 relentlessly pursues the others through the streets of present-day Los Angeles...

Finn made his decision somewhat easier when she brought him a tape of Eddie Furlong. She had discovered the twelve-year-old playing baseball at a YMCA in Pasadena. After interviewing hundreds of candidates and reviewing several dozen tapes, the director saw a certain strength of character in the young man that he had not seen in anyone else. Furlong was ultimately hired to play John, while veteran actor Joe Morton was cast as Miles Bennett Dyson and Earl Boen reprised his role from the first film as Dr. Silberman.

The company began principal photography on October 9, 1990, in the rough terrain of the Mojave Desert near Lancaster, California, which served as survivalist camp. Nearly all the crew from *The Terminator* with James Cameron back in 1984 settled into a relaxed, friendly atmosphere. The production then moved to Reseda, California, for several

weeks of shooting in the flood-control channels all around Los Angeles County. The actual truck-and-motorcycle chase through the channels had been meticulously choreographed by Cameron, visual effects production supervisor Alison Savitch, and stunt coordinator Joel Kramer weeks before with toy vehicles, so when actual filming took place, everyone knew what was required to make the shots successful. Kramer explained:

Jim writes very intricate action sequences. In most scripts, action is thinly outlined and basically left up to the stunt people to choreograph. With this movie, all of the action sequences have been detailed so explicitly that it has been like following a blueprint. And the great thing about this film is that all the action and stunts have been worked into the natural telling of the story.

194

Terminator 2: Judgment Day spent six days at the Sherman Oaks Galleria for the sequence involving John's first confrontation with the Terminators and his subsequent escape. Most of the work did not begin until well after nine each night. Shooting at the Corral Bar, in Venice, California, occupied the crew for several other evenings. (On one night, however, Schwarzenegger, Cameron, and crew turned the tables on a drunken barfly who had wandered into the Corral unsuspectedly by explaining Arnold's near nudity as a special "male stripper night.")

At the beginning of November, the production moved to the San Jose suburb of Fremont (and the Warm Springs industrial area) to film Arnold's fire-fight with the SWAT team and the subsequent deto-nation of the Cyberdyne complex. For months leading up to the shoot, Cameron and his crew had searched sites in both northern and southern California, Houston, and Dallas for the appropriate building. Unable to find exactly what he wanted, Cameron was about to concede to building a minia-ture when an abandoned structure outside San Jose

was discovered. Though the shot would be the most logistically challenging in the film, he confessed that it was his favorite.

I embraced that sequence because it was the first time in the film that you got a real feeling of this being the Terminator you remembered from the first film. I hadn't really had a chance to do any of that yet, and Arnold needed a kicking-ass fix. We did one shot where he put about four hundred rounds into three differ-ent cars and just shot them to pieces. Afterwards, I walked over to him and said, "Now Arnold, you can't tell me that wasn't a rush.

The biggest "rush" for cast and crew actually came several days later when (with the help of Tommy Fisher's explosives) Cameron actually blew the building apart in front of eight running cameras.

The company then moved south to Long Beach for two weeks of night shooting on the Terminal Island Freeway in order to capture the fugitives'

...and later demonstrates his ability to absorb shocks and recon-figure his body.

The Terminator, Sarah, and John watch as the T-1000 is dissolved in the molten steel.

escape from the Cyberdyne complex and the highway battle with the T-1000. The cast and crew spent the subsequent weeks between Thanksgiving and Christmas at an abandoned steel mill in Fontana. (Negotiations to use the facility almost fell apart when a Chinese consortium purchased the mill for relocation, but Cameron prevailed.) Ruins beyond the steel mill provided the backdrop for the war-torn, postnuclear setting of the future. To dress up the shot, production designer Joseph Nemec III borrowed a variety of things, including burned bicycles, trucks, and balcony railings and misshapen steel, from the recent back-lot fire at Universal Studios.

With time running short and several scenes behind, Cameron asked Schwarzenegger to cancel his Christmas plans so that they might catch up. Reluctantly he decided to forego both an appearance at the Shrivers' Christmas party and an agreement he had made with President Bush to visit the troops in

Saudi Arabia. The added shooting time helped get the production back on schedule.

After the holiday break, on January 16, 1991, the cast and crew resumed filming at the Lake View Medical Center in the San Fernando Valley, just north of Los Angeles. Shortly after the center was built in 1970, it suffered significant earthquake damage and was never officially opened. The center was often used for film shooting, and Cameron's people had re-dressed the institution to look like the Pescadero State Hospital. Just moments before filming was to start, a production assistant announced that the Persian Gulf War had started. The somber mood on the set was appropriate for the filming of a dream sequence (later cut) between Hamilton and Michael Biehn as Kyle Reese in which the time traveler tells Sarah, "The future is not set. There is no fate but what we make for ourselves."

Principal photography continued into the second

196

week of March 1991, when the final scenes, involving the interior battle at Cyberdyne, were shot. Cameron was then left with a very short postproduction schedule to add the special effects from Fantasy II and Dennis Muren's crew at Industrial Light and Magic.

> The most important thing was staying on top of it while we were shooting—editing scenes as they were shot. I just had to realize that I wasn't going to get a day off until the film was in the theaters—that was a given. There's a certain thrill in doing something that you know nobody has the balls to do.

Schwarzenegger spoke similar words about the picture's scope and the director's vision.

> The film is much bigger than the first one, and the experience making it has been very intense. But you know, I rarely felt any pressure from Jim. He had worked the scenes already ten times over. It's not like with some directors where you have to second-guess. You don't have to do that with Cameron. There was simply no pressure. He's one of the most professional people I've ever worked with.

With a major financial deficit and facing cash-flow problems, Carolco Pictures was somewhat relieved when Cameron screened a rough cut of the film early in June. Mario Kassar and other studio executives could see not only their investment of $94 million in every frame of the film but also that they had another winner. Conservative estimates suggested that *Terminator 2: Judgment Day* would do double the business that Schwarzenegger's previous vehicle (*Total Recall*) had done. They certainly could not have foreseen the phenomenal landslide of ticket purchases made during the film's first week.

Critical Commentary

Terminator 2: Judgment Day was released on July 3, 1991, and grossed an incredible $70 million in its opening week, easily beating the 1989 *Batman* as the biggest money-maker for a single week. The film opened at number one on the box-office charts, brushing aside its mismatched competition of Kevin Costner's *Robin Hood*, Billy Crystal's *City Slickers*, Ron Howard's *Backdraft*, Ridley Scott's *Thelma & Louise*, and Disney's *The Rocketeer*, and did not

relinquish the much-cherished spot until well into October of that year. Unlike many big-budget movies of the past years, the exorbitant costs of which had raised the ire of critics and general audiences alike, *Terminator 2: Judgment Day* did not suffer the fate of *Hudson Hawk*, the summer's chief casualty. Both Gene Siskel and Roger Ebert gave the motion picture a big "thumbs up"; David Ansen, writing in *Newsweek*, called attention to Schwarzenegger's "impressive, hilarious, almost touching" performance; and Owen Gleiberman in *Entertainment Weekly* gave the film high marks for its state-of-the-art effects, solid performances, and thrilling action. By the end of 1991, as the movie was being released on videocassette and laserdisc, it had grossed more than $240 million and was well on its way to becoming one of the top box-office leaders of all time.

Terminator 2: Judgment Day ended up with five Oscars: for Best Editing, Best Sound, Best Sound-Effects Editing, Best Makeup, and Best Visual Effects. Even though Jonathan Demme's *The Silence of the Lambs* won Oscars in each of the major categories (including Best Picture), the two films effectively tied with five awards apiece. Regrettably, the high-powered performances of Arnold Schwarzenegger and Linda Hamilton were overlooked. Many showed their support for Barbra Streisand, who had been overlooked in the Best-Director category for *The Prince of Tides*, but the single biggest disappointment of the nominating process was that James Cameron's name had been excluded from a list including John Singleton, Ridley Scott, Jonathan Demme, Martin Scorsese, and Barry Levinson.

In *Terminator 2: Judgment Day*, Schwarzenegger, with his portrait of the Terminator as a protective father, again demonstrates considerable acting ability. While he appeared in less than 25 percent of the original (with a total of seventeen lines of dialogue), his presence dominates most of the sequel. (In fact, he appears in nearly every scene.) But Schwarzenegger is clearly much more than the lean, mean killing machine from the first film. He emerges through the time warp as an inhuman, relentless machine that has but one purpose (as in the original); however, the cyborg's relationship with John Connor gradually humanizes him, in much the same way that Arnold's intimate relationship with his audience has helped make him a superstar. He somewhat explained the Terminator's transformation in *Interview*:

(Opposite and above) Director James Cameron works through several action sequences with Schwarzenegger. (Courtesy Tri-Star Pictures/Carolco Home Video)

There are certain feelings that I begin to understand by observing human beings. There is a wonderful scene where the boy cries and I say, "What's wrong with your eyes?" Later I tell him that I have come to understand about crying, though it is something I can never do.

Subtle changes in facial expressions, posture, body language, speech, and humor also help Arnold Schwarzenegger convey the machine's gradual metamorphosis.

Whereas much has been written about the star's patient endurance of prosthetic application by makeup artists Stan Winston, Jefferson Dawn, and Steve LaPorte, very little has been said about his acting challenge from behind the layers of latex. Like Lon Chaney before him, Schwarzenegger conveys many "human" emotions (which the machine has learned) during the film's bloody climax. In spite of the thirty-five sessions during the course of the shoot, he continues to express himself with great skill. Arnold told *T2 Movie Magazine*:

I had to act like a cyborg, which meant I couldn't show any kind of human fear or reaction to the fire, explosions, or gunfire that were going off around me. That can be difficult when you're walking through a door with its frame on fire, trying to reload a gun, and at the same time thinking in the back of your mind that people have accidents doing these kinds of stunts and that it might be my turn.

His T-800 character is considerably more complex than the serial killer Hannibal Leckter, which won Anthony Hopkins an Oscar as Best Actor, and clearly demonstrates his range as an actor.

Linda Hamilton delivers a performance in *Terminator 2: Judgment Day* that arguably was also better than Jodie Foster's Academy Award–winning turn in *The Silence of the Lambs* or Geena Davis's or Susan Sarandon's in *Thelma & Louise*. Little of the vulnerability of her earlier self—the mousy waitress who finds it difficult to accept her role in saving the world—remains in the mature woman, who is driven by nightmares of Judgment Day. Older, wiser, leaner, hard-edged, she walks a tightrope between

199

sanity and impending doom. While Schwarzenegger's Terminator becomes "humanized" by her son, Hamilton's Connor has lost all her humanity on the way to becoming a female "terminator." And somewhere on that path to self-destruction, she ultimately learns the value of human life. Hamilton confessed to *T2 Movie Magazine*:

> A woman who grows and transforms on-screen is always a wonderful thing to play. Sarah went from a vulnerable, normal girl to someone who finds all of her deep reservoirs of strength and comes through it all.

Had her two cut scenes been restored (featuring Sarah and Reese and Sarah as an old woman) to the final release print, no one could have denied her an Academy-Award nomination as Best Actress.

Robert Patrick also succeeds with the daunting task of playing the flashy new Terminator. Boyishly handsome but with catlike features and cold, dead eyes, he provides a powerhouse of pure adrenaline with his performance. Dennis Muren and Industrial Light and Magic's state-of-the-art, visually striking special effects help transform him into the perfect adversary for Arnold's older, more protective Terminator. Edward Furlong is very good as John Connor and shows promise of emerging as one of the brighter young stars of the nineties. But the real star is director James Cameron.

Cameron was involved in nearly every facet of the production, from writing and producing to directing and supervising the special effects, and his genius is apparent throughout the film. Part *tech noir*, part heavy metal, and all humanistic, *Terminator 2* boasts a director who brilliantly leads enthusiastic audiences through a maze of technology and metaphysical time warps to the simple, single revelation that reckless indifference to human life will ultimately cost mankind its place on the earth. "The film is about human value," said Cameron, explaining the theme in one sentence, and that theme is carried forth in every sequence. While he has little difficulty in providing nonstop action that leads to a thunderous climax, Cameron also leaves audiences thinking about his theme long after they have left the theater. In many respects, that type of filmmaking makes James Cameron one of the most important directors of the nineties. (20th Century-Fox also recognized his enormous contribution to cinema and signed Cameron to an exclusive contract that will net him twenty motion pictures and more than a billion dollars over the next few years.)

Finally, as with the original, discussion about another installment in the *Terminator* series has left many people in the industry speculating about a third film. If one is made, 2029 A.D. is the time to place the film, and the logical plot line would involve an interdimensional battle between Skynet (to destroy the alternate time line that Reese and the T-800 have created) and those (Sarah, John, and another protector?) who wish to preserve the time line of peace. Arnold Schwarzenegger has not ruled out his involvement in another installment and told *T2 Movie Magazine*:

> I don't necessarily want to leave the magic of the *Terminator* movies behind, and who says we have to? According to what we know about the future, there were hundreds of Terminators built. The story of the Terminator could go on forever.

Only time, James Cameron, and an incredibly large budget will tell!

Terminator 2: Judgment Day is currently available on videocassette and laserdisc from Live Home Video. A special wide-screen version, which includes an informative special about the making of the film, is available on laserdisc.

(Opposite) The Terminator decides to sacrifice himself for the betterment of mankind.

FIFTEEN

ACTION!

Last Action Hero

1993. Columbia Pictures. *Director:* John McTiernan. *Producers:* Steve Roth and McTiernan. *Executive Producer:* Arnold Schwarzenegger. *Screenplay:* Shane Black and David Arnott. *Based on an original story by* Zak Penn and Adam Leff. *Photography:* Dean Semler. *Music:* Michael Kamen. *Editor:* John Wright. *Starring:* Arnold Schwarzenegger, Charles Dance, Anthony Quinn, F. Murray Abraham, Art Carney, Joan Plowright, Mercedes Ruehl, Robert Prosky, Tom Noonan, Ian McKellen, Tina Turner, and Austin O'Brien. Released June 18, 1993. [130 minutes]

"You're only as good as your last film," said Arnold Schwarzenegger back in 1987. While he has excelled with every performance since *Conan the Barbarian*, he maintains a very simple philosophy about his motion pictures. "If your last film was a bomb, then you were a bomb. If your last film went through the roof, then you went through the roof."

In the summer of 1992, a mere ten years since the release of *Conan the Barbarian*, Schwarzenegger began planning for his twentieth motion picture, *Last Action Hero*. Although his name had been attached to more lucrative productions, including sequels to *Commando*, *Predator*, and *Conan the Destroyer* as well as original projects like *Sgt. Rock*, *Curious George*, *Sweet Tooth*, *The Flintstones*, and *The Watchmen*, he chose his latest because of the challenge it offered him as an actor and its antiviolent theme.

In our business, it's like in the political arena:

(Opposite) Arnold Schwarzenegger—the "last action hero"? (Courtesy Cinema Archives.)

You have to find out what the audience really wants. The country is going in an antiviolence direction. I think America has seen now enough of what violence has done in the cities, and while it was okay for the Arnold of the eighties to kill 275 people on-screen, it is not for the Arnold of the nineties.

The Screen Story

While decidedly a typical vehicle for Schwarzenegger, *Last Action Hero* provides him with another multifaceted character, like John Kimble and Douglas Quaid. He plays Jack Slater, appropriately enough a movie star whose action-adventure films have created a worldwide cult following. Although the on-screen persona of Jack Slater is worshipped by young and old alike, he becomes the particular fascination of Danny Madigan (Austin O'Brien), a youngster with a very vivid imagination. One moment he's watching Laurence Olivier as Hamlet on a television screen in English class, and the next the young fan is daydreaming that Arnold is Hamlet with a MAC-10. Not long after, Danny's daydreams literally allow him to enter the movies that feature his screen idol. Despite objections from his mother (Mercedes Ruehl), Danny cuts school to invest all his emotions and creative energies in the fantasy world of Jack Slater. Then one night, the projectionist (Robert Prosky) at the rundown local movie house gives Danny a "magic ticket" that was once given to him by Houdini. That ticket transports him into the world of his idol's latest movie. One moment, Danny's sitting in the crummy theater, watching *Jack Slater IV*, and the next, he's in the back seat of Jack's rampaging Bonneville convertible speeding toward a series of spectacular adventures.

The two forge a special relationship that seems to transcend the boundaries of film and its mythical worlds, and that relationship allows Slater to step out of the confines of his fictional world into Danny's reality. Unfortunately, several bad guys (including Charles Dance) have also slipped out of the movie world and are determined to kill Arnold Schwarzenegger at the opening of his new film, *Jack Slater IV*. (By killing the actor, they reason, they can destroy their nemesis, Jack Slater.) Summoning all his resources and the tricks that he has learned from making films, "the last action hero" ultimately discovers some things about himself and the influence his films have had on others. With his young friend he races to New York City to prevent the bad guys from winning and to return to the world of motion pictures, where he belongs.

The screen story may seem like an unlikely cross between *The Secret Life of Walter Mitty*, *The Purple Rose of Cairo*, and *Kindergarten Cop*, but the central character of the piece once again offers Arnold Schwarzenegger an ideal opportunity to explore his own superstardom and the elements that have made him a star. "It's bigger than *Terminator 2*," several studio executives insisted while brimming with marketing plans for *Last Action Hero*. Those claims may have been the requisite Hollywood hyperbole, but then again, with a motion picture featuring the world's most successful actor, anything is possible. Each of Schwarzenegger's action-adventure films, with one or two exceptions, have surpassed the previous outings in terms of critical acceptance and box-office receipts.

Last Action Hero provides Schwarzenegger with another opportunity to play a complete, multifaceted character who is a man of action.

When Shakespeare's *Hamlet* does not live up to young Danny Madigan's expectations, he fantasizes action hero Jack Slater in the role of the melancholy Dane.

Production Details

Last Action Hero began in the word processors of two very talented yet inexperienced screenwriters, Zak Penn and Adam Leff. Less than six months after graduation from Wesleyan University, Penn and Leff were working in Hollywood as readers when they decided to write on speculation a screenplay entitled *Extremely Violent*, with Schwarzenegger in mind. It told of a schoolboy who literally enters the movies that feature his idol. Penn and Leff continued to polish their early draft while the script was shopped around to the various studios in October 1991, initially asking $750,000 for the rights. They settled for $150,000 against $350,000 when the film was finally made, and Columbia sweetened the pot by offering an additional $150,000.

Several months later, in January 1992, Peter Guber, Barry Josephson, and studio chief Mark Canton met with Arnold Schwarzenegger at his newly opened Santa Monica restaurant, Schatzi on Main, to discuss the project. The superstar was intrigued by Penn and Leff's concept but expressed certain reservations about the screenplay itself. When Josephson mentioned that Shane Black, who had acted with Arnold in *Predator*, was being brought in to lend the writing talent he had demonstrated with *Lethal Weapon* and *The Last Boy Scout* to the rewrite, Arnold not only approved the production but called on Black to "write me an E ticket." Teamed with his buddy David Arnott, who had written *The Adventures of Ford Fairlane*, Shane Black began creating a magical work that he terms "a cross between *The Wizard of Oz* and *48 HRS.*

"We threw in every action-movie convention we could," Black and Arnott told reporters earlier in the year, "but it's not *Naked Gun*—no one pulls out a bazooka and says, 'Mine's bigger.'" Black was also quick to point out that although the movie has many explosive set pieces, the action is decidedly cartoon-

205

ish, conceived with a PG-13 rating in mind. "This would be a movie that I would take my kids to, if I had kids," he explained.

By late spring, with the new script taking shape, *Extremely Violent* (now retitled *Last Action Hero*) joined a collection of other projects from which Arnold Schwarzenegger could choose. He passed on the big-budget remake of *The Count of Monte Cristo*, worried that his accent would doom the highly literate script, and again dismissed Joel Silver's *Sgt. Rock* as not ready. James Cameron's remake of the French film *La Totale* and Ivan Reitman's *Oh Baby* were also briefly considered. He eventually narrowed the field down to Norman Lear's *Sweet Tooth*, with Ron Underwood (the director of *City Slickers*) in tow, and *Last Action Hero*, both with Columbia Pictures. "We decided that we had the best action script in town," Arnold finally told Columbia about *Last Action Hero*, "but we needed William Goldman to flesh out the relationship between the kid and me."

Slater, accompanied by Danny Madigan (Austin O'Brien), is bewildered by life in the real world on the streets of Manhattan.

Fictional Jack Slater learns what the real world is like from Danny's mom (Mercedes Ruehl).

With Arnold Schwarzenegger's name finally attached to the property, Guber, Canton, and Josephson offered Goldman, who wrote *Butch Cassidy and the Sundance Kid*, *All the President's Men*, *Marathon Man*, and *Misery,* $1 million to complete a four-week polish. At first, Goldman claimed there was little he could do to improve Black and Arnott's work. After Arnold put a little friendly muscle on him he eventually accepted the assignment. Larry Ferguson, who had adapted *The Hunt for Red October* for the big screen, later contributed to the script, as did Charles Dance, who wrote much of his own dialogue. (Much later, when ownership of the screenplay was disputed, the final script was submitted to the Writers Guild of America for arbitration to determine who exactly deserved screen credit.)

Before the cameras could begin rolling, however, the search began for director, cast, and crew. Several directors were considered, including Richard Donner, Penny Marshall, and Joel Schumacher, but contractual obligations with conflicting projects forced Columbia to review other candidates. Fortunately,

Cameo appearances by M. C. Hammer, Jim Belushi, Jean-Claude Van Damme, Sharon Stone (as Catherine Tramell from *Basic Instinct*), Robert Patrick (as the T-1000), Little Richard, Damon Wayans, Tina Turner, Chevy Chase, Maria Shriver, Arnold Schwarzenegger (as himself), and others contribute to the film's overall light tone.

Principal photography on the $60 million production began in the fall of 1992 on the back lot at Columbia (now Sony) Pictures on sets left over from Francis Ford Coppola's 1992 remake of *Dracula*. In fact, Schwarzenegger destroys Dracula's castle (stand-

Outgunned by one of the movie world's most dangerous criminals, Jack and Danny find themselves in a perilous situation.

John McTiernan was available. He also happened to have been Arnold Schwarzenegger's first choice as director—they had worked together five years earlier on *Predator*, and Schwarzenegger was convinced McTiernan could handle the assorted action sequences as well as the complex story setup. Schwarzenegger would also share production duties, as executive producer, with him.

Oscar winners Anthony Quinn, F. Murray Abraham, Art Carney, and Mercedes Ruehl were also brought aboard, along with Oscar nominee Joan Plowright (Mrs. Olivier) and noted British actor Charles Dance, who had played opposite Sigourney Weaver in *Alien 3* and the Phantom of the Opera in the popular miniseries as the villain of the piece. Other key roles went to Tom Noonan as the Ripper, Frank McRae as the chief of police, and Robert Prosky as a movie projectionist. For the central role of sidekick Danny Madigan, eleven-year-old Austin O'Brien was selected from a group of fifty young performers (in much the same way Edward Furlong had been discovered for *Terminator 2: Judgment Day*).

207

ing in as a Danish fortress) in a riotous send-up of Hamlet's famous "To be, or not to be" soliloquy. By late November the production had moved to locations in and around the Los Angeles area (notably in the districts hardest hit by the Rodney King riots). McTiernan's production company rebuilt several neighborhood blocks; they were used as sets, then later left to local area groups. Interiors of Los Angeles's Orpheum Theater stood in for the Pandora Theater. For the complicated scene in which Jack Slater falls into the La Brea Tar Pits, the production crew moved to the Long Beach Hyatt Regency hotel, where a replica (complete with giant models of a *Tyrannosaurus Rex* and *Brontosaurus*) had been built. The tar was actually a mulch made from Oreo cookie dough, and Schwarzenegger was forced to spend several hours submerged in the goop. By February the crew had moved to New York City for shots involving the faux movie premiere of *Jack Slater IV* and the film's extended climax. A seventy-five-foot balloon of Arnold as Jack Slater was inflated in the middle of Times Square to promote the movie-within-a-movie and tied up traffic (and pedestrians) for several days. (On the heels of the World Trade Center bombing, the figure's left hand, which once held dynamite, now sported a badge.) The cast and crew braved real world weather as arctic winds descended on Manhattan midway through the shooting schedule as the blizzard of the decade struck most of the East Coast.

The five-month shoot wrapped

Slater rescues Danny Madigan (Austin O'Brien) from a perilous situation

Director John McTiernan discusses a complex scene with Arnold Schwarzenegger and Austin O'Brien between takes of *Last Action Hero*. (Courtesy Columbia Pictures)

late in March 1993, leaving McTiernan a meager two and a half months for postproduction. In addition to the visual- and sound-effects editing, dialogue looping, and scoring, the script demanded the addition of an animated-cat character, similar to Mark Rogers's "Samurai Cat." Those special effects (which also included the recording of the cat's voice courtesy of Danny DeVito) consumed an enormous amount of time, as did a well-managed publicity campaign, the centerpiece of which was the Cannes Film Festival. Early in May, just six weeks from the premiere and more than five weeks after the film had supposedly wrapped, McTiernan, Schwarzenegger, Dance, and crew were shooting a new chase on a narrow side street in downtown L.A. (standing in as a street in Manhattan). Other action sequences were also filmed, late in May, following a less than enthusiastic preview.

Slated for a late spring 1993 release date, the film faced some fairly stiff competition from Steven Spielberg's *Jurassic Park; The Firm; Dennis the Menace; Hot Shots, Part Deux;* and *Cliffhanger* (with Stallone), but the marketing staff at Columbia left no stone unturned. Besides the traditional tie-ins with toy companies and fast-food chains, the studio tried unsuccessfully to pay NASA $500,000 to put Arnold Schwarzenegger's name and logo of the movie on a rocket headed into orbit in May (later delayed to August). *Last Action Hero* was ready for the summer box-office sweepstakes.

Critical Commentary

Less than one week before the premiere of his new feature, Arnold Schwarzenegger appeared on *Larry*

King Live (CNN) to head off some of the negative publicity that was aimed at *Last Action Hero*. Both *The Hollywood Reporter* and *Daily Variety* had come out with scathing reviews, calling it a "bomb" and criticizing the film's violence, numerous rewrites, and outrageous budget. Schwarzenegger defended himself, saying, "I don't think any one of the people who have written those things have seen the movie, because it was finished a week ago literally." Larry King called the movie "fantastic, a perfect summer movie. If you don't enjoy it, check your pulse—something is seriously wrong," but pressed the superstar for reasons why anyone would wish to sabotage his premiere.

"I think it was something to be expected," Arnold replied to his question very succinctly. "But I have never really done movies for the critics or for some of those inside writers. I always do movies for the movie audience and for the fans out there."

Originally scheduled for premiere on Friday, June 18, *Last Action Hero* was sneaked onto 2,500 screens Thursday evening for the fans in an effort to generate more ticket sales for the weekend sweeps, and took in more than $1 million in the advance showing. The weekend total, which was the fourth biggest opening of the year, was slightly over $15 million, topping the openings of both *Twins* and *Kindergarten Cop*. Unfortunately, *Last Action Hero* could

Heavily armed or not, Arnold Schwarzenegger is clearly a formidable presence.

only manage a small percentage of the grosses for Steven Spielberg's monstrous *Jurassic Park*. (In less than nine days, the dino-epic had topped the $100 million mark on its way to cinematic history.) By its second weekend, Arnold's movie was rapidly losing its muscle, having fallen to fourth place (with a disappointing $8 million take) behind *Dennis the Menace*, *Sleepless in Seattle*, and *Jurassic Park*.

The overall critical response to *Last Action Hero* was also mixed. Most fans and reviewers gave the film high marks for its special effects and extraordinary stunt work but seemed generally disappointed by the film as a whole. David Sheehan of NBC-TV wrote that "this is one phenomenal movie," and Gene Siskel called it "most ambitious," claiming to have "enjoyed chunks" of it, while Roger Ebert "found problems" in its duality, annoyed because the movie "constantly confuses you on the level of emotional involvement." Stephen Hunter of the *Baltimore Sun* called the motion picture the "first one not merely to acknowledge its own ludicrousness but to celebrate it, while at the same time gamely hoping to be the ultimate action movie."

If the final tally of *Last Action Hero* is considered a disappointment, then Arnold Schwarzenegger may have simply fallen victim to expectations raised by his past box-office performances in *Total Recall* and *Terminator 2: Judgment Day* and his own highly publicized predictions that he would top himself. These expectations and predictions are often the kinds of material that generate the negative buzz which sells newspapers. Media critics enjoy flexing their own muscles from time to time with this stuff, discrediting some celebrity one moment and then embracing him in the next. But that seems hardly fair when it is the motion picture (not the lead actor) that should be judged, and then solely on its own merits. Technically, *Last Action Hero* is brilliant, with its unique evocation of cinema's imaginary worlds and heroes and its parody of the action-adventure genre popularized by Schwarzenegger and others. The special effects, which allow Danny, Slater, and Benedict to move from one world to the other, are flawless, and help contribute to our willing suspension of disbelief. Schwarzenegger's appearance in the film as both the fictional Jack Slater and himself provides the actor with some of the best material of his career. As the kick-butt, hard-as-nails amalgam of

Dirty Harry, Martin Riggs, and John McClane, Arnold not only parodies the kinds of roles which have made him famous but also pays tribute to the heroes of our mythic past (immortalized by John Wayne and Clint Eastwood). As the tacky self-promoter who coincidentally happens to be a movie star, Schwarzenegger acknowledges his own limitations and pokes fun at the shallow image the press has created of him. While this movie may not be one of his best, it does rank as one of his most imaginative.

The motion picture also demonstrated a tremendous sense of wit that made it clearly a cut above most of its summer competition. Recognizing that the best genre movie is the one that parodies and criticizes its own conventions, like Clint Eastwood's *Unforgiven*, Schwarzenegger has his film pander to its audience's need for mindless violence while at the same time gaining points for political correctness. Arnold is very aware that the action-adventure films that made him a household hero are relics of a violent era which has passed and that he, like his on-screen persona, must begin "to lighten up." *Last Action Hero* is best when it raises questions about filmgoers' devotion to the genre and then addresses them coherently through (of all people) the movie character of Jack Slater.

With little doubt concerning the final less-than-spectacular receipts of *Last Action Hero*, Schwarzenegger still remains a highly sought after presence in front of the cameras. More than a dozen different projects have been linked to his name, and each one has the potential to break box-office records in the United States and in every major venue in the world. No other actor has had so much clout. His continued presence on the big screen is a welcome one. Unlike many of his screen contemporaries and rivals, including Jean-Claude Van Damme, Dolph Lundgren, Bruce Willis, Steven Seagal, and Sylvester Stallone, Arnold Schwarzenegger makes certain his adventures in film are not the bland artifacts of a production line or the thinly disguised rehash of another movie but rather the fruits of individual invention. The durability of his near-mythic characters and his flexibility as an actor have demonstrated time and again the superstar's appeal. Whether as actor, producer, or director, it's a good bet that Arnold Schwarzenegger will continue to be welcomed by his adoring fans and the moviegoing public.

SIXTEEN

TRUE LIES

1994. Twentieth Century-Fox, in association with Lightstorm Entertainment. Panavision (released in 70 mm, Dolby Stereo). *Director:* James Cameron. *Producers:* Cameron and Stephanie Austin. *Executive Producers:* Rae Sanchini, Robert Shriver, and Lawrence Kasanoff. *Screen Story by* Cameron and Randall Frakes. *Screenwriter:* James Cameron. *Based on characters created by* Claude Zidi, Simon Michael, and Didier Kaminka. *Music Composer:* Brad Fiedel. *Director of Photography:* Russell Carpenter. *Film Editors:* Mark Goldblatt, Conrad Buff, and Richard Harris. *Special Effects by* Digital Domain (under the supervision of Julia Gibson and Mike Chambers). *Special-Effects Supervisor:* John Bruno. *Production Designer:* Peter Lamont. *Stunt Coordinator:* Joel Kramer. *Starring:* Arnold Schwarzenegger, Jamie Lee Curtis, Tom Arnold, Bill Paxton, Art Malik, Tia Carrere, Eliza Dushku, Grant Heslov, and Charlton Heston. Released on July 15, 1994. [145 minutes]

James Cameron's *True Lies,* with Arnold Schwarzenegger perfectly cast in the role of a super-secret agent, is the best James Bond–type film that Albert R. Broccoli and Harry Salzman never made. Like the perfectly blended martini, the motion picture is quite often stirring (through its use of stunning special effects and spectacular stunt scenes) but never shaken. Even though the project was based on a much slighter French farce, the film still managed to transcend its humble origins to become one of the biggest box-office features of the year. It also helped rebuild the Austrian superstar's credibility after the poor reception of *Last Action Hero* (1993). More importantly, the film consolidated Cameron's dominance of the genre by proving that no one knows

Arnold Schwarzenegger is secret agent Harry Tasker, in James Cameron's *True Lies.* (Courtesy Twentieth Century-Fox)

how to stage action-adventure sequences better than he.

La Totale!

Members of an Arabic terrorist faction, known as the Crimson Jihad, threaten to detonate Soviet-made nuclear missiles in several U.S. cities if their extortionist demands are not met, and secret agent Harry Tasker must not only disarm the weapons but also rescue his failing marriage. While *True Lies* may sound like the typical action-adventure picture that only Hollywood and Jim Cameron could devise for the lucrative summer blockbuster season, the film was actually based on an earlier French comedy entitled *La Totale!* Written by Claude Zidi, Simon Michael, and Didier Kaminka, the slight farce was about a mild-mannered telecommunications worker (named François) who pretends to be a boring man when really he's a secret agent. The central conflict is that he's done such a good job of pretending that his wife, Helen, a mousy librarian who dreams of far-flung adventures, is nearly ready to leave him. The plot is further complicated by Helen's affair with Simon, a used-car salesman who poses as a spy to get women (but may well be the international terrorist François has been following). Eventually, the mild-mannered superagent discovers his wife's infidelity and uses her to infiltrate the terrorist group. They are both captured and flown to an Arab country as hostages. When François realizes that they have never left Paris, he devises an elaborate plan for their escape. François then reveals his true identity, and he and Helen live happily ever after.

The French film was not a tremendous success

213

Harry (Arnold Schwarzenegger) and Helen (Jamie Lee Curtis) Tasker share an intimate moment in the Florida Keys; from *True Lies*. (Courtesy Twentieth Century-Fox)

ing *Strange Days,* a futuristic technothriller, for his ex-wife, Kathryn Bigelow, and Twentieth Century-Fox. He was also having a baby with actress Linda Hamilton, his paramour at the time. But Schwarzenegger's interest in the little-known French film intrigued him. Cameron arranged for a private screening of *La Totale!* and liked the film enough to write an original treatment, which he subsequently submitted to Fox. Although the plot seem borrowed from the 1965 James Bond movie *Thunderball* (remade as *Never Say Never Again* in 1983), in which the terrorist group SPECTRE threatens to blow up two U.S. cities (one of them being Miami) with stolen NATO warheads, Cameron felt the story was strong enough and different enough from his previous work to be fun to make.

Jim explained his attraction to the film in a recent interview:

The film is not as big a picture as *Terminator Two*. It's a more complex picture on other levels because of the relationships and humor. But in terms of seeing that sort of stunning science-fiction image that existed only in your dreams previously—like the guy coming out of the linoleum floor in *Terminator Two*—that doesn't exist in this film. It takes our shared cultural fantasy from the sixties of what espionage was all about and has fun with it. It has a pop sensibility—the spy stuff I loved as a kid: James Bond, *The Man From U.N.C.L.E., I Spy.* But it's really a movie about relationships.

when it first debuted several years ago, but *La Totale!* left an indelible impression on Arnold Schwarzenegger when he saw it with his wife, Maria Shriver. He was hoping that James Cameron might be interested. But several weeks after the release of *Terminator 2: Judgment Day* (1991), Cameron told Schwarzenegger about his plans to make *The Crowded Room* with John Cusack. Cameron recalled:

Arnold and I also talked about making another picture together, but I had had my fill of big-budget, science-fiction, action-adventure films. I told him my next few films would not be genre pictures and that I was going to begin with a very modest picture and start broadening my base laterally instead of vertically.

Cameron wanted to be perceived as a filmmaker first and a genre filmmaker second and had purposely mapped out an artistic strategy for the future which included more mainstream films.

Nearly a year later, after failing to get *The Crowded Room* beyond the early stages of preproduction, the Canadian auteur again heard from Schwarzenegger. He called Jim and said, "I have the picture you have to do next." Now James Cameron's latest project may have stalled, but he was far from inactive. He had put the finishing touches on his own special-effects studio (Digital Domain) and was writ-

From the fall of 1992 to the spring of 1993, Cameron expanded on his original treatment, writing several different drafts of the script. While similar to its original source material, the final screenplay was clearly different. In fact, the most discernible difference was in the extensive background of the characters. Early in his development of the story, Jim Cameron concluded that only believable characters would help sell the extraordinary nature of the story. He wanted Harry (changed from François) and Helen Tasker to have a genuine relationship that had become strained because he was needed for these special assignments. Much of the stress that Cameron had experienced in his marriages to fellow professionals Gale Anne Hurd and Kathryn Bigelow provided him with the basis for his story.

Once Arnold Schwarzenegger had completed work on *Last Action Hero* (1993), he met with Cameron to discuss the picture and offer his input. Jim recalled their early strategy sessions about *True Lies:*

> When Arnold and I sat down to talk about this, we said, "We've gotta go big. We're gonna be compared to Bond pictures, and we have to deliver the goods,"

I viewed the film as a "domestic epic." It juxtaposes the guy's home life with his work. His wife doesn't have any clue what he does, but then she kind of gets sucked into that. Ultimately, the movie is about the unknowability of people and how that's a good thing if you are in a relationship.

The Screen Story

James Cameron's final shooting script for *True Lies* begins in Lake Champeau, Switzerland, at a luxurious château (familiar to fans of *The Dirty Dozen,* 1967). Harry Tasker (Schwarzenegger), the number-one operative for the Omega Sector, a supersecret CIA branch that combats nuclear terrorism, emerges through a hole in the ice in a frogman's wet suit, then sheds it to reveal a dapper tux (much like James Bond in *Goldfinger,* 1964). First rigging several explosive distractions, he penetrates the security of the château and infiltrates an exclusive party for rich art collectors and billionaire terrorists. Harry then slips upstairs and taps into a computer network for his partner, Albert "Gib" Gibson (Tom Arnold), and a decoding specialist (Grant Heslov). Suddenly, when Tasker's scuba gear is discovered, all hell breaks loose. Harry calmly drinks a glass of champagne, dances a tango with Juno Skinner (Tia Carrere), a beautiful but deadly art dealer, and walks out the front door. He then shoots and body-surfs his way out and down the snowy slopes, all with the wry detachment of an English poet holding forth on the art of the simile.

Several hours later, Harry arrives home in a sleepy suburb of Washington, D.C., and climbs in bed with his unsuspecting wife, Helen (Jamie Lee Curtis). She

Secret Agent Harry Tasker tangos with luscious but deadly Juno Skinner (Tia Carrere). (Courtesy Twentieth Century-Fox)

thinks that her husband is a boring computer salesman who must occasionally take business trips to Europe. Although they are evidently prosperous, live a solid, decent lifestyle, and have a beautiful fourteen year-old daughter, Dana (Eliza Dushku), his wife has grown bored with their fifteen-year marriage. That boredom apparently extends into the bedroom as well. The frustrated Helen fantasizes about other, more exciting men and soon becomes the *objet d'amour* of a sleazy used-car salesman, Simon (Bill Paxton), whose method of seduction is to tell his targets that he's really a secret agent; that, in fact, he's Harry! (He even takes credit for the handiwork Harry does.)

Meanwhile, back at headquarters, Harry's gruff section chief, Spencer Trilby (Charton Heston), chews out Tasker and Gib for a complete botch of the operation. Even though they were successful in tapping into the computer network, most of the information is useless. They were supposed to have found out who took possession of four stolen Soviet warheads. Harry refuses to accept defeat and reexamines each of the coded files until he discovers a possible link. Juno Skinner's name and art gallery figure predominantly in the terrorist files. He suspects that the terrorists are moving the weapons through her art consignments (mostly ancient Persian), but the only way to know for certain is to search her shop. Tasker pays her a visit under the ruse that he's shopping for antiquities,

215

Determined to stop terrorists from detonating a nuclear bomb in Miami, Harry Tasker (Arnold Schwarzenegger) pilots a "Harrier" jet to the rescue. (Courtesy Twentieth Century-Fox)

but Aziz (Art Malik), the terrorist leader of the Crimson Jihad, suspects Harry is a government spy.

En route home to his own birthday party, which Helen and Dana have prepared, Harry and Gib are followed by Arab hit men. Tasker turns the tables on the assassins in Georgetown in a men's room shoot-out that deconstructs a public facility into Swiss cheese. He then chases a motorcycle-mounted Aziz through Washington on a police officer's horse, through streets, hotel lobbies, and ultimately up elevators and onto rooftops in an astonishing, completely unbelievable but mesmerizing set piece. Finally, cornered on the roof of the Marriot, Aziz jumps his motorcycle into the rooftop pool of an adjacent building. Harry attempts to follow on horseback, but the horse throws him off. The secret agent should have thought twice about trying to jump a horse from one rooftop to the next.

Of course, by the time Harry Tasker does reach home for his party, both Helen and Dana are asleep. Harry has missed yet another special occasion. He tries to make up for the party by surprising Helen with an impromptu lunch date; but the surprise is on him: Helen has a date to meet with her mystery man. But Harry, who has no appreciation for irony, learns the truth about Simon—that he's nothing more than a used-car salesman—and utilizes the full force of his

agency to squash the affair and the little man. He catches Helen and Simon at a broken-down trailer park and uses his power as a secret agent to play an elaborate and extremely sadistic prank on his poor wife. Blackmailing her (through a secret guise) into taking the role, and performing some of the degrading acts, of a prostitute, he sends her on a "mission": She must seduce a double agent in order to plant a miniature transmitter. He then poses as the agent and watches her squirm (from the shadows) as she goes through the motions of a whore. Unfortunately for both Harry and Helen, the terrorists have been watching them very closely. They break into Tasker's suite and take them both hostage.

At first, Helen is shocked to learn the truth about her husband; then, angered beyond words, she strikes out at him, punching him squarely in the nose. Their fifteen-year marriage has been a total lie.

Aziz and Juno Skinner are momentarily amused by the Taskers' little marital spat, but now it's time to get down to business. The terrorist leader and his Crimson Jihad plan to detonate three of the four nuclear warheads in major cities if their demands are not met. And to prove that they mean what they say, the terrorists have armed the fourth one to explode on an island in the Florida Keys in less than two hours. Harry and Helen must save the world; their

216

marriage and mutual dishonesty are now secondary to the lives of millions of people. They expertly break free of their captors but are separated in a massive firefight with AK-47s, UZIs, and grenades. Harry Tasker jumps to safety—presumed dead—and Helen is again taken captive by Juno and Aziz. The terrorist leader quickly marshals his remaining forces, and they leave the island in both trucks and a helicopter. The fourth nuclear warhead is still ticking down to destruction.

Gib arrives with a Special Forces unit and rescues Harry from the island of doom. Once they have evacuated the locals to a safe distance, they concentrate on Aziz and the other terrorists. Two marine Harrier jets follow the terrorist truck convoy along the miles-long bridge through the Florida Keys and blow them apart. Harry, Gib, and a jet helicopter then catch up to Helen, in a speeding, driverless limousine, and pull her to safety (as Juno goes crashing into the water). But there's still one problem: Aziz has reached Miami with one of his nuclear warheads, and he's threatening to destroy the city if his demands are not taken seriously. He has also taken Dana Tasker hostage to ensure his own safety.

Without any thought to his own safety, Harry commandeers one of the Harrier jets and races to Miami to save her. He then manages to take out most of the terrorists with a blast from his weapons and pulls Dana aboard the craft. As the plane drifts in midair above the skyscraper, like a Chris Craft floating in a swimming pool, Harry and Aziz scamper about its dangerous contours for control of the bomb key. Tasker gains the upper hand and sends Aziz blasting into oblivion, attached to one of the jet's missiles.

One year later, the Tasker family is gathered around the dinner table, celebrating Harry's birthday, when the phone rings. The Omega Sector needs both Harry and Helen (using the code names Boris and Doris) to penetrate another posh château. The couple, dressed in formal attire, easily infiltrate the party but are surprised to see Simon, who's supposed to be working as a waiter, once again pretending to be a spy. They quickly dispatch the little man and proceed with their mission,

first drinking champagne and dancing a tango. Harry and Helen Tasker have become Mr. and Mrs. James Bond.

The Crew

Peter Lamont, who had worked with Cameron on *Aliens* (1986), was the Canadian auteur's first choice as production designer. Best known for his work on fourteen James Bond films, beginning as a draftsman on *Goldfinger* (1964) and graduating to production designer with *For Your Eyes Only* (1981), Lamont has been working in the industry for over thirty years. After graduating from architectural school, he was hired as a draftsman on *Waltz of the Toreadors* (1962) and a set designer on *Burn, Witch, Burn!* (1962). Those first experiences in film led to The *Sporting Life* (1963) and brought him to the attention of Albert R. Broccoli and Harry Saltzman. He apprenticed under the legendary Ken Adam on *Goldfinger* and quickly moved to set designer for *On Her Majesty's Secret Service* (1969). He was then nominated for his set-decoration work on *Fiddler on the Roof* (1971). Lamont moved up to art director for

Aziz (Art Malik), leader of the Crimson Jihad, threatens Harry and Helen Tasker (Jamie Lee Curtis). (Courtesy Twentieth Century-Fox)

217

Sleuth (1972), *The Dove* (1974), *The Man with the Golden Gun* (1975), *Inside Out* (1975), *The Seven Percent Solution* (1976), *The Boys From Brazil* (1978), *The Spy Who Loved Me* (1977, for which he was nominated for his second Academy Award), and *Moonraker* (1979). Broccoli recognized his obvious talent and turned him loose as a production designer on four of the last five James Bond movies, including *For Your Eyes Only* (1981), *Octopussy* (1983), *The Living Daylights* (1987), and *Licence to Kill* (1989). Peter was nominated for an Academy Award a third time for *Aliens* and has since completed extraordinary production designs for *Eve of Destruction* (1991) and *The Taking of Beverly Hills* (1991). Robert Laing and Mike Novotny, both art directors, were later called upon by Cameron to assist Lamont with the film.

Jim Cameron's brother Mike, who had worked the past fourteen years as an aeronautical engineer, was brought into the project to manage a number of the more difficult sequences involving the Harrier

In a scene cut from the release print, Helen Tasker (Jamie Lee Curtis) holds a live hand grenade in her lap. (Courtesy Twentieth Century-Fox)

jets. He also appears in the movie as the "citation" pilot. The noted stuntman and stunt coordinator Joel Kramer was also hired by Cameron to make each sequence appear flawless. Russell Carpenter, one of Hollywood's most brilliant cinematographers, was tapped to work as the director of photography.

The composition of the motion picture's music, which was to recall in many ways John Barry's James Bond themes and Jerry Goldsmith's score for *The Man From U.N.C.L.E.,* was awarded to another alumnus of James Cameron's films, Brad Fiedel. Fiedel, who began his career as a keyboard performer with Hall and Oates, had worked primarily in the horror and action-adventure genres before composing for such mainstream films as *The Big Easy* (1987) and *The Accused* (1988). His first score was for *Apple Pie* (1975), and that was eventually followed by scores for *Compromising Positions* (1985), *Fraternity Vacation* (1985), *Fright Night* (1985), *Desert Bloom* (1986), *Let's Get Harry* (1986), *Nowhere to Hide* (1987), *Mystic Pizza* (1988), *The Serpent and the Rainbow* (1988), *Fright Night II* (1989), *True Believer* (1989), *Encino Man* (1992), *Gladiator* (1992), and *Straight Talk* (1992). For Cameron, he had composed scores for both *The Terminator* (1984) and its big-budget sequel, *Terminator 2: Judgment Day* (1991).

True Lies was the first motion picture produced under Jim Cameron and Larry Kasanoff's $500 million deal with Twentieth Century-Fox. Even though Cameron has resisted the label, his film may well be the most expensive picture ever made. Its original budget of $60.5 million quickly escalated to $90 million, then $120 million, and Lightstorm Entertainment was unable to find a completion-bond company to insure them. Cameron and coproducer Stephanie Austin eventually arranged for massive financing from the studio on a production-finance deal. But in order to retain the rights to the film, they were responsible for repayment of cost overruns, while Fox functioned like a bank, extending credit in exchange for the rights to distribute the motion picture. Fox soon learned that the film would nearly double in cost and threw out all the numbers. "Once we learned that there were logistical problems," explained Jon Landau, senior vice president in charge of feature production, "we knew that the production would run well over its estimated budget. We also knew we weren't going to make that schedule."

Cameron and Austin faced not only escalating costs but also production delays. They soon found themselves having to negotiate for additional time.

Trapped in a Georgetown men's room, Agent Tasker shoots it out with enemy agents. (Courtesy Twentieth Century-Fox)

Twentieth Century-Fox did not want a repeat of *The Abyss* and insisted the film be ready for release early in the summer of 1994, possibly the lucrative Fourth of July weekend. Landau eventually relented, extending the release date by two weeks. (That extension was also calculated to give Fox's other big release, *Wyatt Earp,* enough time to recoup its enormous budget.) They had originally agreed to a shooting schedule of twenty weeks, but Cameron needed (at least) twenty-four weeks, with a minimum of five months for post production. Jim actually shot 130 days, although sources close to the production claim that that number is actually very conservative. (The rumor is 180 days.) The location shooting was divided between Rhode Island, Georgetown and Washington, D.C., Miami and the Florida Keys, and Los Angeles.

During the early stages of preproduction, Arnold Schwarzenegger's *Last Action Hero* was released and died a horrible death at the box office. The movie was savaged by critics and was a major box-office disappointment to the Austrian superstar. James Cameron confessed that he was

> At first ... a little nervous. But then I started thinking about why *Last Action Hero* didn't work. My current theory is that it totally stopped outside and looked in on and made fun of the audiences who were willing to invest in Arnold—essentially, it was ridiculing the very fans it was hoping to attract.

Jim was determined that he didn't want to make that same mistake.

The Special Effects

Even though *True Lies* was not touted as a big special-effects film, like *The Abyss* (1989) or *Terminator 2: Judgment Day* (1991), there were, in fact, an extensive amount of visuals. Nearly six months of special effects, matte paintings, and model photography were completed by several facilities in California, over three thousand miles away from his locations in the East. James Cameron decided to divide the visual effects between several different facilities because they were not only so extensive but also because Twentieth Century-Fox wanted the film ready for a summer release. He relied on his old friends at Fantasy II to complete a number of key effects and called upon Image, Pacific Data, Cinesite Digital, and Boss Film Corporation for specific sequences.

Because his favorite facility, Industrial Light and Magic, was already engaged in a number of projects, including *Forrest Gump* (1994) for Robert Zemekis, Cameron gathered a group of technicians together to form his own special-effects company called Digital Domain. The notion of "domesticating the highfalutin digital effect" so that even the most technophobic filmmaker could use it, Jim recalls, came to him while he was driving one of his fast sports cars. He hired Scott Ross, one of Industrial Light and Magic's com-

Helen Tasker (Jamie Lee Curtis) models the latest in secret-agent apparel. (Courtesy Twentieth Century-Fox)

puter whizzes, and offered IBM a share of the company. The famous computer company leaped at the opportunity and pitched in both money and machines. Digital Domain's first assignment was *True Lies* (1994), for which it provided miniatures, mattes, composites, and digital enhancements of the visual effects. Nearly all of the special effects were supervised by John Bruno and his team, including Julia Gibson and Mike Chambers of Digital Domain and Cameron himself. Bruno had worked for Jim on *The Abyss* and won the coveted Academy Award for special visual effects that year. His highly complex understanding of effects and his technical wizardry contributed to many of the breathtaking sequences that took place in the motion picture. Bruno had worked for both Industrial Light & Magic and the Boss Film Corporation (on *Ghostbusters*, 1984), and he was very capable of coordinating the various effects units.

The Cast

Arnold Schwarzenegger was still the number-one box-office draw in the world when he and Cameron decided to make *True Lies*. Schwarzenegger had first

met the Canadian amateur nearly ten years before, during the preproduction phase of *The Terminator* (1984), and they hit it right off. In the intervening years, he had become one of the most successful actors in Hollywood, with a string of action-adventure pictures. Two of his most recent films, *Total Recall* (1990) and *Terminator 2: Judgment Day* (1991), had become moneymaking bonanzas. He had also successfully demonstrated his penchant for comedy with *Twins* (1988) and *Kindergarten Cop* (1990). Even though his previous film, *Last Action Hero* (1993), had been a major disappointment at the box office, Schwarzenegger still had enough clout in Hollywood to green-light his own pictures. He had, in fact, already committed to two other potential blockbusters (Ivan Reitman's *Junior,* with Danny DeVito, and Paul Verhoven's *Crusades*). When he first approached Jim Cameron with the remake of *La Totale!* there was no question (at all) who would play the lead.

The part of the secret agent's loving but essentially unaware wife went to Jamie Lee Curtis, who had been one of the leading actresses considered for the role of Lindsey Brigman in *The Abyss* (1989). Curtis, the daughter of Janet Leigh and Tony Curtis, was born on November 22, 1958, in Los Angeles and educated at the University of the Pacific, in Stockton, California. She worked on a double major in prelaw and drama and easily made the transition to the big screen. Her first big break as a performer was in John Carpenter's *Halloween* (1978); she continued playing the terrified but capable heroine in a series of low-budget horror films, including Carpenter's *Fog* (1980), *Prom Night* (1980), *Terror Train* (1980), *Halloween II,* and *Road Games* (1981). Jamie proved that she could play both an attractive and capable leading lady by starring as the ill-fated *Playboy* centerfold in the made-for-television movie *The Dorothy Stratten Story* (1982). After that film debuted on television, she began to get offers for more prestigious projects, and her career took off. She made *Love Letters* (1983), *Trading Places* (1983) (with Eddie Murphy and Dan Aykroyd), *The Adventures of Buckaroo Banzai Across the Eighth Dimension* (1984) (with Peter Weller and Jeff Goldblum), *Grandview,* U.S.A. (1984), *Perfect* (1985) (with John Travolta), *Amazing Grace and Chuck* (1987) (with Gregory Peck), *A Man in Love* (1987), and *Dominick and Eugene* (1988) (with Ray Liotta). Curtis demonstrated that she could handle comedy opposite John Cleese in *A Fish Called Wanda* (1988) and drama as a policewoman who gets romantically involved with a psychotic killer in Kathryn Bigelow's *Blue Steel* (1990). She reteamed with Dan Aykroyd for *My Girl* (1991) and its sequel and was featured with Mel Gibson in *Forever Young* (1992). Her role in *True Lies* not only provided Jamie Lee Curtis with the opportunity to combine comedy and drama opposite Schwarzenegger; it also gave her the chance to perform her own stunts.

Tom Arnold also brought an impressive body of stage and television work to his characterization of Gib, Schwarzenegger's wisecracking sidekick. Arnold was a rising star in the late seventies and eighties at various clubs on the Los Angeles comedy circuit. The stand-up comedian then met and married Roseanne Barr in 1989 and made the transition from nightclubs to television with *The Jackie Thomas Show* (1993) and *Tom* (1993). Regrettably, Tom and Roseanne's turbulent marriage and highly publicized divorce cast a pail over his impressive work for Jim Cameron.

The well-known character actor Bill Paxton was cast, partially for comic relief, in the role of Simon, Jamie Lee Curtis's mystery man. Paxton (like Schwarzenegger, Michael Biehn, and Lance Henriksen) had worked with Cameron several times before and over the course of several years had become very good friends with the Canadian director. In fact, Cameron had recently shot a music video, featuring Kathryn Bigelow, for Bill in his backyard in order to promote Paxton's band. At one point, he even used an ultralight plane to get a dangerous but extremely effective shot. Born in Fort Worth, Texas, Paxton first began working in motion pictures as a set decorator for Roger Corman on *Big Bad Mama* (1974) and *Darktown Strutters* (1975). He was working behind the scenes when Jonathan Demme offered him a bit part in *Crazy Mama* (1975). Other roles in a handful of forgettable motion pictures followed. Cameron remembered his face from several of those films and cast him as a street punk in *The Terminator* and a wisecracking soldier in *Aliens* (1986), which earned him much critical praise. Paxton would later star opposite Henriksen in *Near Dark* (1987) and Biehn in *Navy Seals* (1990) and *Tombstone* (1993). Other featured performances have included *Predator 2* (1990), *The Dark Backward* (1991), and *Future Shock* (1993).

For the pivotal role of Spencer Trilby, the Omega Sector's eye-patched administrator, Cameron called upon one of the silver screen's great actors, Charlton Heston. Born on October 4, 1924, and educated at Northwestern University, in Chicago, Heston has been a commanding male lead in motion pictures for over fifty years. His righteous, highly driven, and intelligent roles in several biblical epics, most notably *The Ten Commandments* (1956) and *Ben Hur* (1959), for which he won an Academy Award as Best Actor, made him a star in the late fifties. Other turns in *The Greatest Show on Earth* (1952), *The Naked Jungle* (1954), *The Far Horizons* (1955), *The Big Country* (1958), *El Cid* (1961), *55 Days at Peking* (1963), *The Agony and the Ecstasy* (1965), *The Greatest Story Ever Told* (1965), *Major Dundee* (1965), *The War Lord* (1965), *Will Penny* (1968), *Julius Caesar* (1970), *The Three Musketeers* (1974), *The Four Musketeers* (1975), and *Midway* (1976) demonstrated not only his versatility as an actor but also his longevity as a performer who has reached across many generations. He started directing in 1972 with *Anthony and Cleopatra* and was a six-term president of the Screen Actors Guild. Like Schwarzenegger, Charlton Heston has remained active in politics as a staunch Republican and served as cochairman of Ronald Reagan's Task Force on the Arts and Humanities. Science-fiction fans remember his superb work in such genre favorites as *Planet of the Apes* (1968), *Beneath the Planet of the Apes* (1970), *The Omega Man* (1971), *Soylent Green* (1973), *Earthquake* (1974), *The Awakening* (1980), *Call From Space* (1989), and *Solar Crisis* (1990). Heston's role as the cantankerous, one-eyed bureau chief of the supersecret agency in *True Lies* may well be one of his most remembered performances.

Exotic Tia Carrere, fresh from her featured role opposite Sean Connery and Wesley Snipes in *Rising Sun* (1993), was the perfect choice for the mysterious art dealer Schwarzenegger is called upon to seduce. Art Malik, who had appeared as an Afghanistan freedom fighter in *The Living Daylights* (1987), was cast as Aziz, the Muslim terrorist and bad guy. Grant Heslov and Eliza Dushku helped round out the cast and provided fresh new faces to important roles.

Production Details

Principal photography on *True Lies* was scheduled to begin late in May 1993 at studios in Santa Clarita, a facility thirty miles outside Los Angeles, with fairly routine shots in the Tasker household. But when word reached the production office that *Last Action Hero*—currently in postproduction across town at Sony Studios with Arnold Schwarzenegger—was in trouble and would require additional photography, Jim Cameron naturally became concerned about his production. Schwarzenegger could not make the film's starting date and would now be unavailable for the first few weeks of principal photography. (Cameron had experienced a similar delay with Sigourney Weaver during his work on *Aliens*.) Stephanie Austin reminded Jim that in order to be ready for an early summer 1994 release, they needed to begin shooting no later than the middle of June 1993. Since so much of the project revolved around Arnold's participation, the Canadian auteur was left in a real quandary. He revised his carefully worked out shooting schedule, postponing his start for several weeks.

When Schwarzenegger finally arrived on the set, shortly after the release of *Last Action Hero*, he did not appear to be bothered by the disappointing returns of his latest film. The Austrian superstar was, in fact, well toned and anxious to begin work on the new project. Cameron told Joshua Mooney of *Movieline:*

> The only reaction I could perceive from Arnold—and I've worked with him for ten years—was that he decided he wanted to go less toward comedy and more toward hard action, which was basically a retrenchment for him. Now, my only interest in *True Lies* was to do comedy. Action to me is boring, in and of itself, unless it can be contextualized. So I said no, we have to go for it. We have to pop the jokes.

Arnold Schwarzenegger trusted his opinion and knew intuitively that he was right. Because *True Lies* had been billed as an action-comedy, he agreed to play it Jim's way.

Actual filming began during some of the hottest days on record in Santa Clarita with some interior scenes between Schwarzenegger and his costar Jamie Lee Curtis. "[The first scene] was just two people getting ready for work, that wonderful dance that married people do where they're oblivious to each other," Curtis recalled. But even though the air-conditioning units were working at full capacity, the heat wave actually affected conditions on the set. For three weeks, while they established Harry and Helen's relationship in a linear collection of scenes, the shooting captured the perspiration and exertion Schwarzenegger and Curtis felt on the set. That edgy, nervous tension may have actually worked to their benefit to convey the tension in their screen marriage.

For four days in a row, Jim Cameron also had Jamie Lee Curtis prepare for her striptease. In the movie, Helen is blackmailed by her husband (in a secret guise) into taking the role, and performing some of the degrading acts of a prostitute; she then is sent on a "mission" to seduce a double agent in order to plant a miniature transmitter. Harry poses as the agent and watches her squirm (from the shadows) as she goes through the motions of a whore. The actress told *Entertainment Tonight* that she prepared herself for the striptease: "I did what anybody would do if they were going to dance around in a G-string and bra in front of fifty men for four days in a row: I didn't eat very much for a month!" The kinky scene is one of the most hilarious pieces in the movie, and Cameron's crew shot the sequence like a trashy piece that had been inspired by the classic works of film noir.

Early in the fall, the immense production moved to Washington, D.C. (specifically Georgetown) in a traveling-circus caravan of trucks. Fans lined the streets for hours waiting for an opportunity to watch Schwarzenegger and his costars work. A major sequence photographed during this period was the chase scene. "It was not an ordinary scene with car crashes," Schwarzenegger reminded his public. "Imagine riding a horse through a hotel lobby and into an elevator, going up the elevator with the horse and people in tuxedos and dresses, then going onto the roof." Outside the men's room, where Harry has managed to turn the tables on assassins, he races after Aziz. He ends up chasing the motorcycle-mounted terrorist through Georgetown on a policeman's horse, through the streets and into the lobby of the Mayfair Hotel and Marriot Marquis. Joel Kramer and his stunt crew were largely responsible for staging this sequence, with Arnold performing most of his own stunts. Subsequent scenes, featuring Tom Arnold (as Gib), were also filmed on some of the same locations, including the Georgetown Park Mall. All of the sequences were also filmed with a video camera so that Jim could personally review each shot. If the shot was less than perfect, he would order another take, sometimes working long hours into the night.

As the scope of the film expanded and the production began falling behind its shooting schedule, the stress level began to rise. Cameron demanded that his crew give more than 120 percent of their time, attention, and creativity. He would order his people together and talk to them via a loudspeaker, like a drill sergeant. To keep things moving, he even forbade them to take restroom breaks, which caused additional tension. One day, the production crew arrived wearing T-shirts with the semihumorous slogan You Can't Scare Me—I Work for Jim Cameron. Jim knew that he was expecting a great deal from them, but he was also aware of the stakes if they failed to deliver the project on time. "I did not actually sanction this," he responded. "I found out about it after they'd been wearing them, and I thought, Well, I don't want to draw attention to it by pulling them off the field." He was very good-natured about the joke, and he allowed them to continue wearing the shirts for the rest of the shoot.

After several weeks of intensive shooting in the nation's capital, Cameron and his crew moved to Florida to film two important set pieces: the chase scene on Florida's Seven-Mile Bridge and the Harrier jet attack on a Miami high-rise. To complete the actual filming, the production was forced to close off sections of the bridge, which connects Miami with the Keys, for two weeks. During the sequence, Helen Tasker must free herself from the Arab terrorists, climb onto the roof of an out-of-control limousine, and take the hand of her husband, who is hanging out of a moving helicopter. A stunt woman was hired for the most dangerous parts of the sequence, but for the final stunt Cameron convinced Curtis to perform it herself. "It" involved dangling from a wire under the helicopter a hundred feet off the water. "Will you be up there with me?" she asked, and his reply was that he would be the one shooting the scene. Both of them ended up "hanging out of the helicopter with nothing but the Seven-Mile Bridge and lots of water and manta rays" below.

The massive assault on the Miami high-rise by the Harrier jet was the production's most difficult shoot in the entire project. But the stunningly authentic illusion was done entirely on camera (with no computer morphing or special effects). By suspending an actual Harrier aircraft from a crane thirty stories up, they produced one of the best pure adrenaline sequences of all time. For three weeks, Cameron and his crew filmed with every camera and piece of equipment they had. "The first time I saw that, my jaw dropped," Jamie Lee Curtis said. "They took a real Harrier jet and mounted it on top of a hydraulic–it looked like an upside-down spider, with all there legs moving up and down." The numerous setups went flawlessly, without a single production glitch. When filming wrapped for the Christmas holiday break, the cast and crew were in very high spirits, having rebounded nicely from the earlier tension of the shoot.

By the time the cast and crew returned from their holiday break, the production was ready to move from Florida to Newport, Rhode Island. Unfortunately, many local activists, led by Maureen O'Neil, complained to the press that they didn't "particularly want [their] neighborhood simulating Sarajevo." They protested the violence inherent in Schwarzenegger films and made the final months of shooting difficult. In fact, the city council had to call for a special vote to grant an exemption from the city's noise ordinance. The vote was very close, but in the end, Jim Cameron and his project prevailed.

Finally, in March 1994, with the final shots of Schwarzenegger penetrating the château having just been completed, principal photography on *True Lies* wrapped. A week later, Cameron and his three editors (Mark Goldblatt, Conrad Buff, and Richard Harris) went to work. Jim knew that he not only had to cut thousands of feet of raw film down into a workable, two-hour time frame; he also had to combine the special-effects footage seamlessly into the whole. He also knew that he had less than three months to complete his postproduction work.

Critical Commentary

True Lies sent its competition running for cover when it first hit theaters on July 15, 1994. In its initial week of American release, the movie knocked Disney's *Lion King* and Robert Zemekis's *Forrest Gump* off the top of the charts, grossing an incredible $25.9 million. The action-adventure comedy also inflicted serious box-office damage on the summer's other big winners, including *Speed, Blown Away, I Love Trouble, The Shadow,* and *The Flintstones.* Audiences and critics alike praised the film for its high-energy sequences and welcomed Arnold Schwarzenegger's return to the genre that made him famous. David Ansen of *Newsweek* called the movie "a gargantuan thrill machine," and Jim Ferguson of KMSB-TV/FOX claimed that it was "the roller-coaster ride of the decade." Stephen Hunter of the *Baltimore Sun* was perhaps the most astute of critics, writing, "What compels [this movie] is the stunning dynamism with which it is delivered. Arnold is not only Arnold, but a good director, such as James Cameron, is a smoke." In spite of negative criticism from certain Arab groups, which objected to being portrayed as stereotypical, fanatic terrorists, *True Lies* continued to do bang-up business throughout the rest of the summer movie season.

This comic suspense thriller is, with little doubt, a superbly crafted pastiche of the James Bond films as well as other spy series. In fact, its high-powered plot is really an amalgram of the most familiar elements from the espionage fantasies of the 1960s. The opening sequence, in which Harry penetrates the defenses of a château in a frogman's wet suit, then sheds it to reveal a dapper tuxedo, seems borrowed (almost frame by frame) from *Goldfinger* (1964), while the subsequent chase down the snowy Swiss slopes combines the acrobatic nihilism of *On Her Majesty's Secret Service* (1969) and *For Your Eyes Only* (1981). The nuclear weapons' threat by a terrorist organization is also a familiar plot device from *Thunderball* (1965) and a dozen other series, including *The Man From U.N.C.L.E.* (1965). One of the best gags, and totally irrelevant to the story, is the shoot-out in a Georgetown men's room; it recalls an earlier confrontation between Derek Flint and enemy agents in *Our Man Flint* (1966). The screwball zaniness of a Hepburn-Tracy comedy, *Romancing the Stone* (1984), and *Jewel of the Nile* (1985) also provide the template for Harry and Helen's struggle with the terrorists. And finally, the dizzying finale, in which Tasker and Aziz scamper about the dangerous contours of the Harrier jet in midair for control of the bomb key and Dana's life, seems cribbed from Alfred Hitchcock's *North by Northwest* (1959), *Octopussy* (1983), and *A View to a Kill* (1985).

What compels this homage to the superagent clichés of the 1960s is the stunning dynamism with which it is delivered by Jim Cameron. Cameron knows how to stage action sequences better than any other director, and he moves audiences from set piece to set piece with a smooth, sophisticated visual style that is clearly light-years ahead of his contemporaries. But no matter how spectacular each set piece is, Cameron always manages to top himself with the next. His final sequence is literally unbelievable, yet we know that the illusion is stunningly real (done entirely on camera, without the aide of special effects). The brilliance of his imagery and skillfully controlled rhythm is all-absorbing. He also manages to tell an interesting story about two people who are married to, but know very little about, each other. The story of Harry and Helen Tasker may well be an extention of his marriages to Gale Anne Hurd and Kathryn Bigelow or his relationship with Linda Hamilton; but there is still something in the core of the piece that resonates with universal truth. For example, when the Taskers are imprisoned on the tropical island, the audience intuitively understands that there's something much more at stake than the deaths of millions of innocent people—the outcome of Harry and Helen's marriage.

Cameron's film is also cleverly constructed around its oxymoronic title; "true lies" is, in fact, a pointedly foolish, contradictory phrase that often reveals a deeper insight. At first glance, the story may appear to be simply a send-up of spy thrillers, but it is also a biting commentary on the many incongruities that exist in a person's life and relationships. Each character in the film lives a secret life, and the lies they tell about themselves are also true. Harry Tasker appears to be the archetypal loving husband and father, and computer geek; in reality, however, he is also a government agent. Helen is a loving wife and mother who dreams of a little excitement in her life; her illicit romance with the used-car dealer and the subsequent penance she must pay when that affair is discovered provide her with a secret life. Dana Tasker also masquerades as a loving daughter when, in fact, she is a thief. Simon, the used-car dealer, carries on the most ridiculous charade of all, pretending to be a secret agent in order to sleep with lonely housewives. When each of the masks are finally stripped away, the "truth" behind the lies reveals that all of us—to one extent or another—build constructs (or fictions) so that our lives seem much more interesting than they really are.

The complexity of the central character in *True Lies,* who is both a hero and a common man, requires Arnold Schwarzenegger to demonstrate his considerable talents as an actor. Harry Tasker is an incredibly complex character whose personal and private lives are slowly merging into one. For the role of Tasker, Arnold must not only be fearless but also slightly vulnerable, average, and boring. In one sequence, he is asked to turn the tables on a trio of assassins in a men's room shoot-out in Georgetown. Then, less than a few minutes later, he must appear in his suburban home as an overworked computer salesman who has just missed his birthday party. This moment, somewhat lightened by Tasker's response to his wife's love pats, places the actor squarely in a difficult situation that other, lesser talents would not have played as convincingly. Tasker, the loving but neglectful husband, is not really certain how he's supposed to be responding to his wife, as if his actions are, in fact, beyond his secret-agent persona, and Arnold manages to convey his confusion, his awkwardness, and his uncertainly with considerable skill.

In a rare behind-the-scenes photograph, Director James Cameron jokes with Arnold Schwarzenegger and Jamie Lee Curtis prior to a take. (Courtesy Twentieth Century-Fox)

And when Harry Tasker is called upon to combat nuclear terrorists, Schwarzenegger combines the subtleties of his killer robot from *The Terminator* with his characters from *Raw Deal* and *The Running Man* to create a memorable secret agent. It again takes a certain amount of skill to play the darker side of an essentially good character. Ironically, while Arnold was making *True Lies* for Jim Cameron, his name was being considered (perhaps tongue in cheek) with a group of other actors for the role of Ian Fleming's James Bond. Most Bond fans, of course, did not take him seriously, and Pierce Brosnan ultimately won the role, beating out Liam Neeson, Ralph Fiennes, Hugh Grant, Sharon Stone, Sylvester Stallone, and Schwarzenegger. But after seeing Arnold in action, and in a dapper tuxedo, as Harry Tasker (his role as secret agent Douglas Quaid in *Total Recall,* 1990, notwithstanding), he would have made a superb 007.

Jamie Lee Curtis, in the role of Helen Tasker, also succeeds with the daunting task of playing opposite Schwarzenegger and thousands of exploding bombs. When we first meet Helen, she is a mousy legal secretary who dreams of a more exciting life. Later, after she has been caught and blackmailed by her husband, Helen clumsily discards her demure suburbanite for a hilariously sexy prostitute. When she is finally liberated by the truth, she teams up with Harry and demonstrates her ability to outshoot and outpunch her husband. Curtis is both delightful and believable in the role. Similar kudos belong to Tom Arnold, in a winning role as Schwarzenegger's sidekick, and Bill Paxton, as the sleazy used-car dealer who seduces women by pretending to be a spy.

True Lies is truly a winner for both Schwarzenegger and Jim Cameron, and that is no lie. The film was released on both videocassette and laser disc by Twentieth Century-Fox Home Video early in 1995.

FROM IVAN REITMAN, THE DIRECTOR OF "GHOSTBUSTERS," "TWINS" AND "DAVE."
ARNOLD SCHWARZENEGGER
DANNY DEVITO
EMMA THOMPSON
Nothing is inconceivable.
AN IVAN REITMAN FILM
JUNIOR
UNIVERSAL PICTURES PRESENTS A NORTHERN LIGHTS PRODUCTION ARNOLD SCHWARZENEGGER DANNY DEVITO EMMA THOMPSON "JUNIOR" FRANK LANGELLA PAMELA REED MUSIC BY JAMES NEWTON HOWARD COSTUME DESIGNER ALBERT WOLSKY CO-PRODUCERS NEAL NORDLINGER GORDON WEBB EDITED BY SHELDON KAHN A.C.E. WENDY GREENE BRICMONT A.C.E. PRODUCTION DESIGNER STEPHEN LINEWEAVER DIRECTOR OF PHOTOGRAPHY ADAM GREENBERG A.S.C. EXECUTIVE PRODUCERS JOE MEDJUCK DANIEL GOLDBERG AND BEVERLY J. CAMHE WRITTEN BY KEVIN WADE AND CHRIS CONRAD
PG-13 PARENTS STRONGLY CAUTIONED
DUE NOVEMBER 23RD
PRODUCED AND DIRECTED BY IVAN REITMAN A UNIVERSAL PICTURE
UNIVERSAL

SEVENTEEN

JUNIOR

Universal Pictures, in association with Northern Lights Entertainment. *Producer-Director:* Ivan Reitman. *Screenplay:* Kevin Wade and Chris Conrad. *Starring:* Arnold Schwarzenegger, Danny DeVito, Emma Thompson, and Frank Langella. Released on November 23, 1994.

Junior (1994), Arnold Schwarzenegger's third collaborative effort with producer-director Ivan Reitman, reteamed the superstar with his *Twins* costar Danny DeVito for deliciously hilarious results. Based on an original story by Kevin Wade and Chris Conrad, it also provided Schwarzenegger with another opportunity to flex his comedic muscles. His role as the misguided geneticist who becomes pregnant in order to test a new drug required him to walk a fine line between self-parody and genuine comedy. Although the motion picture was released into the crowded field of holiday favorites, *Junior* proved to be a genuine crowd pleaser and box-office giant.

Arnold told reporters during his publicity tour for *Junior:*

> The only one who could do this is me. I really felt that. If Billy Crystal does it, it would be expected of him. You see comedians like Billy Crystal try to be pregnant, and way after that there is *Mrs. Doubtfire* and Robin Williams. That's the typical way of going—you give it to one of those guys. To really make it unique, to make it funny, it had to be someone like me who does it.

Poster from *Junior,* an Ivan Reitman film starring Arnold Schwarzenegger, Danny DeVito, and Emma Thompson. (Courtesy Universal Pictures, in association with Northern Lights Entertainment)

The Screen Story

Dr. Alexander Hesse (Arnold Schwarzenegger), a distinguished scientist in his mid-forties, has developed a new drug called Expectane, which assists tissue adherence in miscarriage-prone women. Together with his diminutive partner Dr. Larry Arbogast (Danny DeVito), a gynecologist, he tries to convince the Food and Drug Administration (FDA) to grant him approval to test the drug on humans. The Investigational Board, chaired by a woman, is not convinced the antimiscarriage drug is ready for human testing and refuses to grant their request. Hesse is gravely disappointed and returns to Leland University in Southern California a broken man.

Upon his return to the Stanford-Lufkin Biotechnology Research Center, Hesse learns from Dr. Adam Flusser (Frank Langella), the head of the center, that his grant has been terminated. Alex must vacate the premises immediately to make room for Dr. Diana Reddin (Emma Thompson), a beautiful geneticist in her mid-thirties, formerly of the Genome Atlas Project. Flusser is not only convinced that her research into the genetic makeup of unfertilized human eggs will bring the research center much prestige; he has also simply grown tired of Hesse's work. Unwittingly, Hesse rescues his new rival from a mishap in the laboratory and falls madly in love with Reddin. She, too, is quite taken with the scientist and offers to share the valuable lab space with him. Hesse is noncommittal. Meanwhile, Larry has learned some disturbing news of his own. His ex-wife, Angela, is pregnant by some stranger (after many years of trying to impregnate her himself), and she wants Larry to be her doctor.

227

Danny DeVito plays Arnold Schwarzenegger's partner Dr. Larry Arbogast, a gynecologist who is helping market an antimiscarriage drug in *Junior*. (Courtesy Cinema Archives)

Still distraught over the hearing, Hesse makes several unsuccessful attempts to kill himself, but Larry literally pulls him back from the edge. They decide to test the drug without FDA approval, and Alex volunteers to act as the guest host. The two scientists plan to implant a fertilized egg on the omentum in Dr. Hesse's abdomen, dose him with Expectane, and record the results through only the first trimester. (Edward Jenner, after all, infected himself with smallpox in order to test his vaccine, and he won a Nobel Prize.)

Larry Arbogast breaks into Reddin's freezer at the research center and steals a test tube labeled "Junior." Then, unthawing the unfertilized egg, he injects a sample of Alex's sperm. The two naturally join, and he implants the now-fertilized egg into his partner. Hesse is placed on a regimented "diet" of female hormones and Expectane. Over the course of time, Alex begins complaining about morning sickness, cramps, nausea, lethargy, repeated trips to the bathroom, and swollen nipples. He also starts to gain excessive weight and begins experiencing nightmares in which he gives birth to a one-to-one copy of himself. Diana Reddin recognizes how distracted Alex seems all of the time and asks if she can help. Larry makes up an elaborate story to explain Hesse's condition, calling it "Gelandesprung syndrome," a condition of "fatness" which strikes only men from his native country. Satisfied, Reddin complains that men are such babies and that they could never survive the rigors of womanhood.

As the end of the first trimester nears, Alex begins to express doubts about ending the pregnancy; in fact, he is actually determined to keep the baby. Larry tries unsuccessfully to discourage him. At Arbogast's office, Alex's determination to have the child carries into the waiting room and startles his patients. He has to tell the other expectant mothers that he's really treating a mental patient. The ladies try to humor Alex, asking him if he wants a boy or a girl. At the research center, Flusser has discovered irregularities in the manufacture of Expectane.

The romance between Alex and Diana begins to heat up as they meet for dinner, then drinks, and finally lovemaking at the home he now shares with Arbogast. Their romantic interlude is cut short, however, when Angela arrives to speak with Larry. Diana leaves, feeling very embarrassed by her carnal behavior. The next day, Hesse and his partner are interrupted at the mall, shopping for maternity clothes, by Dr. Flusser. He suspects they have disobeyed the FDA and are experimenting with the antimiscarriage drug on a human subject. He doesn't want to turn them in to the FDA; instead, he seeks cocredit. Alex and Larry deny they are working on anything.

Later, over an intimate candelit dinner for two, Hesse tries to tell Diana Reddin the truth about his condition, but she mistakes his overtures for subtle inquiries about her own fertility. The geneticist reveals that she has frozen one of her own unfertilized eggs, under the code name "Junior," for future fertilization. This revelation nauseates Hesse. (Apparently, Alex has been lied to by Larry, who claimed to have taken "Junior" from a UCLA colleague.) He finally finds the courage to tell her that he's pregnant with her egg, and she explodes: "You lie to me, you steal from me, you take away my dignity and mock my womanhood .... This is just so male!" Flusser bursts in on them and triumphantly grabs Alexander Hesse for tests. He now intends to take sole credit for what he calls the greatest discovery of mankind, but the scientist is much too slippery for him to hold. The pregnant man escapes two musclebound orderlies and, with the help of Larry Arbogast, checks into a prenatal retreat in Carmel under the alias "Alexandra." He plans to remain there throughout the pregnancy and, with the help of Larry and Angela, hide his true identity. But Alex can't seem to get Diana off his mind; he's in love with her and fears that she may no longer want to have anything to do with him.

Eventually, Diana Reddin thaws. She realizes that Alex was duped by his friend and would have never purposely hurt her. Once the geneticist arrives at the retreat, she spells out the rules for cosharing the baby and keeping it a secret from the world. She also insists on having sex with Alex: "Call me old-fashioned, but I'll be damned if I'm having a kid with a man I've never slept with." The two scientists consummate their relationship, at last, and wait out the pregnancy.

During the next few weeks, several events happen almost simultaneously. Based on their preliminary data, Larry arranges for a Canadian pharmaceutical firm to purchase the rights to Expectane. Dr. Adam Flusser continues with his investigation and alerts the media with news that a man has become pregnant (thanks in large part to *his* discovery of a new drug). And Alex, in disguise as a woman, goes through labor classes, with Diana at his side, at the prenatal retreat. (The other patients suspect "Alexandra" and Diana are a lesbian couple.)

When Larry Arbogast returns from Vancouver with his news, Flusser's spies follow him to the isolated clinic and discover Alex's hiding place. Both Hesse and Angela suddenly go into labor, and Larry hurries them to the emergency ward. Flusser and members of the news media converge on the hospital in a feeding frenzy, but the diminutive gynecologist pulls a brilliant switch. Instead of admitting Alex to the hospital, he wheels his wife into the emergency ward. (At the same time, Diana helps Alex through the service entrance.) Reporters descend on Larry and his pregnant ex-wife and are surprised to learn that she is really a "she." Flusser has lied to them all and forever damaged his credibility.

Alexander Hesse successfully delivers a fourteen-pound, six-ounce baby girl, and Angela gives birth to a baby boy who looks just like Larry. (She is forced to confess that Larry, and not some stranger, is the father.) Nine months later, "Junior" and little Larry are happily playing together in a crib. But when Junior cries out for "Mama," both Alex and Diana respond.

The runaway success of both *Twins* (1988) and *Kindergarten Cop* (1991) encouraged Arnold Schwarzenegger to work again with producer-director Ivan Reitman. Not only had the Austrian superstar established a good professional relationship with the popular filmmaker; he had also made a lifelong friend in this fellow immigrant. Like himself, Reitman had been born abroad (in Czechoslovakia) and was lured to the United States by the American dream of riches and success. First educated in Canada at McMaster University, Reitman began his career as a stage and television producer. Among his early, low-budget efforts were two films, *Foxy Lady* (1971) and *Cannibal Girls* (1973), which he both produced and directed. He later collaborated with David Cronenberg on *The Parasite Murders* (1975) and *Rabid* (1977) before venturing to Los Angeles. Reitman made a big impression on Hollywood, producing the blockbuster *National Lampoon's Animal House* (1978) and directing the critically acclaimed *Meatballs* (1979). The phenomenal box-office appeal of *Stripes* (1981) and *Ghostbusters* (1984) firmly established him as one of the most successful filmmakers in the business. Subsequent turns as either a producer or director (or both) of *Legal Eagles* (1986), *Big Shots* (1987), *Casual Sex?* (1988), *Feds* (1988), *Ghostbusters* II (1989), and *Beethoven* (1992) helped to place him in the same company as Steven Spielberg, George Lucas, and other Hollywood power brokers.

Following a less than stellar collaboration with he-man Sylvester Stallone on *Stop! Or My Mom Will Shoot* (1992), Reitman enlisted Schwarzenegger's aid for a two-minute cameo in his satire about presidential politics, *Dave* (1993). In the film, Arnold (appearing as himself) works out with Kevin Kline, a man masquerading as the top executive when the real president has a stroke during an illicit liaison with a female aide. Naturally, Schwarzenegger's own personal friendship with several U.S. presidents helped to lend credibility to the story, and the irony that George Bush had just lost the presidency to a man like "Dave" was not lost on most audience members. During the ten-day shoot, the two men joked and kidded each other about their next production together, but neither of them had a clear idea what it might be.

Several months later, while Reitman was completing postproduction chores on *Dave,* he received a script from Chris Conrad and Kevin Wade. Originally titled *Oh, Baby!,* the screenplay focused on two male scientists who, when prohibited by the FDA from testing an antimiscarriage drug, decide that one of them must serve as a guinea pig by becoming, of course, pregnant. While the story itself was highly original, the premise (and some of the better jokes) seemed to be borrowed from Joan Rivers's low-budget farce *Rabbit Test* (1978), with Billy Crystal. At about the same time, Schwarzenegger had produced a home movie in which he imitated Maria Shriver in her seventh month of pregnancy as a practical joke for his wife's baby shower. Later, when Reitman (and a host of Arnold's other intimate friends) saw his video, the producer-director realized the comic potential behind making Schwarzenegger pregnant. He then optioned Conrad and Wade's script, based on a substantial rewrite, and set up an exclusive deal with Universal Pictures for *Junior.*

"The strangest part of Arnold being pregnant—or any man—is he doesn't have breasts. The proportions are all wrong. It's interesting aesthetically," Reitman said in a bemused manner. "All that aside, he does have the potential to become one of the great comic actors."

Opposite the Austrian oak, producer-director Ivan Reitman cast Schwarzenegger's *Twins* costar, Danny DeVito, as the crude, fast-talking gynecologist. The diminutive, chunky character actor had demonstrated over the years a flair for demonically comic roles; in fact, his role as Louie DePalma, the tyranical dispatcher on the hit television series *Taxi* (1978, ABC), was a character that audiences had best loved to hate. Born on November 17, 1944, in Asbury Park, New Jersey, DeVito first studied hairdressing before turning to acting. He began his career with a number of small but memorable performances onstage and in movies like *Dreams of Glass* (1968), *Lady Liberty* (1972), *Scalawag* (1973), and *One Flew Over the Cuckoo's Nest* (1975). Following *Taxi,* his big screen career was rejuvenated with featured roles in *Terms of Endearment* (1983), *Romancing the Stone* (1984), and *Jewel of the Nile* (1985). He added directing to his repertoire with the comedic *Throw Momma From the Train* (1987) and the acclaimed *War of the Roses* (1989). His star turn as the "Penguin" in Tim Burton's *Batman Returns* (1992) seemed to mark

the pinnacle of his success. Danny DeVito's last few films, including *Hoffa* (1992), in which he both directed and costarred, *Jack the Bear* (1993), and *Renaissance Man* (1994), had all done poorly. *Junior* marked a return to the kind of roles which made him famous.

For the part of the brainy, if somewhat clumsy, geneticist, Reitman selected Academy Award–winning actress Emma Thompson. Even though the producer-director had failed to secure Thompson for the Sigourney Weaver role in *Dave,* he was very anxious to work with this multitalented actress. Born in 1959, Emma Thompson began writing and performing her own comic material while still a student at Cambridge University. After costarring in the hit West End musical *Me and My Girl,* she joined the Renaissance Theatre Company and met founder Kenneth Branagh (whom she later married). Her film career began in 1989 with *The Tall Guy* and Branagh's award-winning *Henry V.* Star turns in Branagh's *Dead Again* (1991), *Impromptu* (1991), and *Peter's Friends* (1992) as well as the popular BBC variety series *Thomson* helped establish her as one of England's leading ladies. But it was her Oscar performance as the forthright heroine of the Merchant-Ivory film *Howards End* (1992) that forever changed the way Hollywood would consider her. She has since appeared in Branagh's *Much Ado About Nothing* (1993), *Honor Thy Father* (1993), and *Remains of the Day* (1993). *Junior* was not only her first big-budget comedy; it also gave Thompson the chance to break away from the stuffy roles that had made her famous.

"The relationship between Arnold and the very British Thompson is something to behold," revealed Ivan Reitman. "We giggled from the first to the last day of shooting." In fact, during most of the filming, both Danny DeVito and Schwarzenegger kept playing practical jokes on Thompson. There was plenty of kidding, and she became—like the Three Stooges—one of the boys.

To round out his cast, Reitman relied on Frank Langella, the tall, dark, and handsome character actor who had been so memorable in *Dave.* Born in 1940, Langella had performed in a number of stage and screen roles before he burst onto the scene in 1977 with the definitive stage performance as the Transylvanian count in *Dracula* (made into the 1979 film by Universal Pictures). Subsequent turns in *Those Lips, Those Eyes* (1980) and *SPHINX* (1981) proved disappointing to audiences. Five years later, he mounted a major comeback with *The Men's Club* (1986), *And God Created Woman* (1987), and *Masters of the Universe* (1987) and received only satisfactory reviews. Since then, he has played in a number of supporting roles in *True Identity* (1991), *1492* (1992), and *Body of Evidence* (1993) but has never really shaken the curse of that one great role as Dracula. His portrayal of Dr. Adam Flusser in *Junior* provided him with yet another meaty role with overtones of campiness.

The high-concept comedy began its principal photography during the last week of June 1994 on locations in and around the Los Angeles area (including an upscale shopping mall in Santa Barbara). Early in the shoot, Arnold took a few weeks off to promote *True Lies* for James Cameron and Twentieth Century-Fox. By midsummer they had moved onto the Universal back lot for most of the scenes inside the Stanford-Lufkin Biotechnology Research Center, at the gynecologist's office, and in Arbogast's apartment. Exteriors for Leland University were filmed at the University of Southern California. Additional shots in the city of Carmel and on the road were completed by Ivan Reitman and his second unit.

At times during the ten-week shoot, *Junior* was a producer's dream come true as the small cast and crew came together within the relatively limited budget of the motion picture. Schwarzenegger, DeVito, and Thompson, and Reitman's crew, became known as the team, and small as that may sound, it helped create an atmosphere that was both fun and highly imaginative. The Austrian superstar had nothing but praise for the other members of the team, but his sentiments were best summed up by one of the crew: "[Reitman] builds a creative environment, assembles a team of the most creative folks in the industry, and then gives everyone the freedom to contribute their ideas." On August 31, *Entertainment Tonight* caught up to the production while Schwarzenegger was being measured for maternity clothes and learned that the former bodybuilder felt "so humiliated. I've lost control over my body...." Of course, Arnold was simply being Arnold, kidding everyone involved while struggling to remain in character.

Several weeks after the production had wrapped, Danny DeVito ran into Schwarzenegger and Maria Shriver in a little cafe. The diminutive actor couldn't

Emma Thompson is Dr. Diana Reddin, a beautiful but daffy geneticist. (Courtesy Cinema Archives)

pass up the opportunity to remind his costar of all the fun they had had while making the film and decided to play just one more practical joke on him. "Arnold didn't see me," DeVito told reporters, "so I had my waiter send him a big quadruple scoop of vanilla ice cream with a note that read: `From the father of your child.'" Schwarzenegger realized immediately who was the culprit and hunted around the restaurant "like a shark," Danny DeVito said, finishing his story. "I finally just walked over to him and said, `Happy Labor Day.'"

Critical Commentary

Junior was released on November 23, 1994, the Wednesday before Thanksgiving, amid a flurry of other holiday comedies, including *The Pagemaster, Livesavers, The Santa Clause, Richie Rich,* and the big-budget remake of *Miracle on 34th Street.* The motion picture fought its way to the top of the box-office charts and remained there in the top ten for months. Critical reaction to the film was generally favorable, with reviewers crediting Reitman, Thompson, and Schwarzenegger for a hilariously good time. By the end of the season, the film had grossed a respectable figure (considering its modest budget) and held its own against big studio projects like *Mary Shelley's Frankenstein, Interview With the Vampire, Little Women, Disclosure,* and *Star Trek: Generations.*

In a role much different from any other and probably the most difficult in his career to play, Arnold Schwarzenegger turns in a fine performance as Dr. Alexander Hesse. Not only is his character one of the most fully realized of all his silver screen personas; it also provides him with a wonderful opportunity to expand his acting repertoire. Arnold demonstrates that he is so much more than a he-man wielding a sword or firing an automatic weapon. On one level in *Junior* he is an intelligent scientist, dedicated to bringing his discovery to the world; on another, he is a love-struck professor, confounded by feelings that he has never before experienced, and on still another level, he is a nervous, expectant mother, overwhelmed with morning sickness, mood swings, and sore nipples. Like Dustin Hoffman, Robin Williams, Jaye Davidson, and Billy Crystal, Schwarzenegger takes a huge risk, exposing himself to tremendous ridicule if the gender bender fails to work, particularly at a time when his box-office appeal was in flux. After suffering a critical beating for his work on *The Last Action Hero,* he could have just as easily retrenched in the familiar action-adventure genre. But the risk pays off big time, and it's not simply because the Austrian superstar looks pretty in pink.

Arnold owes much of his success as an actor to two directors, James Cameron and Ivan Reitman. Both of these filmmakers were willing to work with the relative unknown. Cameron took a chance casting Schwarzenegger as the killer robot in the first *Terminator* film, and the risk paid off, launching both of their careers. Since then, the Canadian auteur has worked with him on two other highly successful motion pictures, *Terminator 2: Judgment Day* (1991) and *True Lies* (1994). By the same token, Reitman gave the Austrian superstar his first chance to play a comic role in *Twins,* and Arnold ably acquitted himself as Julius Benedict and displayed great comic timing. His second outing for Reitman, as the titular character in *Kindergarten Cop,* proved that he could carry a comedy on his

own and made him an even bigger star among non-genre audiences. (Schwarzenegger has since returned the favor by appearing in a two-minute cameo as himself in the producer-director's satire about presidential politics, *Dave* [1993].) *Junior* marks another milestone for him. Not only is the film his third for Ivan Reitman (*Dave* notwithstanding); it is also a daring step into unknown territory once alone reserved for funnymen like Robin Williams and Billy Crystal. Schwarzenegger has long since proved that he is a great action-movie star (like John Wayne and Clint Eastwood), but *Junior* firmly cements his reputation as a comedian who, unlike the great actors of our time, is not afraid to take chances.

Future Productions

"Someday I would like to do a romantic comedy. I would also like to do a hard-core Western and a good, traditional war movie—any of those things would be appealing," Arnold Schwarzenegger told reporters during his press junket for *Total Recall* in 1990. Beyond that, however, the star refuses to be more specific. As this book goes to press, his only definite plans have both run into unavoidable production delays. Following *Junior,* he was to have starred in Paul Verhoeven's big-budget *Crusades* (alternately known as *Crusader*), for which he had contracted to receive $20 million. The story of a ruthless knight who is enlisted by the pope to find the cross of Christ (in the Holy Land) and subsequently undergoes a religious transformation might have been his greatest role to date; but Carolco studio chief Mario Kassar, fearing bankruptcy and cost overruns, decided to back Renny Harlin's *Cutthroat Island* instead. (Ironically, the pirate epic with Geena Davis ran into its own production delays when Michael Douglas withdrew from the project and was replaced by Matthew Modine.)

Similarly, Norman Lear's *Sweet Tooth,* with Ron Underwood (the director of *City Slickers*) attached, might have offered Arnold another genuinely comedic role as none other than the "tooth fairy." But the Austrian superstar wasn't quite satisfied with the script and passed on the project to make *Last Action Hero.* With Underwood's recent defection, the future of that motion picture remains in question. Now, instead of *Crusades* and *Sweet Tooth,* Schwarzenegger may well reprise his role as Douglas Quaid, Martian secret agent, in the sequel to his blockbuster *Total Recall.* He prefers not to look that far ahead and would rather leave the future open for whatever strikes his fancy. But the former bodybuilder's name does continue to be mentioned in connection with several interesting, if somewhat unlikely, projects.

Charles Lipponcott, the publicist behind the *Star Wars* trilogy, wrote *Judge Dredd* specifically with Arnold in mind for Twentieth Century-Fox. Based on the satirical comic-book series, the story is set in a far-flung future in which police officers have the power to both judge and execute criminal offenders. Judge Dredd, the most ruthless of the law enforcers, is framed for a crime he didn't commit and must use his extraordinary abilities to clear of himself of any wrongdoing. Schwarzenegger was lukewarm on the project, in light of his recent disaster with *Last Action Hero,* and passed on it in order to make *Junior.* The producers then hired Sylvester Stallone to take his place. The motion picture was set to debut in the summer of 1995.

Joel Silver, Schwarzenegger's producer of *Commando* (1985) and *Predator* (1987), has also lined up several projects for him, including the lead in *Sgt. Rock* (D.C. Comic's World War II hero) and *The Watchmen.* The much-troubled *Sgt. Rock* has been in studio turnaround for nearly five years, with several other names attached, including Bruce Willis, but it still remains a viable project for the Austrian superstar. "I have also talked to Arnold about the possibility of playing Dr. Manhattan in *The Watchmen,*" Silver told reporters in 1987. "I told him I wanted him to take off all his clothes so I could paint him blue." Created by Alan Moore and Dave Gibbons, *The Watchmen* promises to be the flip side of *Batman* (1989) by examining the negative effects of costumed heroes on society as the world counts down to nuclear Armageddon. But because of the film's potential scope, the project has never gone beyond the preproduction phase. Arnold Schwarzenegger's involvement in *Sgt. Rock* or *The Watchmen* still remains a matter of discussion and two of Hollywood's most closely guarded secrets.

While the Austrian superstar turned down the role of Edmund Dantes in the big-budget remake of *The Count of Monte Cristo* to make *Last American Hero,* he continues to negotiate several other future projects, including an all-star feature about the folk hero Paul Bunyan, an adaptation of the children's story *Curious George,* and a movie adaptation of "Big Bad John," based on Jimmy Dean's musical ballad about "a giant of a man" and his sacrifices during a mine cave-in. Schwarzenegger and John Milius have a long-standing agreement to produce a Viking film together, in the tradition of Richard Fleischer's *Vikings* (1958), and Paul Verhoeven and Ron Shusett have also recently agreed to work with the former bodybuilder on a big-budget science-fiction film (tentatively titled *Tri-Planetary*) based on Homer's tale of Odysseus.

"I make a point of always leaving my next picture open until I've finished the one I'm doing," Arnold said, dismissing various speculations about his next film. "Some actors like to secure themselves with jobs two years in advance because they're afraid maybe they'll go downhill in the next year. They sign up with every studio in town, make deals, and feel comfortable this way. By the time they end up doing the picture, two years later, they hate it. So, I never want to get into that position."

Whatever his film future holds, beyond *Junior,* Arnold Schwarzenegger will continue to excell through hard work and determination, the very cornerstones which have made him the most successful actor in the world.

As this book goes to press, Arnold Schwarzenegger's on-again, off-again eleventh-century epic *Crusade* may well have found new life with one (or more) of the major studios. In May 1994, after Mario Kassar, of the financially shaky Carolco, pulled the plug on Schwarzenegger's costly dream project, rumors began circulating in the industry that both Warner Brothers and Universal were interested. Chief executive Mark Canton, at Columbia Pictures, revealed that he was willing to team up with one of the other studios to share costs on the $100 million film just to acquire the overseas rights. Even though Canton lost a fortune on Arnold's *Last Action Hero,* he could still see enormous potential in this project. Discussions continue at the present time among the three studios, while director Paul Verhoeven completes his work on *Showgirls* and Schwarzenegger basks in the popularity of *True Lies* and *Junior.*

SCHWARZENEGGER
He will erase your past to protect your future.
ERASER
WARNER BROS. PRESENTS
AN ARNOLD KOPELSON PRODUCTION A CHARLES RUSSELL FILM ARNOLD SCHWARZENEGGER "ERASER" JAMES CAAN VANESSA WILLIAMS JAMES COBURN
AND ROBERT PASTORELLI MUSIC BY ALAN SILVESTRI CO-PRODUCERS STEPHEN BROWN CAROLINE PHAM EDITED BY MICHAEL TRONICK, A.C.E. PRODUCTION DESIGNED BY BILL KENNEY
DIRECTOR OF PHOTOGRAPHY ADAM GREENBERG, A.S.C. EXECUTIVE PRODUCERS MICHAEL TADROSS CHARLES RUSSELL STORY BY TONY PURYEAR AND WALON GREEN & MICHAEL S. CHERNUCHIN
SCREENPLAY BY TONY PURYEAR AND WALON GREEN PRODUCED BY ARNOLD KOPELSON AND ANNE KOPELSON DIRECTED BY CHARLES RUSSELL
R RESTRICTED
UNDER 17 REQUIRES ACCOMPANYING PARENT OR ADULT GUARDIAN
READ THE SIGNET PAPERBACK
WARNER BROS.
OPENS JUNE 21 EVERYWHERE

EIGHTEEN

RELAX—YOU'VE JUST BEEN ERASED

Eraser

1996. Warner Brothers. Panavision (released in 70mm, Dolby Stereo). *Director:* Charles Russell. *Producers:* Arnold Kopelson and Anne Kopelson. *Executive Producers:* Michael Tadross and Charles Russell. *Coproducers:* Steven Brown and Caroline Pham. *Screen Story by* Tony Puryear and Walon Green & Michael S. Chernuchin. *Screenwriters:* Tony Puryear and Walon Green. *Music Composer:* Alan Silvestri. *Director of Photography:* Adam Greenberg. *Film Editor:* Michael Tronick. *Special Effects by* Industrial Light and Magic (under supervision of John Sullivan). *Production Designer:* Bill Kenney. *Stunt Coordinator:* Joel Kramer. *Starring:* Arnold Schwarzenegger, James Caan, Vanessa Williams, James Coburn, James Cromwell, Andy Romano, Roma Maffia, Danny Nucci, and Robert Pastorelli. Released June 21, 1996. [120 minutes]

BIFF! POW! BAM! Arnold Schwarzenegger's high-octane action film *Eraser,* directed by Charles Russell, can easily be summed up by those three campy expletives. This thriller is big on *big* action, special effects, and incredible eye-popping stunts—the kind of material that first established the Austrian as a superstar—but the story itself lacks the chills and suspense of a truly first-rate thriller. Some of the sequences—two in particular involving a lost parachute and a reptile house full of angry alligators—look like they've been borrowed from a Chuck Jones cartoon featuring Wile E. Coyote and the Road Runner, but Schwarzenegger somehow still manages to make them believable. While the film isn't likely to prove as indelible as Arnold's earlier successes *The Terminator* and *Total*

One sheet poster, featuring Schwarzenegger and Vanessa Williams, from *Eraser,* Warner Bros., 1996.

Recall, the motion picture is a rowdy, crowd-pleasing absurdity that burned up the summer box office and consolidated Arnold Schwarzenegger's dominance of the action-adventure genre.

"In the summertime when I come out with a movie," said Schwarzenegger, "it's natural to come out with a movie that is for the summer audience. They need to see big spectacles, movies that are large in scale and that have great visual effects. And I like to go all out to give the audience something new and something different that's bigger than before and better."

The Original Screenplay

After the box office success of *True Lies* and the warm critical reception of *Junior,* Arnold Schwarzenegger decided to take a year off from making motion pictures. His wife Maria Shriver had just given birth (in 1994) to their third child, a boy—Patrick, and the Austrian superstar wanted to kick back and study his options. Planet Hollywood, his business venture with Bruce Willis and Sylvester Stallone, was adding a new host city every few months, and he was making millions in other lucrative stock options. If he had decided to retire from show business in 1994, Arnold would have been one of Hollywood's richest men. But he had no interest in retirement. Oliver Stone was pressuring him to star in his remake of *Planet of the Apes;* Joel Silver had several action-adventure projects lined up; Norman Lear wanted Arnold to headline his comedy *Sweet Tooth,* and Schwarzenegger himself had an option to produce and star in *Crusade.* He was also interested in working with Charles Russell after taking in his blockbuster *The Mask* at the local multiplex. Years before, he had been favorably impressed

Caught in the crossfire, U. S. Marshal John "Eraser" Kruger fights his way free.

by Russell's directional debut, *A Nightmare on Elm Street 3: Dream Warriors.*

When he first approached Russell with a remake of the Errol Flynn swashbuckler, *Captain Blood,* the director was intrigued. But shortly after they started work on revising the original screenplay, Renny Harlin's *Cutthroat Island* came out and sank at the box office. Ironically *Cutthroat Island* was the film that producer Mario Kassar decided to make instead of Schwarzenegger's *Crusade,* and that one decision made the difference between the success and bankruptcy of Carolco Productions, which went under shortly after *Cutthroat's* release. There was no question that pirate movies were dead in the water. Schwarzenegger liked Russell and wanted to work with him. Both looked around for a project to do instead of the swashbuckler, and they finally settled upon *Eraser.* Russell thought it would provide a solid foundation for some "wild genre ideas" he'd been filing in his head for years, and more important, he knew that the role of John Kruger was ideal for Schwarzenegger.

"It was Arnold's suggestion to look for something contemporary," Russell explained, noting that the script seemed tailor-made for Schwarzenegger. "I see Arnold the way a lot of people do—as a mythic, bigger-than-life character—and that's who Kruger is. The character and scenario are based firmly in reality, but I liked the mythic proportions of this man with a strong sense of duty, a strong sense of honor, who will literally do anything to protect a witness. I was excit-

ed about doing a film that had heroic proportions."

Actually, Tony Puryear's action-packed, character-rich original screenplay for *Eraser* was brought to Russell and Schwarzenegger by Arnold and Anne Kopelson, the producing team that had brought both *Outbreak* (1995) and *Seven* (1995) to the screen. The other Arnold, as he is affectionately known in Hollywood, earned the 1986 Best Picture Academy Award for *Platoon,* and produced *Triumph of the Spirit* (1989), *The Fugitive* (1993), and *Falling Down* (1993) before creating Kopelson Productions with his wife. "For many years, Schwarzenegger and I have talked about working together," Kopelson revealed. "I knew that *Eraser* was perfect for him. . . . He contributes to every aspect of the project. Working with Arnold has been one of the most pleasurable experiences of my filmmaking career."

The reality-based screenplay by Tony Puryear told the story of a man nicknamed "Eraser" because he aids people in the Justice Department's Witness Protection Program by "erasing" their pasts, who must protect a female witness from the Mafia. In the course of forty-eight hours, several other protected witnesses from highly visible criminal cases turn up dead, and Eraser falls under suspicion as the traitor. He sets out to prove his innocence to Samaritan, his former mentor, and to Beller, the head of WITSEC. He soon finds himself on the run with the female witness, who holds key information that can clear his name and implicate Samaritan in dirty underworld dealings. When she is grabbed by Samaritan and held

236

hostage, Eraser recalls a similar tragic event that cost him his wife, and vows that he will do anything humanly possible to save the female witness. He becomes a force totally committed to just one thing and succeeds in rescuing her from Samaritan. Later, in federal court, Samaritan and his underworld cronies are put away once and for all by her testimony.

While Puryear's original script for *Eraser* may sound like the typical action-adventure picture that only Hollywood and Arnold Schwarzenegger could devise for the lucrative summer blockbuster season, the story was actually deemed far too simplistic. Both Russell and Schwarzenegger agreed that the concept was a winner, but felt that the story needed some revision to make it a winner at the box office. From the fall of 1995 to the spring of 1996, more than a half dozen scribes were brought in to take a whack at the script, making the finished screenplay a rainbowlike composite of Hollywood's writing-by-committee practice. Screenwriting veteran Walon Green, who had written the screenplay for Sam Peckinpah's *The Wild Bunch* (1969) and had worked for the last couple of years on the NBC television series *Law and Order*, was brought on board personally by Schwarzenegger to replot much of the story. Green had also written the script for *Crusade,* and was high on Arnold's favorites list (considering that he held the option to make the medieval epic). Green and *Law and Order* colleague Michael Chernuchin transformed the Mafia villains into defense contractors, and they added the science fiction element of the high-tech weaponry. They also added a key action sequence involving menacing crocodiles at the Bronx Zoo.

Frank Darabont, the Oscar-nominated screenwriter of *The Shawshank Redemption* and the man hired by George Lucas to write the first film in the new *Star Wars* trilogy, was also brought aboard to write dialogue and scenes with his friend Charles Russell. Darabont was largely responsible for shaping a pivotal abduction scene, and he helped to enhance the role of the Mafia gang that aids Eraser in an important sequence near the end of the movie. His work with Russell was uncredited. Similarly, William Wisher, who cowrote *Terminator 2* with James Cameron, worked uncredited on several sequences. In the past, Wisher had coined such Schwarzenegger catchphrases as "I'll be back" and "Hasta la vista, baby" and was responsible for a number of Arnold's quips in *Eraser* including "Relax (or smile), you've just been erased." And finally, Christine Roum, another *Law and Order* writer, was hired by Kopelson to

Arnold Schwarzenegger asU. S. Marshal John "Eraser" Kruger

punch up much of the dialogue.

Officially, according to the final screen credits, *Eraser* was written by Tony Puryear and Walon Green, with story credits going to Puryear, Green, and Michael Chernuchin.

The Screen Story

The final shooting script for *Eraser* begins as John "Eraser" Kruger (Schwarzenegger), arrives in the nick of time to rescue Johnny Casteleone (Robert Pastorelli) and his wife from Mafia hitmen. As a member of an elite group of United States marshals assigned to the Federal Witness Protection Program, Eraser has but one goal—to protect federal witnesses

237

Arnold Schwarzenegger and Vanessa Williams pinned down in *Eraser*

at all costs. His particular specialty is erasing the identities of his charges, relocating them, and protecting them from being killed. He plants two bodies that bear a resemblance to Johnny C. and his wife, torches their home, and whisks them off to safety.

Meanwhile, Lee Cullen (Vanessa Williams), having seen what she wasn't meant to see, has gone to the FBI as a patriot to tell them what she knows. While working as an executive secretary at Cyrez, one of the nation's leading defense contractors, she has inadvertently discovered a scheme to sell advanced super-weapons ("rail guns," which shoot aluminum rounds at just below the speed of light) to a foreign power. What she doesn't know is that the conspiracy reaches to the highest levels of government, in particular to the undersecretary of defense (Andy Romano), and that the conspirators will stop at nothing to keep her from exposing the truth. Lee makes a disk with evidence that will support her testimony and tries to deliver it to waiting FBI agents. She is caught and taken to the CEO of Cyrez (James Cromwell), who threatens to have her killed if she doesn't give the evidence to him. Within moments FBI agents arrive, and he is forced to kill himself rather than let the government men take him alive.

Several hours later, Lee is introduced to Eraser by the FBI agents. She has no interest in having her identity erased by him, and she returns home to try to confront a boyfriend who has supposedly left her. Assassins working for the undersecretary arrive at her rustic retreat with orders to kill her and return the evidence that she stole. John Kruger arrives just in time to save Cullen from an assassin's bullet. The assassins use prototypes of the rail gun to perforate Cullen's house, and all hell breaks loose. But Eraser is so dedicated to his job that he puts his life on the line to save her. Like a one-man death squad, he takes out each assassin, then whisks Cullen safely away and hides her at his home, then, having determined that they're safe, places her in protective custody in New York's Chinatown.

Meanwhile, back at headquarters, Kruger's gruff section chief, Beller (James Coburn), reveals that within the last forty-eight hours, several "protected" witnesses have been killed. Robert Deguerin, also known as Samaritan (James Caan), thinks that the remaining witnesses, including Lee Cullen, should be moved, and he enlists Eraser's help. Kruger owes Deguerin his life, and looks upon him as a mentor; but when Deguerin's witness is killed during a routine move, Kruger begins to smell a rat, and he gives his mentor a false lead. Aboard a 727 jet to Atlanta, Deguerin shoots a rookie marshal (Danny Nuci) and makes it look like Kruger was responsible. Kruger is

238

forced to leap from the jet without a parachute in order to save his life. Freefalling from twenty thousand feet, Eraser cleverly snags a passing parachute and makes it safely to the ground.

Kruger then alerts Cullen to make a run for it, but she gets trapped in the reptile house at the Central Park Zoo with assassins all around her. Eraser rushes into the building, taking out a few of the men as he crashes through the exit door, and slides across the floor to her side. Knowing that he and Lee are dead unless he can think of something, he shatters the glass of an eight-thousand-gallon reptile tank with his last bullet. This unleashes a torrent of alligators upon the pursuing goons, who escape only after a very close encounter with one of the gators.

En route to safety, Kruger puts an alligator's lights out. Then he calls Beller to warn him about Deguerin, but it's too late. Deguerin has already convinced their boss that John Kruger killed the rookie marshal and that he is involved with Lee in a plot to bring down the whole Witness Protection Program. Eraser now has little choice: He must find out what's on the disk that Cullen is carrying, and the only way to do so is to break into Cyrez and use their computer to decode the files.

With the help of Johnny C., Eraser and Lee manage to penetrate the tight security of Cyrez. There they learn that the hypervelocity weapons are to be sold to the Russian Mafia that very night. Ownership of the rail gun can disrupt the balance of power, and putting it into the hands of terrorists could spell a death blow to society. This weapons deal must be stopped at any cost. Unfortunately Deguerin has been waiting for them, and he uses their breach of Cyrez security to capture Lee and trap Eraser behind an impregnable wall of Plexiglas. When he finally does get free, Deguerin is gone, and Lee Cullen has become his hostage.

Eraser commandeers an ambulance and races to save Cullen. Johnny C. insists that they contact his cousin, a mob boss who controls the Baltimore docks. With a handful of dockworkers, Kruger manages to take out some of Deguerin's men—but Deguerin quickly marshals his remaining forces, and they set out to erase the Eraser. But Kruger, taking two heavy rail guns in hand, gives them a blast from their own weapons, wiping out the traitors. Eraser then leaps atop one of the shipping containers, wrests Lee from Deguerin's clutches, and sends him crashing to the

Schwarzenegger, as U.S. Marshal John "Eraser" Kruger, stalks his prey on the docks of Baltimore harbor.

ground in disgrace. In a world where allies could be enemies, Kruger now trusts only the woman he was assigned to protect.

Weeks later, outside a federal courtroom in Washington, D.C., John Kruger escorts Lee to a limousine while Deguerin and the undersecretary look on. Suddenly the car is blown to bits, but the female witness is not dead. Thanks to some fancy pyrotechnics and a well-placed sewer grate, John Kruger has managed to make both his witness and himself disappear. Deguerin and his cronies think that they're safe now that the witness is dead. But Eraser has his own plans for them, as moments later he appears, like some spectre of death, and extolls, "Relax, you've just been erased." He has arranged for their limousine to meet a similarly unpleasant end.

The Cast and Crew

Arnold Schwarzenegger's presence in *Eraser* meant that the Kopelsons had to find both a villain who was, if not an athletic match, at least a complement to his large physical bearing, and a leading lady who would not get lost amidst all the explosions and special effects. James Caan, who had received an Academy Award nomination for his performance as Sonny Corleone in *The Godfather* (1972), was the ideal heavy.

The part of Lee Cullen, the female witness that Eraser must protect after she decides to turn state's evidence, went to singer and actress Vanessa Williams. She first came to the attention of the Kopelsons when Maria Shriver suggested her for the part. After testing scores of other actresses, Russell and Kopelson realized that Shriver was right, and they chose Williams not only for her exotic looks and appeal but also because of the screen chemistry between her and Schwarzenegger. *Eraser* marked Vanessa Williams's first leading role in a major motion picture, and it gave her the opportunity to work with some of the best in the business.

Robert Pastorelli also brought an impressive body of stage and television work to his characterization of Johnny Casteleone, the wisecracking mob informant who Schwarzenegger's Eraser saves in the early scenes of the film. For the pivotal role of WITSEC's silver-haired administrator, Beller, the Kopelsons called upon one of Hollywood's great tough guys, James Coburn. Austrian-born but Italian-raised Danny Nucci, fresh from his featured role with Sean Connery and Nicholas Cage in *The Rock* (1993), was the perfect choice for the role of the rookie U.S. marshal who Caan shoots in order to frame Schwarzenegger's character. James Cromwell, who had just appeared opposite a talking pig in *Babe* (1995), was cast as the dangerous and deadly CEO of the Cyrez corporation. Roma Maffia and Andy Romano helped round out the cast.

Bill Kenney, a veteran of countless action adventure films, was production designer. Best known for his work on *Rambo: First Blood Part II* (1988), Kenney counts among his other credits as a production designer work on *The River* (1984) and *Under Siege* (1992). Michael Tronick was hired as editor based upon his breakneck-paced films *Under Siege II: Dark Territory* (1995) and *Day of Thunder*

(1990).The score was composed by Alan Silvestri, who had just received Academy Award and Golden Globe nominations for his stirring music in *Forrest Gump* (1994). Silvestri had previously scored Schwarzenegger's 1985 hit *Predator.* The noted stuntman and stunt coordinator Joel Kramer was also hired by the Kopelsons. He had worked on thirteen of Arnold Schwarzenegger's many films, and he'd often doubled for the Austrian superstar.

Special Effects

Even though *Eraser* was not touted as a big special-effects film, like *Terminator 2: Judgment Day* (1991) or *True Lies* (1994), there were, in fact, considerable numbers of visual thrills. Nearly six months of special effects, matte paintings, CGI, and model photography were completed by Industrial Light and Magic in northern California under the supervision of John Sullivan. The most complicated and sophisticated visual challenge for Sullivan, director Charles Russell, and cinematographer Adam Greenberg was the breathtaking aerial sequence in which Schwarzenegger must jump out of a jet without a parachute. "How we put this sequence together was fascinating," Russell explained. "These things are jigsaw pieces not only within shooting sequence but within each shot. You had elements that were live action, elements that were miniature, sometimes computer-generated, and they're all married together in the final processing." Arnold was suspended sixty-five feet in the air on a harness for seven days, so that the camera could record his image falling then performing a back flip against a green screen. Later, Sullivan and the specialists at ILM added the sky, clouds, and smoke from the jet's damaged engine to create the composite of one of the film's most compelling sequences.

Another of the film's exciting sequences is the shoot-out in the reptile house at the Central Park Zoo. "I knew that this would be a problem going in, but I felt it world be spectacular scene," Russell concluded. "We couldn't endanger our actors by putting them too close to the animals, so KNB EFX Group built several animatronic ones and CGI ones were created by ILM, in postproduction." The combination of the live alligators with the "robo-crocs" and computer-generated images makes the sequence truly spectacular. Sullivan and ILM also created believable effects involving the hypervelocity rail guns and their x-ray scopes.

240

Arnold "Eraser" Schwarzenegger comes through the floor.

Production Details

Principal photography on *Eraser* began the second week of September 1995 in New York City—during one of the hottest autumns on record. Sequences shot during this period included Schwarzenegger's unorthodox arrival by parachute at the Harlem Rail Yard in the South Bronx at the Willis Avenue Bridge, and the setup for the Zoo sequence in Central Park's Sheep Meadow. Other location shots included one in the quiet neighborhood of Whitestone, Queens, one in Chinatown, and one near Brooklyn's Borough Hall. Charles Russell followed his carefully worked-out shooting schedule and moved the cast and crew through each sequence with great directoral finesse and expertise.

Early in the fall, the immense production moved to Washington, D.C. (specifically to the 17th Street Rainbow Pool and the Phoenix Park Hotel). Fans lined the streets for hours waiting for an opportunity to watch Schwarzenegger and his costars work. Several sequences were photographed during this period, but a major scene at the Central Intelligence Agency was revised at the last moment and cost the production some valuable time. "We went to D.C. to shoot the interior of the CIA," Joel Kramer said, "and for whatever reasons, the scene was rewritten, and it

no longer needed to be shot there. If they hadn't rewritten it just then, though, we would have wasted a week or two filming there, and it would have cost the studio that much more money." Such thirteenth-hour changes occurred throughout the Washington shoot, as the screenplay underwent additional changes. Subsequent scenes, some scheduled for shooting at some of the best known D.C. locations, including the Rainbow Pool, were dropped in favor of sequences to be filmed later on the backlot.

As the scope of the film expanded and the production began falling behind its shooting schedule, Russell soon found himself the focus of scathing articles in the press, many claiming that he alone was responsible for the film's escalating $105-million budget. "That's dramatically high," the director dismissed much of the criticism. "I'm proud of how much the movie is costing. We're within ten percent of our original budget." The press reports also included rumors that the Kopelsons were thinking about a replacement for Russell. But Schwarzenegger stayed loyal to his director. "If we needed more time and money to pull something off, Warner Brothers and Arnold Kopelson supported us completely. They, like the rest of us, wanted the best, most thrilling action movie possible, and they were confident Russell could deliver."

Following a brief sequence shot in New Jersey, the

John "Eraser" Kruger about to blow away the opposition with two of the top secret Cyrez E. M. pulse guns.

production moved to Los Angeles to utilize key locations in California. To complete the sequence in which Lee Cullen's house is beseiged by Caan's henchmen, the production closed off a rustic lodge in Topanga Canyon and filmed at night for several weeks. Additional locations included Los Angeles City Hall, which doubled for the Federal Court Building in Washington, and a nightclub in West Hollywood, which was the gay bar that Pastorelli works. Arnold's dockside assault was partially filmed in the warehouse district in downtown Los Angeles. The remainder of the shoot was moved to San Pedro. For three weeks, Russell and his crew filmed with every camera and piece of equipment they had in order to make up lost time.

In December, while shooting the film's climactic showdown at the docks of Terminal Island in San Pedro, California, one action sequence became dangerously real. Three stuntpeople, representing Schwarzenegger, Caan, and Williams, were injured when a huge shipping container shifted from its harness and sent all three flying to the ground. Stunt coordinator Joel Kramer attributed the mishap to the misfiring of an exploding bolt (which had been designed to sever one of the chains suspending the container). "We tested the rig four times," he explained, "but you never know." The mishap caused everyone in the production

company to pause and think; in a motion picture so heavily dependent on live action stunts a mishap reminds the cast and crew that accidents can even cost people their lives. The Christmas holiday break presented a chance to ease the tension of the shoot.

When the cast and crew returned, the production was ready to move from San Pedro to the unused portion of the Griffith Park Zoo. There, the filmmakers had constructed exteriors to match with New York's City Zoo. For the spectacular action sequence in the reptile house, an elaborate interior set was built on the soundstages of the Warner Brothers Studios in Burbank. The uncompleted sequence involving the shipping container was relocated to Stage 16, the largest structure on the backlot (it had housed sets from the Batman movies and *Jurassic Park*). The last few weeks of shooting on the production took place there.

Finally, on March 15, 1995, after seven long months of production, the final shots of Schwarzenegger rescuing Williams from atop the shipping container were completed. Principal photography on *Eraser* wrapped. A week later, Russell and editor Michael Tronick had relocated from Warner's Burbank sprawl to the studio's cramped downtown Hollywood postproduction facility. They had less than three months to cut thousands of feet of raw film down into a workable, two-hour time frame but also to combine the special effects footage seamlessly into the whole. Two and a half months later, with less than two weeks until the premiere, Russell received word from the suits in the front office that corporate executives from Cyrix, a real semiconductor company, had learned that *Eraser* featured a corporate name (Cyrex) very similar to their own, and were threatening to sue Warners unless the name was changed. At a cost of $1 million, Russell and the technicians at Industrial Light and Magic performed their own form of erasing, digitally altering 1,800 frames of film, so that the name Cyrex would read Cyrez instead. The work was completed in record time, but a mere thirty-six hours before showtime.

Critical Commentary

Eraser debuted in the number-one spot on June 21, 1996. In its initial week of American release, the movie delivered a one-two punch to Disney's *Hunchback of Notre Dame* and Jim Carrey's *The Cable Guy,* grossing an incredible $24.6 million. The action-adventure also dispatched several other box office champs, including *Mission Impossible, The Rock,* and *Twister,* all three of which had already passed the $100 million mark. Most audiences members loved the movie and praised Arnold for making such a crowd-pleaser. Siskel and Ebert gave the film two thumbs up, and Jack Mathews of *Newsday* called the movie "spectacular. A good time," and Bob Polunsky of KENS-TV claimed "*Eraser* is *Terminator* and *True Lies* rolled into one!" Pat Collins of WWOR-TV, perhaps the most astute of critics, wrote "WOW! The summer-action-date movie! With a punchline for every punch, Schwarzenegger tops himself." A few other critics were less than enthusiastic, denouncing the filmmakers for placing so much emphasis on the stunts and special effects at the expense of a coherent plot. But *Eraser* continued to do bang-up business throughout the rest of the summer and emerged as one of the season's winners.

"When I do a film, I don't want to just do a job—I want to do the best job. And whenever you do a film with stunts and special effects in it, you have to make sure that you really use them to entertain people as much as you can," Schwarzenegger responded to the harsh criticism about the stunts and special effects:

You don't want to do the same thing you've done before over and over—you don't want to keep punching a guy in the face or drawing a gun—that gets old. So there's always the challenge to make it better, to make the action bigger, the stunts more unique and more special . . . to give the audience something new and something different that is bigger and better than before. We're not just doing this for ourselves, but for all those people looking to be entertained. They deserve the best product on the screen.

Much to the pleasure of his many fans, Arnold is back in top form as the movie's title character. *Eraser* is a superbly crafted and highly entertaining motion picture. No other actor is better in this type of high-octane, adrenaline-pumping action-adventure, and he deserves additional praise for keeping the film's comic-book plot moving. While several of the movie's key stunts, including Schwarzenegger's freefall without a parachute, may well remind viewers of scenes from certain James Bond films and other thrillers, the material nevertheless seems fresh and realistic. The shootout in the reptile house alone is worth the price of admission. And when Arnold picks up the rail guns at the end and starts blasting, it's vintage Schwarzenegger.

Vanessa Williams and James Caan acquit themselves with skill playing opposite Schwarzenegger and thousands of exploding rail guns. Lesser actors would barely register. Similar kudos belong to Robert Pastorelli and James Coburn.

Although we've seen the plot before—in Harrison Ford's *Witness* (1984) and in countless episodes of *Miami Vice, Magnum P.I.,* and other cop shows, in which a helpless witness must be protected by a jaded detective on the lam from his own employer or from fellow agents, the filmmakers have dressed up the story with eye-popping stunts, state-of-the-art special effects, and the talent of the world's most popular actor and superstar. While *Eraser* is a bit more than just a formula film, some genuine tension and suspense, like that in *Mission Impossible* and *The Rock,* would have improved the final product.

With *Eraser*'s release during the summer of 1996, the videocassette and laser disc versions from Warner Brothers were not available until the winter of 1997.

NINETEEN

THE NEWEST TERMINATOR

Terminator 3-D: Battle Across Time

1996. Lightstorm Entertainment, in association with Carolco Pictures and Universal Studios–Florida. Panavision (released in 70mm, 3-D, Digital Stereo). *Producer and Director:* James Cameron. *Screen Story by* Cameron and William Wisher. *Based on characters created by* Cameron and Gale Anne Hurd. *Music Composer:* Brad Fiedel. *Special Effects by* Digital Domain. *Special Effects Supervisors:* Stan Winston and John Bruno. *Starring:* Arnold Schwarzenegger, Linda Hamilton, Edward Furlong, and Robert Patrick. Released May 1996. [13 minutes]

After nearly five years in a forgotten junk heap, the Terminator returned to the forefront of pop culture in the spring of 1996 with the debut of *Terminator 3-D: Battle Across Time.* Director James Cameron and superstar Arnold Schwarzenegger again teamed to bring the most famous killer robot to the screen. Only this time state-of-the-art, interactive special effects, digital composite computer graphics, one-of-a-kind cinebotics, and live-action stunt work have been combined with 3-D cinematography to produce an entertainment experience like none other. Costing more than most mainstream feature films (at a whopping $12 million), the thirteen-minute short marked the first time that a feature film's creative production team joined together to bring a motion picture concept to life in a theme park attraction.

"When Bill Wisher and I were first plotting *Terminator 2: Judgment Day,* we briefly thought of playing the whole thing in the future—or at least to play more of it in the future war," Cameron said in explaining the genesis of his new project. "So, when the opportunity came to make this theme attraction

for Universal Studios–Florida, I returned to some of my original notes."

The Screen Story

Terminator 3-D: Battle Across Time begins, like most interactive theme attractions, with your group's visit to the attraction. In this case, Cyberdyne Systems has arranged for a big press gathering, and your group has been invited to tour its new facility and see the new products being promoted. With a thick smile that belies the company's evil intentions, Cyberdyne's public relations representative meets you at the entryway. (August 29, 1997—*Judgment Day* is after all only a few short months away.) Then, while you're watching a promotional video, the program's signal is interrupted by John (Edward Furlong) and Sarah Connor (Linda Hamilton). They warn everyone in your group that you have five minutes to get out of the Cyberdyne complex before they attack. But the P.R. rep dismisses them as lunatics and continues babbling on with his sales pitch.

Your group is then led into the Miles Dyson memorial auditorium and given special glasses in order to see a demonstration of the newest Cyberdyne product—the first artificial soldier, the Terminator Model 80. But before you can study the new model, smoke begins to pour out from the side of the room, and six Terminator Model 70s rise from the floor and start firing their mini-guns at the crowd. (The T-70 is actually a more primitive version of the T-800 endoskeleton, but the six robots nevertheless seem fairly sophisticated. At about eight feet in height, they are comprised of a high carbon steel substructure and covered with a polyresin/glass fiber "skin.") Mass

244

chaos quickly ensues, and then, suddenly, John and Sarah Connor burst out of the ceiling to save you.

They start blasting away at the T-70s, taking them out one at a time. A T-1000, the shape-changing terminator from *Terminator 2,* slithers out of the back screen and changes into a familiar human form (Robert Patrick). But just as he's about to kill John and Sarah, the Terminator (Arnold Schwarzenegger, who else?) races onto the stage on a custom built Harley-Davidson. The Terminator snaps John Connor up onto the motorcycle, and struggles with the T-1000 just long enough to give Sarah a chance to escape. He then revs up the Harley, and he and John roar down a darkened highway to safety. Moments later, the T-1000 has climbed back to his feet and is in pursuit.

The balance of the action-adventure is an extended chase in which Arnold's Terminator is pursued by the T-1000 and a hunter-killer aircraft. The Terminator knows that if they can reach Skynet, the master computer that controls the nation's defense system, they can stop the machine from launching World War III. But their journey is dogged every step of the way by the T-1000, the H-K, and several of the T-70s John and Sarah failed to destroy. Eventually the two heroes reach Skynet's computer processing center, and there they face an incredible battle with a liquid-metal spider that can take a plasma bolt at point-blank range. But John and the Terminator prevail, emerging nearly intact from a mind-blowing and ear-shattering explosion. In the end, Arnold's Terminator turns to your group and exclaims, "*I Promise,* I'll be back. Now go!" All that's left for your group is to exit the ruins of the Cyberdyne Building and buy Terminator merchandise at the concession stand.

Production Details

Back in 1991, after completing work on *Terminator 2: Judgment Day,* James Cameron and Arnold Schwarzenegger promised audiences that they hadn't seen the last of the Terminator. Schwarzenegger said that "according to what we know about the future, there were hundreds of Terminators built." However, bringing the killer robot back to life required a tremendous commitment of time, resources, and talent, and Cameron wasn't certain that he was up to the challenge of another motion picture. "Every time I start a film, I have a fantasy that it will be like a big family, and we'll all have a great time," he explained, "but that's not what filmmaking is—it is a war." Besides, Cameron was interested in making some mainstream projects, including a big budget film on the *Titanic,* and he didn't want to be typecast as a sci-fi director.

The wide popularity of theme park attractions, such as the Pyramid adventure at the Luxor in Las Vegas and the *Back to the Future* ride at Universal Studios–Florida (both designed by Douglas Trumbull) gave Cameron an idea. In order to satisfy all those millions of fans who still hungered for another Terminator movie and provide his own special effects facility (Digital Domain) with a unique opportunity to experiment with some new techniques, the Canadian auteur had discussions with Universal Studios–Florida about his plan for a *Terminator 3-D* attraction. The Universal executives loved the idea, and ground was broken for the new attraction in 1995. Originally the plan was to feature the T-800 chrome endoskeletons, seen in *Terminator 2.* But Cameron was not interested in simply covering old ground; he wanted to create something that fans had never seen before. Besides the T-800s came from a different place in time (around the year 2029), and therefore could not exist in the attraction during the present day. As a result, Cameron designed, exclusively for the attraction, the T-70 robot, a totally new, more primitive series of the mechanical soldier. But the project would not have been the same without the original Terminator that started it all.

Shortly after the success of *True Lies,* Cameron convinced Schwarzenegger that the theme park attraction couldn't be done without the Austrian superstar. Despite his decision to take a year-long sabbatical after his back-to-back work on *True Lies* and *Junior,* the actor agreed to a two-week shoot. His costars from *Terminator 2: Judgment Day,* including principles Linda Hamilton, Robert Patrick, and Edward Furlong, also signed on for the unique project. Even though Linda Hamilton had just had a child with Cameron, she was totally in shape and prepped for the shoot. In fact, for most of the cast and crew of the new movie, it was as if five years hadn't passed since they had last worked together. Jim Cameron's fantasy of a family reunion was gradually coming together for *Terminator 3-D.*

Academy Award–winning special-effects wizards Stan Winston and John Bruno were also brought on board to help realize Cameron's new vision. Part of Winston's work required him to bring the six new cinebotic T-70 soldiers to life. He designed these animated figures with a wide range of motions, including movement in their arms, torso, and head. He also built a smaller, fully animated version for the special effects shots that would be digitally composited later. While Winston worked to bring Cameron's original sketches to life, Bruno supervised the construction of gigantic sets at Universal Studios–Florida and scouted location shots where most of the filming would be completed. To perfect the set's devastation, he worked from photographs of Britain after the Blitz. Attention to detail didn't stop there, though. Modern toppling structures had to be studied, as well as "newer buildings [that] blow up quite differently than old ones." The surrealism was necessary because the wreckage in the film's background was genuine—real buildings were blown up just for the shooting.

Additional location shooting took place at the deserted steel mill in Fontana, California, where much of the climax of *Teminator 2* was shot. Cameron and his crew shot the film's live action scenes during an exhausting two-week schedule, mostly at night. The assistant director claimed "it was so bright that people in the next town, twelve miles away, were going to get up and go to work." Computer graphics, digital composite imagery, and other special-effects shots were mixed with the live footage at Digital Domain just across town.

While the Canadian auteur and his talented cast and crew worked to create the magic of the two previous motion pictures, Universal Studios–Florida constructed a façade of Cyberdyne Systems on the Hollywood Boulevard set of its backlot. Behind the façade, they built both the press room of Cyberdyne Systems and a seven-hundred-seat auditorium. A complex web of over a hundred miles of cable was woven throughout the attraction to activate the various audio, video, computer, and show-support systems. A series of theatrical rigging linesets, motors, and controllers to fly scenery in and out on cue were also custom designed and installed by Scenic Technologies, whose work appears in the Broadway versions of *Miss Saigon* and *Phantom of the Opera*.

For the film itself, a specially-designed set of three interlocking projection screens, twenty-three feet high and fifty feet wide, were created so that guests to the attraction would feel surrounded by 180 degrees of in-your-face excitement. NASA scientist Dr. Ken Jones, from Pasadena's Jet Propulsion Laboratories, was enlisted to help align the six fully automated 70mm Iwerks projectors in such a way that the 3-D effects would literally jump off the screens. A state-of-the-art sound system, created especially for the project by Soundelux, was installed to pump a total of

45,620 watts through 141 speakers, making the complex one of the most technically advanced in the world.

Working closely with Winston and Bruno, James Cameron was able to complete the thirteen-minute film for roughly twelve million dollars in approximately six months.

Critical Commentary

Terminator 3-D: Battle Across Time debuted at Universal Studios–Florida in May 1996 to long lines of fans willing to wait hours in the hot Florida sun just to glimpse Cameron's new project. *Terminator 3-D* was deemed an immediate success, and it continues to draw more than two thousand guests per hour, making it the most widely seen of all of Arnold Schwarzenegger's movies. While the film takes far less time (precisely 12:41 minutes) than it does to stand in line to see it, it is worth the wait. The explosive special effects and interactive nature of the short make you feel like you're actually part of the action. And for any fan who has ever yearned to take part in a Terminator movie, this virtual experience is the closest you can presently get. So, don't spend another second reading this book. Pack your bags and head to Orlando, Florida, today. This is one film attraction that won't be arriving at your video store or appearing on cable television.

Naturally the success of Jim Cameron's 3-D attraction gives rise to speculation about another Terminator film. Rumors about *Terminator-3* have been flowing wildly since the 1991 release of the last Terminator film. And Arnold does promise at the end of the new film-attraction to "be back." For any reader who doesn't remember the last film—Cameron did leave himself wide open for another sequel. When the Terminator broke off his own arm in the battle with the T-1000, the limb was left behind in the steel mill. It was not dissolved, as were the Cyberdyne arm or the two Terminators, and the arm is still there, waiting to be discovered by someone who can use it in the creation of Skynet. So, who, except perhaps Cameron, knows what may happen on August 29, 1997?

TWENTY

JINGLE BELLS, JINGLE BELLS . . . AND FUTURE PRODUCTIONS

Jingle All the Way

1996. Universal Pictures. Panavision (released in 70mm, Dolby Stereo). *Director:* Brian Levant. *Producer and Writer:* Chris Columbus. *Starring:* Arnold Schwarzenegger, Robert Conrad, Sinbad, Phil Hartman, Rita Wilson, and James Belushi. Released November 15, 1996. [120 minutes]

After the success of family films like *Twins* (1988) and *Kindergarten Cop* (1990), Arnold Schwarzennegger was eager to make another comedy. His next venture with Ivan Reitman, *Junior* (1994), was something of a misfire for most moviegoers. However, the Austrian superstar returned to high comedic form as the errant dad who winds up in a snowballing series of wild adventures just to buy his son a "Turboman" he's promised for Christmas. Written and produced by Chris Columbus, the creative force behind *Adventures in Babysitting* (1987) and *Home Alone* (1990), the film was sure to be a crowd pleaser. Arnold Schwarzenegger revealed his simple but winning philosophy of moviemaking:

> In the summertime when I come out with a movie, it's natural to come out with a big spectacle. But at Christmas time, I like to come out with nice beautiful stories. They are very important to me." *Jingle All the Way* is an ideal movie. What makes it nice, especially since I have kids, is to do more movies that are for the whole family.

The screen story for *Jingle All the Way* is simple enough. Arnold Schwarzenegger plays a single parent who has put off his holiday shopping until the day before Christmas. His son wants a Turboman, the latest craze in a line of action figures. Naturally all the toy stores are sold out. But in his mad scramble to find that last available Turboman, Dad gets into a series of snowballing comical mishaps, enlists several strange characters to help him, and gradually learns the true meaning of Christmas.

Jingle All the Way was directed by Brian Levant and featured several newcomers to Schwarzenegger films as well as a few familiar faces. Levant had previously made three comedies, including *Problem Child 2* (1991), *Beethoven* (1992), and *The Flintstones* (1994), he was eager to work with the Austrian superstar. The cast included stand-up comedians Sinbad and Phil Hartman, tough-guy Robert Conrad, beautiful Rita Wilson, and James Belushi. Conrad plays the motorcycle cop who pulls Arnold over for speeding, then finds his cycle run over by the star's car. Sinbad plays the postman who competes with Schwarzenegger in his quest for the elusive toy action figure. Phil Hartman and Rita Wilson appear in the film as Arnold's eccentric neighbors, who take holiday decorating to excess. And Jim Belushi has a cameo in a scene involving a Christmas parade.

Principal photography was completed between April 15 and the first week of May in 1996, in Minneapolis and St. Paul. Additional filming in the Mall of America, site of one of Schwarzenegger's Planet Hollywood restaurants, in Bloomington, Minnesota, was done during the second week of May. Maria Shriver and their three children (who ended up playing at Camp Snoopy), and his friend Bruce Willis stopped by to wish Arnold and his production crew well. It was during this time that Schwarzenegger spent $772,500 for the Rockwell printing of JFK, the

247

former president's golf clubs and desk set, items at the Jacqueline Kennedy Onassis auction. He was apparently pretty confident that *Jingle All the Way* would be a big success, and eager to spend some of the early profits of the Christmas release. While these auctioned items were much more easily acquired than the elusive Turboman, the Austrian superstar does intend to give them as gifts.

"I'm only going to keep them until my kids get older, then I'm going to give them one of each," Schwarzenegger divulged. "I think it would be great for the kids to have something from the Kennedy legacy, to know where part of their blood came from."

Batman and Robin

1997. Warner Brothers. Panavision (70mm, Dolby Stereo). *Director:* Joel Schumacher. *Producer:* Tim Burton. *Based on characters created by* Bob Kane. *Music Composer:* Danny Elfman. *Starring:* Arnold Schwarzenegger, George Clooney, Chris O'Donnell, Michael Gough, Alicia Silverstone, and Uma Thurman. To be released June 20, 1997. [120 minutes]

Batman and Robin, the fourth movie in the highly successful Warner Brothers franchise, was guaranteed to be a blockbuster, presold by reports in the trade magazines nearly a year before its debut. Most of those reports centered not around the replacement of Val Kilmer by George Clooney but by the casting of Arnold Schwarzenegger as the main villain. For the role of Mr. Freeze, the former Austrian muscleman reportedly received $20 million and a cut of the merchandising for six weeks of work. He followed the recent trend set by Hollywood superstars who have played Batman villains, including Jack Nicholson as the Joker in *Batman* (1989), Danny DeVito as the Penguin and Michelle Pfeiffer as Catwoman in *Batman Returns* (1992), and Jim Carrey as the Riddler and Tommy Lee Jones as Two-Face in *Batman Forever* (1995).

"Mr. Freeze reminded me very much of the Terminator except with a different attitude," Schwarzenegger said. In an early draft of the film Mr. Freeze is portrayed as a tragic character. When his wife is diagnosed with a rare fatal disease, Mr. Freeze attempts to find a way to freeze her body until a cure can be found. But his experiment literally blows up in his face, killing her and transforming him into a human who can live in only the coldest temperatures. Naturally he blames society for her death, and he sets

in motion an elaborate plan of revenge that includes turning the Dynamic Duo into frosty freezies. In the role of the coldblooded Mr. Freeze, Arnold follows in the footsteps of George Stevens, Otto Preminger, and Eli Wallach, who played the role on the television series. Of course the superstar would be the first to deny comparisons between the old and the new *Batman,* including comparisons concerning Val Kilmer. Schwarzenegger was certain he could have worked with Kilmer, but thinks that George Clooney "without a doubt" will be the best Batman yet.

"Clooney is the new cool guy on the scene. He is a very hip guy," Schwarzenegger said. "It has nothing to do with the performance; it has to do with what's in, what's refreshing for the kids to see. I said to Joel Schumacher that I welcome the change."

In addition to Clooney, Arnold Schwarzenegger will have a chance to play opposite some of the finest talent under the age of twenty-five, and perhaps reach a new age group of fans. Chris O'Donnell will return to the role of Robin that he had originated in *Batman Forever,* and Alicia Silverstone will essay the role of Batgirl. To aid him in his quest to destroy the Dynamic Duo, Uma Thurman was hired to play the evil Poison Ivy. This dark and intense variation of Bob Kane's comic book creation promises many fine, rich performances, some truly dazzling production work, mind-boggling stunts and special effects, and many twists and turns, even occasional cleverness. How could it miss?

Upcoming Productions

Return of the Apes

1997. Twentieth Century-Fox. Panavision (70mm, Dolby Stereo). *Director:* Chris Columbus. *Producer:* Oliver Stone and Jane Hamsher. *Screenwriter:* Terry Hayes. *Based on the novel* Monkey Planet *by* Pierre Boulle. *Special Effects by* Stan Winston. *Starring:* Arnold Schwarzenegger. Possible release date in summer 1997. [120 minutes]

Oliver Stone's decision to remake *Planet of the Apes* (1968) has received a tremendous amount of negative publicity since it was first announced a few years ago. The original movie, Twentieth Century-Fox's stunning and profound science fiction thriller, hurtled viewers into the strange simian civilization where man was regarded as a savage brute to be controlled and ultimately exterminated. The Arthur P. Jacobs production opened so big in New York that for the first three weekends the motion picture not only beat out previous record holders but also bettered the records it had previously set. Eventually the film emerged as the second-highest-grossing, nonroadshow feature in the studio's history. Critical reaction to *Planet of the Apes* was also very favorable. Liz Smith in *Cosmopolitan* called it "a blockbuster movie! A genuine fourteen-carat film. Big, fascinating, and totally entertaining." Pauline Kael, one of the genre's harshest critics, proclaimed in the *New Yorker* that it was "a very entertaining movie" as well as "one of the best science-fiction fantasies ever to come out of Hollywood." She urged potential ticket buyers to "see it quickly" as it had "the ingenious kind of plotting that people love to talk about." Joseph Gelmis in *Newsday* wrote that it was "a first-rate adventure with serious moral, theological and social implications."

Although well able to stand on its own as a first-rate science fiction adventure with plenty of action, suspense, thrills and intrigue, *Planet of the Apes* was also an intelligent allegory. The questions that the film raises about man's warlike habits and his threat to the natural balance of the universe have the flavor of Jonathan Swift or Aldous Huxley. The motion picture proved to be a surprisingly successful film, and inspired four sequels, a short-lived television show, a Saturday morning cartoon series, and a whole collection of tie-in books, comics, and toys. The film was very well directed, and provided winning performances from Charlton Heston, Kim Hunter, Maurice Evans, and Roddy McDowall. It also demonstrated that science fiction films could deal with very difficult and often profound subjects, and still be extremely entertaining. In retrospect, in spite of its singular major flaw (that all the apes seem to speak perfect English), *Planet of the Apes* is a classic. Credit for its enduring legacy belongs clearly with the original novel, *Monkey Planet* by Pierre Boulle (1963), the bold determination of producer Arthur P. Jacobs, and the inspired screenplay by Rod Serling and Michael Wilson.

Return of the Apes (also known as *Return to the Planet of the Apes*), Oliver Stone's new version as adapted by Terry Hayes, seems to invite criticism for daring to revise a motion picture that most people accept as a classic. But plans for this new version, until recently, have never included a direct remake. Just as the first movie was not a faithful adaptation of Boulle's novel, Fox's new *Apes* is neither a remake of the first nor another adaptation of the book. It is instead a retelling that will, with luck, reintroduce today's younger audiences to that upside-down world where intelligent apes rule and man is considered the beast.

Terry Hayes, who wrote *The Road Warrior* for George Miller, crafted a story that sends us hurtling back into another time rather than forward. As the millennium approaches, children are being stillborn, and scientists race to find an explanation before the population of man becomes extinct. One scientist, who once experimented with dangerous chemicals and cost a woman her life, strives to redeem himself. Masquerading under the name Will Robinson (while his name is really Robert Plant), he advances a theory that the stillbirths are somehow connected to mitochondrial DNA. A fellow scientist, Billie Rae Diamond, who is pregnant, concurs. But to track the genetic material back to its source would mean going back nearly a hundred thousand years into the past.

Dr. Robinson feels that he has nothing to lose, and travels back in time using a sensory deprivation chamber. When he arrives in Africa, circa 100,000 B.C., he discovers that intelligent apes with advanced weaponry rule primitive man. He tries to even the balance of power by teaching the primitive humans how to use gunpowder, but is soon captured by a sadistic ape leader named Drak. Drak wants to kill all humans, and has convinced a veterinarian named Dr. Zora to invent a disease that can stop humans from procreating. Robinson is brought to her with injuries that she heals. Eventually he finds an opportunity to communicate with her and he demonstrates that not all humans are savages.

Zora attempts to keep him as a pet, but Ma-Gog, the apes' religious leader, exposes Robinson as a mutant threat to be destroyed. Nazgul, the President and leader of the Council of Elders, reluctantly agrees. Robinson will be executed to serve as an example to all primitive humans. But with help of a friendly ape named Strider and the leader of the seven human tribes, Aragorn, the scientist manages to escape. The three slip into the woods and head for the mountain fortress of the humans.

Back in a twentieth-century lab, Diamond discovers an important detail that Robinson must have overlooked, and she travels back to him. Aiv (pronounced "Eve"), the first woman, was apparently injected with Dr. Zora's disease, but it didn't work right away. Instead it became integrated into her DNA, and was passed on, in mutated form, along the thousands of years human history, like a time bomb. The good guys must prevent Aiv from receiving the injection, and thus protect the many generations that follow. Several bloody battles, numerous escapes, and rescues later, Diamond and Robinson emerge victorious with the young first woman in custody. They have no way to return to their own time, and in turn help the primitive humans win back their valley from the killer apes. In a tribute to the original, Robinson sculpts a replica of the Statue of Liberty in the sand: "It's to make sure we never forget where we came from." And they live happily ever after.

Return of the Apes has languished for several years on the drawing boards at Twentieth Century-Fox while the studio has been waiting for Schwarzenegger to commit. "We met with Arnold, and he definitely wants to do it," said coproducer Jane Hamsher, claiming that the deal has really hinged on the availability of Philip Noyce, the director of *Clear and Present Danger,* with whom the former body-builder had expressed a great desire to work. Schwarzenegger's agent would not confirm or deny his client's involvement in the project, and only said (in 1994) that the start date was far off in the future.

The Oliver Stone–produced project received a green light to begin preproduction in January 1995, once a start date had been agreed upon by both Schwarzenegger and Noyce, but concerns from some high-level executive at Fox over the film's $60- to $70-million budget brought production to a halt. Revisions to key sequences in the script, including several depicting bloody battles between the apes and the primitive human tribes, were recommended to Terry Hayes in order to help bring down some of the film's projected costs. Hayes worked for a few months on a new draft but was later dismissed, and a new screenwriter was brought on board to deliver a script that was actually closer to the original film. Lips are tightly sealed at Twentieth Century-Fox as to what direction the new script takes and how high the final projected budget will be for the film. "It's going to be an expensive movie, and everybody's playing it close to the vest because of what happened to *Waterworld,*" Hamsher added, referring to the most recent megabucks movie disaster.

As this book goes to press, Arnold Schwarzenegger remains very committed to the project and plans to work toward a new start. He has read the new script and is ready to step into a part not unlike the one made famous by Charlton Heston. Even though Philip Noyce has since left the project to begin working with Val Kilmer on the big-screen version of *The Saint,* and Chris Columbus has stepped in to take his place, Arnold is ready to kick some serious ape-butt. *Return of the Apes* will probably be ready for release sometime in the summer of 1997 or the spring of 1998.

Crusade

1998. Warner Brothers, Universal Pictures, or Columbia. Panavision (70mm, Dolby Stereo). *Director:* Paul Verhoeven. *Producer:* Oliver Stone. *Screenwriter:* Walon Green, with revisions by Gary Goldman. *Starring:* Arnold Schwarzenegger. Possible release date in summer 1998. [120 minutes]

Crusade is another Schwarzenegger project that has languished in development hell, faced with a similar collection of setbacks as those bedeviling *Return of the Apes.* The story of a ruthless knight who is enlisted by the Pope to free the cross of Christ (and the Holy Land) from Muslim infidels and subsequently undergoes a religious transformation has been a dream project of the former bodybuilder since he read the screenplay back in 1993. Estimated at a cost between $90 and $120 million, the project was first scheduled to go into production in the summer of 1994. In fact, the cast and crew, under the leadership of director Paul Verhoeven, were just about ready to travel to the Holy Land when Mario Kassar pulled the plug. Fearing cost overruns and bankruptcy, Kassar decided to back Renny Harlins's *Cutthroat Island* (with Geena Davis as the pirate queen) instead of Schwarzenegger's *Crusade.* Ironically the pirate epic sank at the box office, pulling Carolco Productions along with it into bankruptcy and oblivion. As part of a play-or-pay settlement with Kassar, Arnold has retained the rights to the story, but so far he has failed to find alternative financing for the project.

Written by Walon Green with revisions by Gary Goldman, the story takes place in medieval Europe in 1095, and tells about an outlaw knight and lovable rogue named Hagen who has been cheated out of his birthright by the evil Count Emmich of Bascarat. Driven to criminal behavior (like another famous medieval character, Robin Hood) to relieve those who suffer under Emmich's rule, Hagen is caught and sentenced to be hanged. In prison, he meets Aron Ben Zvi (Ari), a seller of religious artifacts, and learns about the Pope's crusade to free the one true cross from the Muslim infidels. Hagen quickly concocts a scheme to gain his freedom. To escape the sentence of death, he claims to have had a dream of the Church of the Holy Sepulchre in Jerusalem, and he pleads with Pope Urban I to let him join the Holy Father's crusade to free the Holy Land from the infidels. The Pope regards Hagen's dream as the work of divine inspiration, and pardons him of his crimes. (Hagen has actually made up this dream as part of a ruse to gain his freedom, but much later in the story the "dream" proves indeed to have been divinely inspired.)

Under the command of Count Godfrey, an honorable man who has sold all his riches to finance the crusade, Hagen leaves with the other knights to free the one true cross from the city of Jerusalem. But Hagen's enemies, including the sex-crazed Abbot, Count Emmich, and the count's cousin, Waldemar, conspire to have the knight and his newly made squire Ari killed by assassins along the journey. After several harrowing escapes, Hagen and his sidekick are finally captured by Muslim corsairs, and taken to be sold into slavery. But after Ari reveals to his captors that he is in fact a Muslim, he arranges for his uncle to purchase Hagen as a bodyguard. This arrangement doesn't escape the watchful eyes of Djarvat, a zealous Muslim, who believes that Jihad (Holy War) is the only way to rid the world of nonbelievers like Hagen.

Meanwhile, Pope Urban's crusade has reached the city of Antioch, not far from Jerusalem, and the crusaders reduce the city to ruin, sacking, raping, and pillaging all that remains. Count Emmich and Waldemar are among the worst of the crusaders, but the true leader, Count Godfrey, doesn't have the strength to oppose them. They continue to march on Jerusalem.

In the Holy City, Hagen makes numerous attempts to escape, but each one fails. His handsome face and powerful physique attract the attention of Princess Leila, the daughter of a wealthy Muslim named Ibn Khaldun. She would like to marry the Christian, but Muslim law states that she must be given to Djarvat, whom she doesn't love. Djarvat knows Hagen is a threat, and he plans to sell him to the crusaders as a traitor. But not before Hagen meets Theodosius, the long-bearded patriarch who has guarded the true cross of Christ all his life. The old man recognizes Hagen as the knight from his dreams, dreams in which a knight has been sent to free the one true cross.

Entangled in Djarvat's web of deceit and finally outwitted by other men that he trusts, Hagen is brought to Emmich and Waldemar in chains. Godfrey orders him freed from his bondage, but Emmich manages to convince the trusting knight that Hagen has betrayed them to the Muslims. (Around his neck, Hagen even wears the Hand of Fatima, a Muslim amulet given to him by Leila.) The rogue knight is sentenced to die at first light, but his sentence is postponed by an attack of advancing Muslim armies. In the course of battle, Hagen manages to win his freedom and prove that he's not a traitor. All the knights soon

rally around him, and march toward Jerusalem in umph. Count Emmich quickly realizes that the o way to beat Hagen is to find the true cross and use to consolidate his power as governor of Palestine.

The story reaches a shattering climax as Hagen must confront his two enemies, Emmich and Djarvat, and rescue the cross from the fiery wrath of the invading armies. Transformed by the power of the cross, the knight succeeds in dispatching them both. Count Godfrey, who is crowned the new governor, offers Hagen a special commission in his service, but Hagen responds, "Take a look around. Take a deep breath and with the stench of death in your nose, go tell God you've restored His kingdom." Hagen no longer wants any part of killing, and he escapes with Leila and Ari into the mysterious regions of the East. The epilogue reveals that "even under torture, the monks of the Holy Sepulchre refused to reveal the hiding place of the true cross. It was never found."

As this book goes to press, Arnold Schwarzenegger's on-again, off-again eleventh-century epic may well have found new life with one (or more) of the major studios. Following the financial and critical successes of other historical epics, like Mel Gibson's *Braveheart* (1955) and Liam Neeson's *Rob Roy* (1995), Warner Brothers and Universal have expressed interest. Columbia Pictures chief executive Mark Canton revealed that he was willing to team up with one of the other studios to share costs on the $100 million film just to acquire the overseas rights. Even though Canton had lost a fortune on Arnold's *Last Action Hero*, he could still see enormous potential in this project. Discussions continue among the three studios, while director Paul Verhoeven completes his work on *Starship Troopers* and Schwarzenegger basks in the popularity of *Eraser*. If *Crusade* does go before the cameras in the next few months, fans can expect a release in the summer of 1998.

Future Productions

With little doubt of the final box office tally of *Eraser*, the Austrian superstar remains a highly sought after presence in front of the cameras. More than a dozen different projects have been linked to his name, and each one has the potential to break box-office records in the United States and in every other major venue in the world. No other actor (currently performing or in the history of the cinema) has had so much clout. Unlike many of his rivals, including Jean-Claude Van Damme, Dolph Lundgren, Bruce Willis, Steven

Sylvester Stallone, Arnold Schwarzen-
... in film are not the bland artifacts of
the thinly disguised efforts of
but are instead the fruits of indi-
...he durability of his mythic charac-
...bility as an actor have demonstrated
...e and again. No matter what parts he
...uture projects he attempts (as either an
...ucer, or director), Arnold Schwarzenegger
...doubt maintain his superstar status.

...omeday, I would like to do a romantic comedy.
...ould also like to do a hardcore Western, and a
...ood, traditional war movie—any of those things
would be appealing," Arnold Schwarzenegger told
reporters during his press junket for *Total Recall* in
1990. Beyond that, however, the star refuses to be
more specific. He doesn't like to look too far ahead,
preferring to leave the future open for whatever
strikes his fancy. But over the years, the former bodybuilder's name has been mentioned in connection
with several interesting projects.

Joel Silver, Schwarzenegger's producer for
Commando (1985) and *Predator* (1987), has lined up
several projects for him, including the lead in *Sgt. Rock*
(Based on D.C. Comic's World War II hero), and *The
Watchmen*. The much-troubled *Sgt. Rock* has been in
studio turnaround for nearly five years, with several
other names attached, including Bruce Willis's, but it
remains a viable project for the Austrian superstar. "I
have also talked to Arnold about the possibility of playing Dr. Manhattan in *The Watchmen*," Silver told
reporters in 1987. "I told him I wanted him to take off
all his clothes so I could paint him blue." Created by
Alan Moore and Dave Gibbons, *The Watchmen*
promises to display the flip side of *Batman* (1989), by
examining the negative effects of costumed heroes on
society as the world counts down to nuclear
Armageddon. But for various reasons the project has
not gone beyond the pre-production period. Arnold
Schwarzenegger's involvement in *Sgt. Rock* and *The
Watchmen* remain matters of conjecture, two more of
Hollywood's closely guarded secrets.

Charles Lipponcott, the publicist behind the *Star
Wars* trilogy, wrote *Judge Dredd* for Twentieth
Century-Fox specifically with Arnold in mind. Based
on the satirical comic book series, the story is set in
the far-off future where police officers have the power
to judge and execute criminal offenders. Judge Dredd,
the most ruthless of the law enforcers, is framed for a
crime he didn't commit, and he must use his extraordinary abilities to clear himself. Schwarzenegger was
lukewarm on the project, and he passed on it in order

to make *Junior*. The producers then hired Sylvester
Stallone, Arnold's former nemesis and current business partner, to replace him. *Judge Dredd* debuted in
the summer of 1995, and received a lukewarm reception at the box office.

Similarly Norman Lear's *Sweet Tooth*, with Ron
Underwood (the director of *City Slickers*) attached,
might have offered Arnold another genuinely comedic
role as none other than the "tooth fairy." But the
superstar wasn't satisfied with the script, and he
passed on this one to make *Last Action Hero*. With
Underwood's recent defection, the future of *Sweet
Tooth* remains in question. Now, it seems possible
that Schwarzenegger may well reprise his role as
Douglas Quaid, Martian secret agent, in the sequel to
his blockbuster *Total Recall*.

While Schwarzenegger turned down the role of
Edmund Dantes in the big-budget remake of *The
Count of Monte Cristo* to make *The Last Action
Hero*, and the role of the doctor-turned-swashbuckler
in *Captain Blood*, he continues to negotiate several
other future projects, including an all-star feature
about the folk hero Paul Bunyan, an adaptation of the
children's story *Curious George*, and a movie adaptation of "Big Bad John," based on Jimmy Dean's musical ballad about "a giant of a man" and his sacrifices
during a mine cave-in. Schwarzenegger and John
Milius have a longstanding agreement to produce a
Viking film together, in the tradition of Richard
Fleischer's *The Vikings* (1958), and Paul Verhoeven
and Ron Shusett have also recently agreed to work
with the former bodybuilder on a big-budget science-
fiction film (tentatively titled *Tri-Planetary*) based on
the *Odyssey*. Arnold also wants to make the World
War II drama, *With Wings as Eagles* and he may backburner all of the other offers (including *Crusade*) just
to green light that one film project.

"I make a point of always leaving my next picture
open, until I've finished the one I'm doing," Arnold
said, dismissing various speculations about his next
film. "Some actors like to secure themselves with jobs
two years in advance because they're afraid maybe
they'll go downhill in the next year. They sign up with
every studio in town, make deals, and feel comfortable this way. By the time they end up doing the picture, two years later, they hate it. So, I never want to
get into that position."

Whatever his film future holds, beyond *Batman
and Robin, Return of the Apes,* and *Crusade,* Arnold
will continue to excel, through hard work and determination, the very cornerstones which have made
him the most successful actor in the world.

TWENTY-ONE
ARNOLD SCHWARZENEGGER—DIRECTOR

Arnold Schwarzenegger is not only a gifted actor but also a budding film director. In the early nineties he had directed a short for HBO Home Entertainment and a made-for-cable film for Ted Turner's TNT. For years Schwarzenegger had dismissed questions about directorial aspirations, but he did recant those earlier statements in 1990. When asked whether he would like to direct, he said:

> Oh, yeah. That's for sure. Again, it's finding a project that I'm really in love with that is small enough that I would feel confident enough that I could do it. Maybe a little story that takes place on location, something where you can concentrate more on the shots and the actors, rather than on special effects and all that stuff.

His directorial work, first on HBO's *Tales From the Crypt* (1990) and then on TNT's *Christmas in Connecticut* (1992), represents an important step in his film career.

Tales From the Crypt: "The Switch"

1990. HBO Home Entertainment. *Director:* Arnold Schwarzenegger. *Producer:* William Teitler. *Executive Producers:* Richard Donner, David Giler, Walter Hill, Joel Silver, and Robert Zemeckis. *Teleplay:* Richard Tuggle and Michael Taav. *Based on an original story that appeared in* Tales From the Crypt *comics by* William Gaines. *Starring:* William Hickey, Rick Rossovich, Kelly Preston, and Roy Brocksmith. [25 minutes]

For Arnold's first taste of directing, friend Joel Silver enlisted him to do an episode of the now-cult HBO series *Tales From the Crypt*, which he (Silver) was producing with four producer-director colleagues: Walter Hill, Richard Donner, David Giler, and Robert Zemeckis. Schwarzenegger lined up former costars Kelly Preston (from *Twins*), Roy Brocksmith (from *Total Recall*), and Rick Rossovich (from *The Terminator*) to help make his directorial debut an impressive one.

"The Switch," based on an original story that appeared in "Tales From the Crypt" comics by William Gaines, tells the ironic story of a rich old man who has everything but youth and the woman of his dreams. Carlton Webster (William Hickey) has fallen for Linda (Kelly Preston), a woman nearly forty years his junior. He doesn't lavish expensive gifts on her because he wants her to love him for who he is and not his money. Because he thinks that she prefers someone with a younger face and an athletic body, Webster gives a mad scientist (Roy Brocksmith) his entire fortune to have him transfer onto him the looks of Hans, a younger man (Rick Rossovich). The now impoverished Webster returns to Linda a new man, only to learn that Hans (who has received his riches and appearance) has married her. Apparently Linda wasn't really bothered by his looks; she was simply looking for a wealthy man to take care of her.

The episode aired shortly before the release of *Total Recall* and proved Schwarzenegger's eye for camera angles and pacing.

> I had a great, great time, and I felt very comfortable with directing actors. I will do much more of that. Maybe next will be a full two-hour show for television, and then a movie.

(Schwarzenegger also appeared in the humorous

Kris Kristofferson, Dyan Cannon, and Tony Curtis star in Schwarzenegger's made-for-cable remake of Christmas in Connecticut (Courtesy Turner Home Video

opening teaser as the Crypt Keeper's personal trainer, spouting the line "Do you want to be a ninety-pound corpse for the rest of your death?")

Christmas in Connecticut

1992. Turner Home Entertainment. *Director:* Arnold Schwarzenegger. *Executive Producer:* Stanley M. Brooks. *Producer:* Cyrus Yavneh. *Teleplay:* Janet Brownell. *Based on the screenplay by* Lionel Houser and Adele Comandini *and the story by* Aileen Hamilton. *Photography:* Chuck Colwell. *Music:* Charles Fox. *Editor:* Michael Jablow. *Starring:* Dyan Cannon, Kris Kristofferson, Tony Curtis, Kelly Cinnante, Gene Lythgow, Jimmy Workman, Vivian Bonnell, and Richard Roundtree. [100 minutes]

Schwarzenegger's warning to critics that "my first movie will not be perfect, but I will do it eventually" regrettably proved accurate. *Christmas in Connecticut* is simply a terrible remake of a 1945 Barbara Stanwyck comedy that hardly called for remaking. After hyping the film for nearly six weeks in February and March, with a very visible Arnold at the helm as director, Ted Turner's TNT debuted the television movie on Monday, April 13, 1992, to lack-

luster reviews and less-than-thrilling ratings.

Bubbly Dyan Cannon plays the hostess of a television cooking show who can't really cook. She's also always telling her fans about her boisterous but imaginary family. She's actually a lonely woman who has never even been married. As a publicity stunt, her producer Tony Curtis arranges for a television special in which a park ranger (Kris Kristofferson) who is a national hero will spend Christmas in Connecticut with Cannon and "family." The very small one-joke story quickly wears on its audience as a bunch of neighbors and friends attempt to fool Kristofferson into believing that Cannon is a happily married and very talented cook.

Lacking the skill that he demonstrated in the *Tales From the Crypt* episode, Schwarz-enegger appears, at least with this movie, much out of his element as a feature-length director. Very clumsily handled, with lots of sloppy slapstick and punch lines that fall flat, it lacks the pacing that had made "The Switch" so innovative. The only element of the film's plot (which degenerates into a standard family sitcom) that is managed with any sophistication is the budding romance between Cannon and Kristoffer-son, which may be attributed to the chemistry between the two rather than Arnold's directing. Curtis, long a deft comedian, appears to be winging it, putting the movie structured by the tyro director at an added disadvantage.

With the enormous talent that Schwarzenegger possesses as an actor and his experience with both success and failure as a director, rest assured he will "be back" behind the camera.

Christmas in Connecticut is currently available on videocassette through Turner Home Entertain-ment.

SELECT BIBLIOGRAPHY

Butler, George. *A Biography of Arnold Schwarzenegger.* New York: Simon and Schuster, 1990.

Churcher, Sharon (interviewer). "Schwarzenegger's Kurt Replies." *Penthouse,* July 1989.

Collins, Nancy. "Pumping Arnold." *Rolling Stone,* January 17, 1985. Straight Arrow Publishers, Inc.

Florence, Bill. "The Making of *Total Recall.*" *Cinefantastique,* April 1991.

Garcia, Robert. "Conan Comes to the Silver Screen." *American Fantasy,* May 1982.

Gleiberman, Owen. "Monster Mash." *Entertainment Weekly,* July 12, 1991.

Goodman, Joan (interviewer). "Interview: Arnold Schwarzenegger." *Playboy,* January 1988.

Leigh, Wendy. *Arnold: An Unauthorized Biography.* Chicago: Congdon & Weed, Inc., 1990.

Lofficier, Randy and Jean-Marc. "Arnold Schwarzenegger: Beyond *Conan* and *The Terminator.*" *The Best of Starlog,* vol. 7. New York: Starlog Communications, 1986.

McDonnell, David, ed. *The Official Conan the Destroyer Poster Magazine.* New York: Starlog Communications, 1984.

————. *The Official Terminator 2: Judgment Day Movie Magazine.* New York: Starlog Communications, 1991.

Sammon, Paul M. "Filming *Conan the Barbarian.*" *Cinefantastique,* April 1982.

Schwarzenegger, Arnold. *Arnold: The Education of a Bodybuilder.* New York: Pocket Books, 1977.

Shay, Don, and Jody Duncan. *The Making of Terminator 2: Judgment Day.* New York: Bantam Spectra Books, 1991.

About the Author

John L. Flynn was born in Chicago, Illinois, in 1954. He started writing his own "Star Trek" and other science-fiction adventures when he was fifteen and published his earliest fiction in fanzines at the age of nineteen. While pursuing bachelor's and master's degrees in English and journalism (as well as working two jobs to pay for his education), he became involved in the Florida Suncoast Writer's Conference (1972–77). That involvement led to workshops with John Barth, Michael Shaara, Damon Knight, Kate Wilhelm, and others and culminated in his first professional sale in 1977 to *Churchman* magazine. He graduated with honors from the University of South Florida, also in 1977, and went to work as a high school English teacher. Finding opportunities somewhat limited in Florida, John moved to Baltimore, Maryland, in 1978 and opened one of the area's first science-fiction bookstores. He also continued to write and has sold more than fifty articles, reviews, essays, and stories, beginning in 1983. His work has appeared in *Starlog, Media History Digest, Monsterland, SF Movieland, SFTV, Enterprise,* the *Annapolis Review, Not of This Earth,* the *Daily Planet, Collector's Corner,* and the *Antique Reporter.* He sold his first book, *Future Threads,* in 1985 and began teaching courses on writing at Anne Arundel Community College that fall. John became a member of the Science Fiction Writers of America in 1986 and was asked in 1987 to serve as the educational consultant on the *Dictionary of Essential English.* He was listed in 1987 and 1988 in *The Who's Who Men of Achievement.* John's second book, *Cinematic Vampires,* was published by McFarland and Company, Inc. His other books include *Phantoms of the Opera, Dissecting Aliens,* and *The Frankenstein Mythos.* He has also appeared on television and spoken on the radio about writing and horror films. Today John lives in Woodlawn, Maryland, and works for Towson State University.